UPON THE RUINS OF LIBERTY

UPON THE RUINS OF LIBERTY

Slavery, the President's House at

Independence National Historical Park,

and Public Memory

Roger C. Aden

 TEMPLE UNIVERSITY PRESS ★ PHILADELPHIA ★ ROME ★ TOKYO

TEMPLE UNIVERSITY PRESS
Philadelphia, Pennsylvania 19122
www.temple.edu/tempress

Library of Congress Cataloging-in-Publication Data

Aden, Roger C. (Roger Craig), 1962–
  Upon the ruins of liberty : slavery, the President's House at Independence National Historical Park, and public memory / Roger C. Aden.
    pages cm
  Includes bibliographical references and index.
  ISBN 978-1-4399-1199-0 (cloth : alk. paper) — ISBN 978-1-4399-1201-0 (e-book) 1. President's House (Philadelphia, Pa.) 2. Washington, George, 1732–1799— Homes and haunts—Pennsylvania—Philadelphia. 3. Adams, John, 1735–1826— Homes and haunts—Pennsylvania—Philadelphia. 4. Independence National Historical Park (Philadelphia, Pa.)—Antiquities. 5. Washington, George, 1732–1799—Relations with slaves. 6. Slavery—Pennsylvania—Philadelphia—History—18th century. 7. Lost architecture—Pennsylvania—Philadelphia. 8. Philadelphia (Pa.)—Buildings, structures, etc. 9. Philadelphia (Pa.)—Antiquities. I. Title.
  F158.8.P86A34 2014
  974.8'11—dc23
                                                                        2014017219

∞ The paper used in this publication meets the requirements of the American National Standard for Information Sciences—Permanence of Paper for Printed Library Materials, ANSI Z39.48-1992

Printed in the United States of America

9 8 7 6 5 4 3 2 1

For Dr. Jack Kay, whose wisdom, insight, and patience encouraged me to grow from a callow first-year college student into a confident professor

Arbitrary power is most easily established
on the ruins of liberty abused to licentiousness.

—GEORGE WASHINGTON,
  Circular to the States, June 8, 1783

Contents

Preface

This has become our Mount Rushmore, our Liberty Bell, our Statue of Liberty.

As the Philadelphia attorney and African American political activist Michael Coard spoke these words in Independence National Historical Park (INHP) on December 15, 2011, he underscored the symbolic importance of the newest commemoration within the park known as "the cradle of liberty," a site called the President's House. Coard's comments, however, spoke not to the nation's early embrace of liberty but to its systematic denial of liberty to the enslaved of the time and their African American descendants. "This site," Coard proclaimed, "is the only site in the history of America on federal property where a slave memorial exists."[1]

How did this place, the site of the executive mansion of George Washington and John Adams, become the Mount Rushmore, Liberty Bell, and Statue of Liberty for Coard and other African Americans? The short answer is George Washington. As Washington prepared to move into the nation's first White House, he arranged to have nine of his slaves from Mount Vernon move into the house as well. But Washington faced a dilemma: Pennsylvania law mandated that any enslaved person who resided within the state for more than six months would be considered free. Washington and his personal secretary, Tobias Lear, hatched a plan designed to mislead both the nine enslaved Africans and the Commonwealth of Pennsylvania: shortly before six months elapsed, the enslaved would be briefly rotated back to Mount Vernon and/or transported across the Delaware River to New Jersey.[2]

When Washington's deceit was unearthed by historian Edward Lawler, Jr., in 2002, the President's House became the battleground for an eight-year controversy in which National Park Service officials, historians, African American activists, and citizens from all places on the political spectrum argued about the role of slavery in America's commemorative landscape, the identity of INHP, contemporary racial politics, and who controls the stories of history. The story of the President's House offers a compelling narrative packed with history, contemporary political intrigue, and conflict among individuals and groups with competing motives and agendas.

As this description suggests, the story of the President's House appeals to several different audiences: scholars in the interdisciplinary fields of public memory studies and African American studies; scholars interested in the cultural, social, and/or political dimensions of our built environment; students of U.S. history; professionals working in the fields of public history and design; and Philadelphia residents who watched the drama unfold in their city over a number of years. As a result, I embraced a writing style that I hope treats each of these audiences with respect. I touch on relevant academic concepts and scholarship in history, geography, rhetoric, environmental psychology, and the like, but I do so in a way that allows these ideas to inform my discussion without dominating the story. My writing in the pages that follow is also informed by the wisdom I gained in visiting with some of the people involved in the President's House story, people who played very different roles in the controversy. Their willingness to share their ideas with me has, I hope, emerged both in the way I tell the story and in the variety of perspectives present in that story. Their openness to speaking with a stranger with no previous attachments to the park, Philadelphia, or the profession of memorial design gave me the necessary knowledge to honor the deep investments they all held in the project.

My distance from the site, and the need to rely on the kindness of strangers, points to a question that some readers may have: how did I get involved in this story? The answer begins with my family's ritual viewing of the musical 1776 on the Fourth of July. I had long been interested in the study of meanings in places and had recently begun to research public memory places as we watched the musical in the summer of 2006. Realizing that I did not know much about Independence National Historical Park, I decided to learn more. I quickly discovered that the park was in the midst of struggling with how to manage the revelations unearthed by Lawler four years earlier.

As I continued to read about Lawler's telling discovery and its aftermath, I learned that the symbolic power of the President's House was astounding. Some public historians were thrilled about the possibility of adding the executive branch to the park's portrayal of the nation's founding. Social historians were excited to see an opportunity to address more fully the complexities of liberty in the country's early years. African American activists eagerly embraced the idea of the federal government commemorating the efforts of the enslaved in general and the nine Africans enslaved by Washington in particular. I was also stunned to find that park officials initially wanted little to do with these ideas.

The story of the President's House, I came to discover, tells us much about the politics of remembering the past, the deep-seated tensions about how the United States defines its history and future, and the daunting challenges of working through those tensions in a public place of memory. It is a story packed with conflict, suspicion, and backstage maneuvering. It features heroes, villains, and fools—some of whom serve different roles for different audiences. And, most of all, it is a story that has revealed the need to face—in the symbolically powerful place of our nation's birth—the secrets of our collective national memory: our heroes weren't saints, and our country was built on the backs of enslaved Africans.

UPON THE RUINS OF LIBERTY

1

Discovering the Truth

The Revelation of Ugly History

The story of the President's House begins, innocuously enough, with a typical tourist moment. One summer day in 1996, Philadelphian Edward Lawler, Jr., was giving an informal tour of the some of the city's historic sites when he was asked, "Where was the White House?" Lawler had already noted the early homes of the nation's legislative branch and judicial branch, but the question threw him; he could not definitively identify the site of the executive mansion where Presidents George Washington and John Adams once resided. Lawler recalled, "I pointed behind me and I said, 'I think it's over there where the women's restroom is.'"[1]

Indeed, a wayside marker indicated that Presidents Washington and Adams lived in a home only one block away from the buildings where the Congress and Supreme Court convened (Congress Hall and Old City Hall) and from Independence Hall, where the members of the Continental Congress declared their independence from Great Britain. Yet the National Park Service (NPS) marker within Independence National Historical Park (INHP) provided little additional information about the long-destroyed building. Although the sprawling historical park offers more than two dozen sites, many of which are the original colonial-era structures, to visitors seeking encounters with tangible signs of the nation's beginnings, the only physical presence of the executive branch, beyond the wayside marker, was Washington's version of Camp David, the Deshler-Morris House, which is located in

Germantown, miles away from the park's heart in Independence Mall—and one of the least popular sites in the park.[2]

Stirred by his realization of this hole in the park's commemorative landscape, Lawler initiated an archival expedition that eventually produced a historical treasure: the exact location and floor plans of the elegant structure that once served as home to the nation's first two presidents—and before them, financier Robert Morris, British general Sir William Howe, and Benedict Arnold.[3] In addition, Lawler's historical excursion uncovered an architectural fact with contemporary repercussions: Washington had ordered modifications to the home before moving in, the most intriguing of which was the installation of a striking bow window in the state dining room. This bow window, which Washington used as a backdrop when greeting guests to the house, very likely served as the inspiration for the design of the Oval Office in the White House. Lawler's discoveries, published initially in the January 2002 issue of the *Pennsylvania Magazine of History and Biography,* provided INHP officials with the information needed to tell park visitors the story of the development of the presidency as well as the legislative and judicial branches.[4] The building—which came to be known as the President's House (as Washington and Adams referred to it in their communication)—could complete the park's story of how the U.S. government took shape in its early years.

The story wasn't that simple, though. Lawler not only identified the structure and location of the home; he also unearthed a generally overlooked historical fact: "Washington held enslaved Africans in the President's House for the whole time he lived in Philadelphia"—willfully violating a 1780 Pennsylvania law that would have released the enslaved from bondage after six months of living in the state.[5] Washington evaded this law by taking those he had enslaved out of the state, typically to Mount Vernon in Virginia, just before six months had passed; he then had them returned to the executive mansion in Philadelphia.[6]

This story, described by one former INHP employee as a "symbolic bombshell,"[7] was brought to the attention of a broader audience by the historian Gary Nash during an interview on a Philadelphia radio station;[8] it was initially not well received by INHP officials. In addition to providing evidence that the nation's ideals were subverted by its most revered founding father, Lawler revealed another troubling, and untimely, fact for the park: the footprint of the part of the home where many of the enslaved slept was a mere six feet from the entrance to the soon-to-be-constructed Liberty Bell Center (LBC)—the $12.9 million crown jewel of a $314 million makeover of the park that had been years in the making (see Figure 1.1).[9]

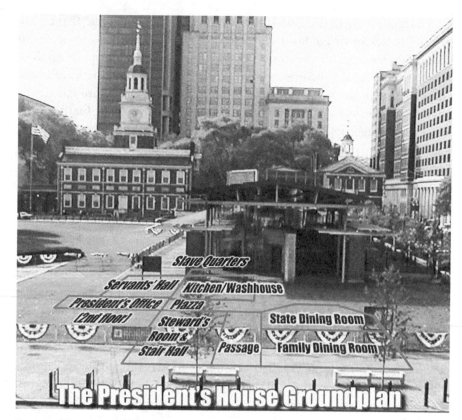

Figure 1.1. The footprint of the President's House, with the Liberty Bell Center and Independence Hall in the background. (Copyright © by, and used with permission of, Edward Lawler, Jr., and the Independence Hall Association; on the web at www.ushistory.org.)

The Liberty Bell is, of course, one of the nation's most iconic symbols. "It is virtually a touchstone of American identity," asserted Nash, "because Americans have adopted it, along with the flag, as the symbol of justice, the rule of law, and the guardian of sovereign rights."[10] Thus, even though abolitionists adopted the bell as their symbol in the 1830s, it has long been treated as a positive and revered symbol of freedom enacted, not denied. Lawler's discovery that Washington kept enslaved Africans only feet away from the entrance to the LBC was more than ironic—it was a threat to the core identity of INHP, affectionately known as "the cradle of liberty." Writing in *The Public Historian*, former park employee Jill Ogline noted that "the responsibility of preserving and interpreting icons of American civil religion such as Independence Hall and the Liberty Bell has been the crucible in which [INHP] has forged its sense of identity."[11]

Lawler's revelations created a quandary for INHP officials. If the park refused to acknowledge his discoveries, it would be seen as evading an indisputable truth (an uncomfortable and ironic prospect given the myth of Washington's reputed insistence on not telling lies). Yet if the park embraced the story he unearthed, the fidelity of the story trumpeted throughout the park's installations and interpretation would be threatened. Ogline aptly summarized the controversy: "The fundamentals at stake have been nothing less than the place of slavery in the American narrative and Independence National Historical Park's own sense of self-understanding and mission."[12]

That mission, of course, is not greatly different from those often found at other commemorative sites across the country and around the world. Put simply, public memory places are the sites in which collective *we*'s mark timeless truths about what we ought to remember. As Kenneth Foote has written, "The very durability of the landscape and of the memorials placed in the landscape makes [memory places] effective for symbolizing and sustaining collective values over long periods of time."[13] Often these sites tell a story that Henry Tudor labels a foundation myth, or "the tale of how a political society came to be founded."[14] These narratives are especially powerful, for they form the bedrock of a nation's identity. They are part of what we informally call our *heritage*. We do not trifle with heritage, for it "attests our identity and affirms our worth"[15] by representing "all that is good and important about the past."[16]

Public memory sites provide only partial glimpses into our collective past, largely because the resources of commemoration are insufficient for sharing a variety of stories, perspectives, and details. So instead of complex, multilayered stories illustrating the messiness of historical moments, events, and figures, we often encounter only one version of how our heritage was represented in this place, at that time, and/or within some person(s). In short, places of public memory typically are made to reaffirm a collective's heritage, a practice that Kristen Hoerl called, in a slightly different context, *selective amnesia*, or "the rhetorical processes by which public discourse routinely omits events that defy seamless narratives of national progress and unity."[17] For example, officials at INHP knew of Washington's slave-holding within the executive mansion when the NPS took control of the land on which it was located in 1974, yet they made no effort to include this story within their interpretation at the park (nor had Philadelphia and Pennsylvania officials before that time, when they were in control of the site) because that story, in Ogline's words, was "considered irrelevant to the park's primary narratives."[18] Even then, park officials knew that to acknowledge Washington's actions, as well as other stories of slavery within the park's sites, would be incommensurate with the scenes of American heritage crafted throughout INHP.

Yet, to the then park superintendent's chagrin, local African American activists and politicians, historians both near and far, and members of the Independence Hall Association (a nonprofit entity that monitors how the park is managed) coalesced to suggest that INHP make a different kind of place on Independence Mall and, in so doing, make a bigger place for African Americans in the nation's commemorative landscape. Operating relatively autonomously, each of these groups agitated for recognition of the President's House within INHP. A collection of prominent historians banded together as the Ad Hoc Historians to raise public awareness of the site and to urge NPS historians in Washington, D.C., to intervene. Philadelphia-area African Americans founded two groups, Generations Unlimited and Avenging the Ancestors Coalition (ATAC); the latter, founded by the Philadelphia attorney Michael Coard, became the more prominent of the two because of its multi-faceted advocacy efforts, including staged protests in the park, collection of petition signatures, and lobbying of elected officials in city, state, and federal government. The Independence Hall Association (IHA) developed a website to catalog the controversy and invited outraged citizens to sign an online petition. Philadelphia's media were drawn to the controversy, as were national media outlets such as the Associated Press, *New York Times, Washington Post, Los Angeles Times, Chicago Tribune, Baltimore Sun, Seattle Times,* and *Milwaukee Journal Sentinel.*

As the controversy exploded, INHP staff received pressure from higher-ranking NPS officials, especially Chief Historian Dwight Pitcaithley, to engage rather than ignore the individuals and groups eager to be heard on the subject of slavery at the President's House. At the same time as Lawler's article was being published and distributed, Marie Rust, who was serving as director of the Northeast Region of the NPS (and therefore supervising the staff at INHP), was leading efforts to encourage the integration of citizen participation at park sites and to diversify the stories told within the parks. The result of her work to make a place for citizen participation in park management became known as the Park Service's Civic Engagement Initiative, which later led to significant community participation in the development of the President's House site.

That participation, of course, was generated for a number of other reasons beyond the site's status as the home of Presidents George Washington and John Adams. First, the arguments about whether and how to acknowledge the house and all its residents highlighted the fact that the U.S. commemorative landscape had long failed to make a place for both slavery and the contributions of the enslaved and their ancestors. The President's House was not just a site where two presidents and nine enslaved African resided; it was also a place that represented the nation's ongoing failure to come to terms with its racial history. Public history generally, argued Derek Alderman, has engaged in "marginalizing if not altogether ignoring the memories, contributions and struggles of African Americans."[19]

The near-absence of African American history from the commemorative landscape is only one part of a larger pattern of the historical exclusion of black Americans from public places. "Slavery," observed the historian Eric Foner, "rendered blacks all but invisible to those imagining the American community."[20] Knowing "their place," in fact, was used as a none-too-subtle code in Reconstruction-era rhetoric to continue the exclusion of black Americans from public life.[21] Nearly a century later, Ralph Ellison confirmed that being black in America still meant being invisible in public places. Whether through Jim Crow laws, violent responses to nonviolent public protests during the civil rights movement, or contemporary phenomena such as "Driving While Black," the descendants of the enslaved have been told to avoid many public places.

Considered in this context, the President's House offered an opportunity to make a place for African American history squarely in the middle of the story of America's founding—an even more potent possibility for recognition than the one that occurred during the controversy surrounding what is now the African Burial Ground National Monument in New York City. There advocates sought recognition of the humanity and economic contributions of the enslaved. In Philadelphia, advocates also had the opportunity to make a place for African Americans in the heart of America's political and philosophical narrative.[22]

Second, the vociferous response from prominent African American leaders in Philadelphia, such as Coard, not only underscored the general unhappiness about the small presence of black Americans in the commemorative landscape; it also illuminated long-standing local tensions. Although "for two generations after the Revolution, Philadelphia was the largest and most important center of free black life in the United States," white residents of the city also increasingly excluded their black counterparts from public spaces during this time period.[23] This process of exclusion continued throughout the 1800s, as W. E. B. DuBois observed in his extensive 1890s investigation of black life in Philadelphia,[24] and throughout the following century. The federal government's 1974 takeover of Independence Mall, whose creation displaced a large number of black Philadelphia residents from the city's center, added a further layer of separation between the city's African American residents and the city's core. Even though INHP held historic structures still owned by the city, many black Philadelphians felt as if the site was in another world.

Thus, the President's House was not just a site in a national historical park; it was also a place that exemplified the ways in which local African Americans felt disenfranchised. A 1994 ethnographic assessment of local groups' impressions of the park confirmed that African Americans "saw a lack of their cultural representation in the park's official history." One black Philadelphia resident observed, "So much for them (tourists, white people) and so little for us (African Americans, working-class neighborhood residents)."[25] INHP's initial response to Lawler's findings so irked local African Americans that Philadelphia mayor John F. Street showed up the park by announcing, at the grand opening of the LBC no less, that the city would contribute $1.5 million toward building a commemorative installation at the site. The President's House controversy thus also pivoted around local African Americans' desire to make a bigger place for the black community within the white-hued confines of INHP.[26]

Third, the intense national reactions surrounding any decision regarding the site backlit the fact that the United States is undergoing inexorable demographic changes in which white residents will soon no longer constitute a majority of the population. In May 2012, the U.S. Census Bureau announced that as of July 2011 over half the members of the nation's population under one year of age were minorities.[27] Then, one year later, the bureau revealed that in 2012 white deaths outnumbered white births in the United States, an unprecedented development. "We're jumping the gun on a long, slow decline of our white population, which is going to characterize this century," William Frey, a Brookings Institution demographer told the *Washington Post*. "It's a bookend from the last century, when whites helped us grow. Now it's minorities who are going to make the contributions to our economic and population growth over the next 50 years."[28] The President's House was not just a site where historical events and figures could be acknowledged; it was also a place where a battle for the nation's future identity would be fought. These battles reflect "the shifting dynamics of the national narrative, of who 'counts' in the unfolding of American history, whose story is most important, who is telling the tale."[29] In short, as Foner asked in the title of his book, the question becomes, "Who owns history?"[30]

In this respect, the President's House controversy represented a widespread concern about how places were going to be made for all Americans in the shaping of the nation's identity. "Debates over American identity," asserted James Oliver Horton and Lois E. Horton, "are often characterized by issues of race and shaped by the urge to forget slavery's long and critically influential history."[31] Thus, for many African Americans, the President's House dispute served as a new test of the nation's willingness to enact its long-stated creed of equality and to face up to its hypocritical embrace of slavery. Would INHP and the NPS acknowledge Washington's duplicity? Would the lives of nine enslaved Africans be recognized in a national historical park where a shining story of liberty enacted is told? In short, would the federal government make a place for an African American narrative? At the same time, for individuals uncertain about the evolving stories and demographics of the United States, the President's House controversy served as a test of the nation's ability to envision itself as a particular kind of country in the face of growing challenges to its traditions. Would Washington's reputation be stained? Would the founding narrative of the nation be threatened? And, most pointedly, would the site of the home of the nation's first two presidents be turned into a slave memorial? In short, would the "cradle of liberty" be redefined, and thus change the traditional story of the United States of America?[32]

Thus, while Lawler's archival excavation unearthed an opportunity to add the presence of the executive branch to INHP, it also revealed long-buried issues about selective storytelling across the commemorative landscape, a city's lack of control of its own core, and a nation's changing identity. The emergence of the President's House reminded us that "no heritage discourse or moment of heritage is necessarily uniformly shared or homogenously constructed; rather, there are always elements of dissent and challenge, and thus the possibility of change within it."[33] For African Americans (not to mention social historians), the President's House offered the possibility of making black history a fundamental part of the nation's founding and development. Such an opportunity was especially tantalizing because, as Nathan Glazer has argued, the United States has been unable or unwilling "to incorporate into its society African Americans, in the same way and to the same degree that it has incorporated so many groups."[34] At the same time, of course, the President's House—as situated in INHP—was perhaps one of the least likely sites at which to attempt this task. "For many Americans," reminded Clarence Lusane in his *The Black History of the White House*, "it is an act of unacceptable subversion to criticize the nation's founders, the founding documents, the presidency, the president's house, and other institutions that have come to symbolize the official story of the United States."[35]

The President's House thus emerged into a murky commemorative landscape, one filled with the shadows of untold stories of bondage, the enduring appeal of a narrative of a noble nation, and a profound uncertainty about how to deal with the contradiction between the two. Given this context, the opening of the President's House commemorative installation on December 15, 2010, represented quite an achievement. "This choice, to foreground the history of slavery, at a federal monument no less, and within just steps of the

Liberty Bell and Independence Hall," wrote the Temple University historian Seth Bruggeman, "surely ranks among the most significant in the history of American public memory."[36] So how did it happen? I answer that question in the pages that follow. Relying on interviews with principal participants and visitors to the completed site, internal documents gathered through both a Freedom of Information Act (FOIA) request and my own expedition in the INHP archives, media coverage thoroughly catalogued and housed on the IHA website, and a wide-ranging reading of scholarship in public memory, I outline how—from beginning to end—a place was made on Independence Mall. This place, whether known by its formal name (The President's House: Freedom and Slavery in the Making of a New Nation), its shorthand appellation (the President's House), or the name preferred by Coard (the Slavery Memorial), illustrates how a place of public memory is the location of discourses and histories present and absent, immediate and distant, past and future.

As I share the story of the making of the President's House, I begin by explaining in Chapter 2 how we can appreciate the variety of perspectives and investments that people bring to places of public memory. This approach, which I have dubbed *re-collection,* recognizes that the work of remembering is done not simply through commemorative markers of some sort but by the people who experience those places of memory. Moreover, because those people bring both shared and disparate experiences with them to the memory site, they are bound to make different kinds of sense of the site. In other words, the President's House—and other places in the commemorative landscape—does not possess a singular meaning; it means different things to different people.

In Chapter 3, I continue the discussion I initiated in this chapter by explaining why the President's House mattered so much to so many people. In so doing, I first outline how the development of INHP marked it as a unique and special place in the commemoration of the founding of the United States as a land of liberty. The amount of intellectual energy and public resources poured into the park over the years makes sense when INHP is considered a place, perhaps *the* place, to remember the birth of the ideas that have formed the foundation of the nation's identity. On the other hand, when viewed from the perspective of those whose stories have been systematically excluded from public recognition over the generations, the revelation that enslaved Africans were held by the father of our country on the same block where the Liberty Bell, inscribed with "proclaim LIBERTY throughout all the land unto all the inhabitants thereof," was housed was cause for the release of years of pent-up anger. As these conflicting stories emerge in Chapter 3, the complexity of remembering at the President's House becomes especially vivid.

The next four chapters of this book represent four distinct stages in the making of the President's House. Chapter 4 explains how advocates for the President's House, especially those who wanted to mark it as a site where white Americans enslaved black Africans, offered public arguments that INHP ultimately could not defuse. As this chapter illustrates, those seeking to change the character of INHP by acknowledging the role of slavery and the actions of the enslaved within the nation's development ultimately relied on arguments that *embraced* the stories told by the park. That chapter concludes with the decision to build a commemorative installation on the site, and the next chapter points out the difficulties in making a place that would satisfy everyone invested in the project. Specifically, Chapter 5 reviews how five semi-finalist designs envisioned the President's House installation and how the designs were assessed by those who encountered them. This chapter demonstrates that the story of the President's House is not entirely black and white; instead, it contains a variety of perspectives—many of them indeed informed by race— about what we should remember and how we should remember it.

Chapter 6 then illuminates the astonishing (and temporary) convergence of those perspectives after an excavation of the site unexpectedly revealed the foundation remains of the kitchen where the enslaved chef Hercules worked, an underground passageway to the main building, and the bow window that Washington had installed in the dining room (and which likely served as the inspiration for the Oval Office). The viewing platform at which hundreds of thousands of people converged became the most powerful place in the entire saga of the President's House and prompted a redesign of the installation. As Chapter 7 points out, this moment was the only time when widespread agreement emerged at the site. After funds were secured to integrate the foundation remains in a revised design, new battles were engaged as the interpretive material for the site was developed and then finalized. Not surprisingly, when the completed commemoration opened, the disagreements continued; the President's House, like any memory site, could not sufficiently contain all that people wanted to remember.

Perhaps, though, as the final chapter ponders, the story of the President's House provides us with the wisdom to recognize the ways in which our own preferences and perspectives color our judgments about how we continue to engage the difficult memories of slavery and race in the United States. The President's House installation is, I conclude, far from perfect, but its lessons offer a means of continuing the dialogue. More specifically, it reminds us that, as the editors of an oral history of enslaved Africans remarked, "the historical memory of slavery remains central to Americans' sense of themselves and the society in which they live."[37]

2

Re-collecting the Past

The Complexity of Public Memory

I don't make objects; I make places. . . . The places set a stage for experience and for understanding experience.[1]

begin this chapter with Maya Lin's statement because both her words and her most famous creation, the Vietnam Veterans Memorial, vividly illustrate how we make places of public memory in many ways. Lin's masterpiece, initially designed while she was still an undergraduate at Yale University, was made not just by her but also by the individuals and entities who selected, funded, supported, and tinkered with her design. The legislative and executive branches of the federal government contributed to the process by making a place for the memorial amid the celebratory structures on Washington Mall. And, as Lin's words indicate, those who experience the place make their own meaningful version of it as they engage the site within a context of personal, cultural, historical, and physical landscapes. Not just one type of place, in other words, is made when a place of public memory takes shape.

To understand the story of how the President's House has been made, then, requires a longer explanation of what I mean by the idea of making places of public memory. Let me begin by providing an example of how a different type of public memory place was made, and how two insightful scholars recognized that focusing on only the physical installation hinders our ability to understand the experience of those who make the place meaningful.

In 1991, President George H. W. Bush dedicated the Astronauts Memorial (now known as the Space Mirror Memorial) at Kennedy Space Center's Visitor Complex (KSCVC). The memorial, which lists the names of all U.S. astronauts who lost their lives on NASA missions, consists of a large, rectangular surface composed of black granite that—thanks to a white corkscrew-and-jack contraption at the base of the memorial—follows the sun's path so that the sun's rays reflect off mirrors to illuminate the names of the deceased astronauts, carved through the black granite slab, throughout the day. Shortly after the president's dedication of the memorial, public memory scholars Carole Blair and Neil Michel undertook three journeys to the site over the course of eighteen days. Moved by the symbolic power of the memorial's design, Blair and Michel praised the site: "It incites contemplation and thoughtfulness rather than decreeing preferred attitudes. It allows for different, even contradictory, answers to the questions it raises, but it indeed does raise compelling issues, about relationships of the deceased astronauts to the living, the future of the space program, and the values and dangers of technology."[2]

This brief summary, of course, does not do justice to Blair and Michel's thoughtful and detailed analysis of the symbolic dimensions of the memorial. It also, as they reflected, did not capture how other visitors to the memorial experienced the installation. "We watched and listened to literally thousands of visitors," they wrote, "and the character and consistency of their reaction (or, more precisely, their lack of reaction) took us by surprise."[3] Specifically, the tourists who visited the site seemed to ignore the gigantic slab of black granite tilted toward the sun. "The few visitors who sat down on the benches on the landing were more interested in discussing a film they had just seen, what time their tour bus was scheduled to leave, the weather, or their fatigue than to attending to the Memorial immediately in front of them."[4] As scholarly critics of public memory places, Blair and Michel found themselves facing a conundrum: should they proceed with their analysis even though others clearly did not share their enthusiasm for the memorial? "We found it very difficult to ignore our reservations, not only because we were curious but also because it seemed so utterly dishonest to pronounce on a public memorial's appropriateness and symbolic virtuosity when we were perfectly well aware that it did not hold similar allure for its public."[5]

Puzzled by the incongruity between the visitors' lack of interest and their scholarly unpacking of the memorial's symbolic power, Blair and Michel tried to make sense of this disconnect rather than plow ahead to write only their critical insights. Their first conclusion? They were odd. Actually, a colleague helpfully pointed this fact out to them. "As one of our colleagues observed astutely, after reading an earlier draft of this essay, 'How many regular tourists stand around for hours looking carefully at inscriptions, thinking about the angle of the object, noting its placement, geography [and] cant . . . ? Face it, you two are odd viewers.'"[6]

Undoubtedly, every scholar who seeks to unpack layers of meaning embedded in places whose appearances are thoughtfully designed and whose inscriptions are carefully worded will likely provide odd or atypical explanations. I came to such a realization about the same time as Blair and Michel were writing, although my work at the time was focused more on places suggested in popular culture narratives than on places of public memory. I asked myself: "How do I know that anyone else understands this set of stories in the same way that I do?" I didn't—and that bothered me. Certainly, the informed, thoughtful, and analytical judgments of trained critics are valuable and necessary; at the least, they prompt those reading their work to think more reflectively about the subjects tackled by the critic.[7] Like Blair and Michel, I "remain convinced that the written, critical performance resulting from a critic's 'odd viewership' is important"—yet I also agree with them that if such work offers "inattention to [others'] experience and reception, it will be trapped in the dilemma of either rendering such a dubious conflation [of the critic's and others' responses] or having little or nothing to say about what discourse does."[8]

Blair and Michel's experiences also provided me, and other scholars of public memory places, with another valuable lesson: places are permeable. In other words, while we like to think of such sites as material containers housing discrete and bounded symbolic phenomena, most of these places can best be understand in relation to the surrounding landscapes that penetrate their borders. For Blair and Michel, that meant an excursion to Disney World. After observing that a number of visitors to KSCVC sported attire adorned with Disney characters, they talked with the KSCVC's then director of marketing, who confirmed that most of the people attending KSCVC had earlier visited Disney World in nearby Orlando. Comparing their experiences in Walt Disney World (WDW) with those at KSCVC, Blair and Michel believed that they had found an answer to their puzzle. In short, they argued, "KSCVC perpetuates WDW's rhetoric, coaxing visitors to remain immersed within the vista of efficiently fun, safe, technologically enabled happy endings."[9] As a result, when the migrants from Disney World encountered the Space Mirror Memorial, "the most comfortable position for visitors [was] to simply avert attention, to retain the considerable rewards offered by the other attractions, and to allow themselves to be distracted or distanced from the text of the Space Mirror."[10]

After reading Blair and Michel's exceptional piece of scholarship, I felt emboldened. I was not alone in thinking that my critical insights, while worthy of sharing publicly, could somehow provide richer and potentially more fulfilling answers to the question that has long driven my research into what I've come to call "places that matter"—if I also placed my insights into conversation with the experiences of others who engaged places in less "odd" ways. That question is, simply, What does this place mean? The answers to that singular question are, of course, plural because we make different sorts of meanings out of the same physical installations.

In the intervening years, I've discovered sympathetic and, from my perspective, compelling arguments from others in my home field of rhetorical studies. Carroll Arnold, inspired by the thinking of Henry Johnstone, suggested that rhetorical scholars "shift the focus of [their] analytical attention from the *structures of messages* to the nature of *self-rhetoric* made *about* messages."[11] That is, as in the Reader Response movement in literature,[12] Arnold argued that rhetorical scholars should focus on meanings not as they are suggested by a message but as they are made by those who attend to the message. More recently, Edward Schiappa argued that—absent the voices of others who also experienced popular culture narratives—critics of such texts should not presume to think that their impressions are widely shared.[13] Michael Middleton, Samantha Senda-Cook, and Danielle Endres have employed the phrase *rhetorical field methods* to describe work that shared both a critic's attention to the text and a qualitative scholar's devotion to discerning the experiences of others.[14]

I have since proposed, while working with some creative and thoughtful graduate students in a seminar on public memory places, a more concrete and discrete way of seeking answers to the question "What kinds of places are made at sites of public memory?" This approach, which I've termed *re-collection*, is inspired by Blair and Michel's work at the Space Mirror Memorial and offers an extension of the ideas they provide in the conclusion of their work. In brief, re-collection is both an account of and a method for understanding how meanings are generated in places of public memory as visitors to those places bring their experiences into their encounters with sites that are themselves embedded with symbols and vulnerable to the importation of other symbols from surrounding landscapes. As a result, my investigation of the President's House site was not exclusively focused on the site itself or on the experiences of those who engaged the installation. Instead, I approached the site with an eye toward understanding the meanings generated by *persons-with/in-places*.[15]

My conceptualization of *persons-with/in-places* recognizes that *both* persons *and* places interact within the complex process of meaning-making at memory sites. Each physical site holds a rich collection of symbolic representations of the past and suggests their relevance to the present, just as those of us who visit the site bring with us our own assemblage of understandings and expectations about how the past should be remembered and used. Moreover, material structures, powerful cultural symbols, and compelling personal and group memories converge in ways that also draw on the landscapes surrounding the site. All told, then, the meanings of memory places emerge from the evocative interplay of the cognitive, kinetic, and sensuous experiences of those who encounter the site *and* through a process in which those individual experiences occur within, and thus are influenced by, the intersecting elements of the design of the memory site, its surrounding environs, and the individual's prior experiences.[16]

Attending to these interrelationships is vital because the designers of public memory places *intend* to move those who visit the sites.[17] Indeed, a significant element of the power of memory sites derives from what Carole Blair, Greg Dickinson, and Brian Ott call visitors' affective investments in the ideas they find represented in the memory places;[18] those investments are located not solely within the memory place but *within the humans who are moved, and touched,* by the stories told, the artifacts displayed, and/or the opportunities provided to engage the stories and artifacts while experiencing the sensuous dimensions of the site.[19] Perhaps the most exemplary memory site in this regard is the Vietnam Veterans Memorial. As several scholars have observed, the memorial evokes profound emotional responses from many of those who visit,[20] so much so that the more than *one hundred thousand* items that have been left at the wall are now stored in a Landover, Maryland, warehouse.[21]

Our work, as the producers of meaning with/in places of public memory, is akin to the bystander who encounters boxes of puzzle pieces strewn across the landscape. We *re-collect* the pieces in ways that make sense to us; we make our own places from the resources available to us. I am drawn to the label *re-collection* to describe my approach because it represents both a process and a product; in other words, through a process of *re*-collecting from among the fragments of memory that circulate through our experiences at a memory site, we generate a recollection of what the past means in that place. In addition, the term implies an ongoing process of negotiating our relationships with the past generally and places of public memory in particular. Barbie Zelizer's descriptions of remembering and recollection have been especially helpful as I've formulated this idea. She wrote: "Recollection is the act of establishing a relationship with some event, issue, or entity of the past," and "Remembering is a processual action by which people constantly transform the recollections that they produce."[22] Zelizer's words underscore both the dynamic and diverse nature of re-collection. Even though the designers of a place of public memory seek to tell a particular story about the past, we possess—and embrace—the opportunity to tell ourselves our own stories in relation to the history acknowledged with/in the site.

As we make these places through what I'm calling re-collection, we simultaneously sift through three collections of pieces. First, we encounter the physical place of public memory as a rich repository of symbols or as a place that was made by designers and contractors. Second, we attend to the ways in which the physical place of public memory contains traces of other landscapes as well, or as a place that becomes meaningful within the contexts that surround it. Third, we bring to bear our own experiences—both prior to our experience at the site and while we engage the site—as we make the site meaningful within our horizons of understanding. As I describe each of these collections of pieces in more detail, I do so with the understanding that we are typically not all that aware of how we are re-collecting.

Places of Public Memory Are Rich Repositories of Symbols

In much the same way that our personal memories require containers such as scrapbooks, photo albums, and shadow boxes, the memories that we share with others in public also need containers to house them. "Every collective memory unfolds within a spatial framework," argued collective memory pioneer Maurice Halbwachs. "Each group cuts up space in order to compose . . . a fixed framework within which to enclose and retrieve its remembrances."[23] Those places—be they museums, monuments, memorials, or markers—are thoughtfully designed and constructed in order to *suggest* meanings.[24] The individuals and firms that design these places, and the private and governmental entities that sponsor them, make choices about color, shape, size, access, media, language, and so forth as they decide how to shape the site.

Each of these design elements offers dazzlingly diverse possibilities of meaning; in concert, those possibilities are multiplied. As they considered the Space Mirror installation, for example, Blair and Michel found a complex conglomeration of symbols embedded within the installation's use of black and white in its technological apparatuses. "The black face of the Mirror," they proposed, "may be read as symbolizing either humanity or morality, in contrast to the white mechanism on its backside that can be taken to represent technology."[25] As they considered the combinations of possible meaning suggested by the confluence of black-white symbolism in a memorial that both represents technology and *is* technology in operation, Blair and Michel called the installation "an engaging set of puzzles . . . [about] the relationships of death, humanity, and technology."[26] The Space Mirror, they initially concluded, did not provide an explicitly clear meaning for its visitors; rather, it offered questions to consider.

Those questions, as well as the musings generated by other memory sites, may also pivot around what is *not present* within the site. Just as scrapbook creators have limitations regarding page size, number of pages, and their own interests in choosing what to remember, memory sites are limited by both the dimensions of the container and the perspectives of their designers and sponsors. When multiple entities are involved in the design and installation of a place of public memory, such as the Vietnam Veterans Memorial and the Korean War Veterans Memorial on the Washington Mall, those perspectives may clash and eventually produce sites that make many of the invested developers unhappy.[27] Fittingly, Marita Sturken argued that the Vietnam Veterans Memorial wall serves as a dual-purpose *screen* in that it both projects memories for visitors while filtering other discursive fragments of memory out of the memorial (e.g., the deaths of residents of Vietnam and other Southeast Asian nations during the war).[28]

Typically, public memory scholars define this dichotomy of inclusion (making present) and exclusion (making absent) as remembering and forgetting, although—as I illustrate in more detail in later chapters—absence does not necessarily mean forgetting.[29] The material absence of these stories from the U.S. commemorative landscape underscores, as noted earlier, the *partiality* of remembering. Every container of memory is insufficient for holding everything that could be remembered about the person, event, thing, and so on. "No single memory contains all that we know, or could know, about any given event, personality, or issue," asserted Zelizer in outlining one of public memory's fundamental assumptions.[30] Decisions about what to include and exclude *must* be made. Those decisions are incomplete and selective, yet the implied permanence and authority stamped on every memory site suggest a misleading wholeness about the place. Accordingly, Zelizer continued, we would do well to remember that "collective memories help us fabricate, rearrange, or omit details from the past *as we thought we knew it*."[31]

In this respect, as I've noted, places of public memory are partial in a second sense: they provide an account of the past that reflects a particular perspective or perhaps bias. Eugene Victor Walter labeled this process, in his discussion of places in general, the doctrine of selective support: "We build the world we suppose by expressing or suppressing specific features of experience."[32] *Any* place, not just a place of public memory, is designed and constructed by individuals and entities to achieve particular ends.[33] All places, including places of public memory, are configured in particular ways for particular purposes, typically involving an attempt to control the experiences of those who navigate within them.[34] Within memory sites, especially, our attention should be drawn to how "the geography of these places also nominates for public audiences very particular views of which people and events of the past are most worthy of memory."[35]

This twofold sense of partiality provides us with much symbolic grist to mill. No wonder, then, that places of public memory such as museums, monuments, and memorials have drawn a great deal of interest from scholars across a wide array of academic disciplines beyond my home field of communication, including American studies, art history, environmental psychology, geography, history, and sociology, to name a few of the more prominent.[36] The focal point of all these efforts is typically, and understandably, the memory site itself. The material and symbolic riches available in these sites provide us with more than enough raw material for a journal-length article, so communication scholars alone have explored everything from the memory site–filled Washington Mall area (e.g., the U.S. Holocaust Memorial Museum, the display of the AIDS Quilt, the National World War II Memorial, controversies over a single exhibit at the U.S. National Air and Space Museum) to the ways in which neighborhoods and communities commemorate the past (e.g., the Harlem music scene, roadside shrines, the naming of streets).[37]

At the same time, they are permeable containers that inevitably admit even more meaningful fragments into their locations. Rather than treat a place of public memory as what Blair and Michel call "an unproblematic container," then, we must also attend to how the landscapes surrounding it seep into the site—just as the Space Mirror, at the least, cannot be considered apart from the landscapes that surround it, including both the KSCVC environs and the larger theme park landscape of central/coastal Florida.[38] Sites, in short, "cannot be understood as inert matter. . . . [T]he features of one site will always implicate another."[39]

Places of Public Memory Contain Traces of Other Landscapes

"Our epoch," observed Michel Foucault, "is one in which space takes for us the form of relations among sites."[40] Edward Casey, who waxed perhaps a bit too enthusiastically in his humanizing of places, nonetheless made an excellent point when he asserted that "minimally, places gather things in their midst—where 'things' connote various animate and inanimate entities. Places also gather experiences and histories, even languages and thoughts."[41] Walter referred to this process as the doctrine of mutual immanence, which "includes all the effective presences influencing one another that abide together in a place."[42] Thus, much as a novel contains traces of different voices through its characters, genre, and setting, a single memory place contains a number of different voices; it is what the Russian literary scholar Mikhail Bakhtin called *polyphonic*, or many-voiced.[43]

Interestingly, the presence of other voices in a memory site can often be ascertained by absences. Just as Blair and Michel discovered that the theme park landscape of central Florida was present in the KSCVC through their initial observation that the Space Mirror was absent from the attention of most visitors, the traces of other landscapes may not always manifest themselves directly and/or concretely in the physical landscape of the memory site. Yet, as Blair and Michel illustrated, the traces of theme park landscapes— from the attire of many of the KSCVC visitors to the displays at the KSCVC installations surrounding the Space Mirror—were present within the physical borders of the memorial, which is why "the analysis of a specific site deepens when it is considered in relation to its spatial milieu."[44] In fact, Greg Dickinson, Brian Ott, and Eric Aoki argue that memory sites are best understood "as constitutive elements of landscapes [rather] than as discrete texts."[45] In the following paragraphs, I point to two types of landscapes whose presence is implicated in any place of public memory: the *physical*, or spatial, landscape and the *historical*, or temporal, landscape. Both of these landscapes help make the memory site, but not always in the most direct or material way.

The Physical Landscape

Visiting a place of public memory requires travel, and travel demands that we enter and move through a variety of landscapes on our way to the memory site. "The experience of museums and memorials does not begin at their entrances," noted Dickinson, Ott, and Aoki. "Visitors must travel to these sites, which are often surrounded by other historical or tourist sites."[46] The terrain immediately contiguous to the memory place is the most apparent landscape that can seep into the site. Sociologists Robin Wagner-Pacifici and Barry Schwartz introduced the idea of a "discursive surround" to demonstrate how the meanings of the Vietnam Veterans Memorial are inextricably linked to the discursive fragments of memory found not just in the memorial site itself but throughout the Washington Mall.[47] Given that visitors to the memorial would undoubtedly have already encountered these surrounding memory sites, whether in person on the same excursion or through mediated forms of some sort, they would bring traces of those physical sites with them as they experienced the wall. Indeed, much of the controversy surrounding Maya Lin's original design for the memorial emanated from its difference from the other memory sites on the Washington Mall (its black color, V shape, and listing of the dead, to name but a few)—so much so, in fact, that an addition to the site was commissioned: a bronze statue of three heroic male soldiers, which was installed near a pole flying the American flag.

Even when the surrounding terrain is not composed of other memory sites, the features of the nearby landscapes may well flow into the place of public memory. Antietam National Battlefield in Maryland, for example, is ensconced within a largely rural landscape that undoubtedly flavors one's experience with those sites. In my visit to Antietam, I was more easily able to imagine the battle scenes, and to be shocked by the scale of the carnage, thanks to the stillness and seeming emptiness of the surrounding landscape. The physical landscape in this case allowed me to focus more concretely on the events acknowledged within the site. In a slightly different vein, Manzanar National Historic Site—the location of one of the euphemistically labeled War Relocation Centers used by the U.S. government to imprison American citizens and immigrants of Japanese ancestry during World War II—lies at the bottom of a valley, a fitting parallel to the shameful treatment of human beings who were held against their will within the site. Moreover, the depth of the valley is due, to some extent, to the nearby presence of the Sierra Nevada, including Mount Williamson, which gives Manzanar an oddly Japanese feel as well, given the iconic Mount Fuji's prominence in the Japanese national landscape.

While these examples point to the largely immediate and contiguous physical landscapes that orbit places of public memory, they also remind us of the cultural meanings embedded within these surrounding landscapes. Blair and Michel's discovery that the theme park landscape of central Florida oozed into the coastal location of the KVCSC is, of course, a prime example of how physical landscapes also contain cultural meanings. The discursive surround of the Washington Mall, too, ensures that themes of patriotism and reverence seep into every memory site located within and near the enormous swath of territory marked by the mall. Similarly, Dickinson, Ott, and Aoki argued that one's encounter with the set of museums at the Buffalo Bill Historical Center in Cody, Wyoming, cannot help but be shaped by the experience of approaching those museums by driving through landscapes seemingly lifted from western films, and by the cultural associations embedded in those films.

The place of a particular memory site, then, hosts not only the symbols of the site itself but also the symbolic resources of the spaces surrounding the place. As these fragments converge within the place of public memory, they are also joined by voices from the near and distant past—for any memory site is also the gathering place for stories collected over time.

The Historical Landscape

In choosing to remember an event or person in a particular place, we are also encouraged to draw on the histories and stories associated with that event or person as we make sense of the place. The interpretive material available at the site, the inscriptions or printed language, and any tours provided all reference the historical activities recognized by the site. In addition, if we as visitors have any familiarity about the history recognized by the site, we bring traces of those understandings with us. My adult experience at the U.S.S. Arizona Memorial in Pearl Harbor, for instance, was informed by not only the history presented at the site but also what I had learned in school and even what I had remembered from the 1970 film *Tora! Tora! Tora!*, which I saw in the theater as a child. Thus, any current experience we have at the site is influenced by our understanding of how the place pulls in narratives relevant to its history.

Moreover, as much as the physical borders of the place of public memory may seem to contain the trove of possible histories that may be present within the site, the permeability of the installation allows other, less directly relevant, histories to intrude on the seemingly self-contained memory. While cataloging this vast swath of possibilities is perhaps impossible, we can briefly consider two ways in which other historical discourses might leak into a memory site. To begin, because most visitors to places of public memory are tourists, they bring with them understandings of history as it has been presented in other places (such as the movie theater). In her thorough exploration of how memory sites were experienced in Nuremberg, Germany, for example, Sharon Macdonald observed that "what happens locally does so in multiple intersections with various elsewheres. . . . How heritage is negotiated in Nuremberg is always, though to varying extents, conducted in relation to how heritage is done in other places."[48] This sense of meaning in relation to other places may take another form, such as when the historical discourse of one site prompts recollection of other histories; for example, a visit to the U.S.S. Arizona Memorial might prompt one to recall how the Japanese attack on Pearl Harbor triggered the internment of Japanese Americans in remote outposts throughout the western United States.

Finally, as Blair, Dickinson, and Ott pointed out, "Memory places themselves have histories."[49] Given that one of the foundational beliefs of public memory studies is that memory sites draw on the past to serve the needs of the present, we can assume that some sites will have served different purposes in the past, been renamed or otherwise altered to adapt to changing times, and/or constructed in response to existing memory sites as a type of counter-memorial. For example, the Lincoln Memorial has served as both a tribute to the deceased president and the site of civil rights performances,[50] the National Park Service changed the name of Custer Battlefield National Monument to Little Bighorn Battlefield National Monument, and the National World War II Memorial on the Washington Mall was developed and designed, at least in part, as a more celebratory counterpoint to the somber Vietnam Veterans Memorial.

Overall, the presence of traces of both physical and historical landscapes in a place of public memory ensures that an encounter with the site should not be reduced to an accounting of only the characteristics of the site itself. Instead, "monuments can be usefully known in relation to their connections with the ever-changing 'outside,' instead of being understood solely in terms of what is supposedly intrinsic and exclusively of the text."[51] Even then, however, academics such as me still run the risk of providing "odd" interpretations of a memory site simply because I enter the site having traveled not just *through* a physical landscape but *from* a *cultural landscape*—that of academia. I wonder, for example, what other visitors to the Space Mirror think of an installation that they do not pause to admire or discuss. Surely they must notice it. If they were asked about the memorial, would their responses confirm or complicate Blair and Michel's compelling argument that a theme park landscape permeates the site?

Given that the presence of cultural landscapes, such as academia or a theme park, is that much more difficult to notice within a place of public memory than a physical or historical landscape—each of us maintains innumerable, changing, and complex cultural affiliations—even a dedicated, thoughtful, and lengthy examination of the site may not reveal the rich tapestry of cultural perspectives we bring to bear in our experiences there. Ultimately, the meaning or meanings of a memory place lie not solely in the elements of the site itself, nor even in combination with the presence of surrounding historical and physical landscapes, but in how we sort through these two sets of symbols from the perspectives that accompany us on our travels to and through the site. Meanings, after all, are human creations; a place of public memory—indeed, every place of human experience—does not mean anything until *we* assign meaning to it. As D. W. Meinig argued, "Any landscape is composed not only of what lies before our eyes but what lies within our heads."[52]

Unfortunately, as several public memory scholars have noted, most approaches to the study of memory sites slight, or outright ignore, the experiences of those who engage the sites. "The actual experiences and perspectives of tourists who visit these sites are conspicuously absent in these studies," complained the anthropologist Joy Sather-Wagstaff.[53] "Collective memory studies have also not yet paid enough attention to the problem of reception both in terms of methods and sources," echoed the historian Wulf Kansteiner.[54] With these thoughts in mind, along with the lessons of Blair and Michel's discoveries at the Space Mirror Memorial, let's turn to how we experience places of public memory—and make places filtered by the cultural landscapes from which we have traveled.

People Making Meanings

Decades ago, the distinguished communication theorist Sam Becker encouraged us to consider how our individual sense-making was influenced by our presence in what he called a communication mosaic, or the accumulated conglomeration of messages to which we had been exposed. "This mosaic consists of an immense number of fragments or bits of information on an immense number of topics," wrote Becker. "Each individual must grasp from this mosaic those bits which serve his needs."[55] These fragments could include interactions with others, memories of news reports, recollections of popular culture narratives, snippets of visual images, and the like. For instance, popular culture narratives—such as my imperfect recollections of *Tora! Tora! Tora!*—often contribute mightily, although not always accurately, to how we remember the past.[56] Or, as the anthropologists Eric Gable and Richard Handler noted, "collective memory (at least in the contemporary world) is fostered in socially complex interactions involving written documents and orally transmitted stories, occurring in a variety of contexts, from a sole individual reading a text, to a school group listening to a teacher tell historical stories, to a group of tourists experiencing three-dimensional but nonetheless 'documented' history at places like Colonial Williamsburg and then telling stories about those experiences."[57]

One of Becker's colleagues at the University of Iowa, Michael McGee, revisited Becker's idea almost twenty years later to provide a foundation for his argument that scholars of public communication should move away from their focus on studying texts such as speeches, images, and artifacts as containers of meaning and instead remember that "text construction is now something done more by the consumers than by the producers of discourse."[58] In McGee's approach, traditional texts should be considered "*ap-*

parently finished discourses" because they are seemingly self-contained but, in practice, are completed by individuals who finish, or make meaning from, the texts using their own interpretive practices. Both McGee and Becker emphasized that this consumer- or reception-oriented approach to meaning occurs within cultural contexts; in other words, our abilities to create meaning are constrained and influenced by the social and cultural situations that have shaped our understanding of the world.

Jean Nienkamp offered a compelling explanation of how this process involves both individual latitude and cultural constraint in her book *Internal Rhetorics.* Nienkamp proposed that each of us possesses a *rhetorical self* that manages a "repertoire of inner voices that people have to draw on at any particular time, in all situations, in their lives."[59] This "agora of the psyche" is the site in which we "work out which attitudes and actions [we] will take."[60] These internal deliberations are shaped by two sets of voices, one that constrains our options and another that provides us with a means of sorting through the available options. Nienkamp calls the former *primary internal rhetoric,* or the lifelong accumulation of "societal messages about whom we should be as teenagers, physical bodies, women or men, consumers, citizens, workers, and so forth," and the latter *cultivated internal rhetoric,* or a more conscious conversation in which we consider "certain values, interests, and behaviors over others."[61] Thus, while Nienkamp's formulation of the rhetorical self underscores an individual's unique capacity to make meanings out of what Becker and McGee call the communicative fragments we encounter, all three scholars point to the ways in which our accumulated interactions with others, occurring within social and cultural frameworks, both shape and limit our meaning-making capacities.

Practically speaking, how do we make places of public memory through our experiences? First, we uniquely experience a place of public memory within our social and cultural frameworks. What do we notice and how do we notice it? How do our places of orientation, developed over years of interactions and mediated encounters, contribute to our ways of noticing? Second, our individual experiences likely overlap and/or converge with others' experiences. The pioneer of collective memory studies, Maurice Halbwachs, asserted, "While the collective memory endures and draws strength from its base in a coherent body of people, it is individuals as group members who remember."[62] And, when we do remember together, not *everyone* in the same place will remember the same things or in the same ways together. Instead, the same place of public memory may contribute toward the formation of several groups remembering *distinctly* together.[63] Let's address these two elements of meaning-making in turn.

Individuals Experiencing Memory Places

"A place," claimed Walter, "is a location of experience. It evokes and organizes memories, images, feelings, sentiments, meanings, and the work of imagination."[64] In other words, we do not encounter memory places in a vacuum; we bring our personal histories with us. Environmental psychologists propose that we travel with our own cognitive maps, or spatial representations of our personal histories.[65] These personal maps, imprinted on our psyches, serve as guides for our life's travels and offer points of comparison when we find ourselves in new places. "There is for virtually everyone a deep association with and consciousness of the places where we were born and grew up, where we live now, or where we have had particularly moving experiences," noted Edward Relph, and "this association seems to constitute a vital source of both individual and cultural identity and security, a point of departure from which we orient ourselves in the world."[66] Indeed, in their national survey of Americans' uses of the past, Roy Rosenzweig and David Thelen discovered that we tend to think of historical events in our lifetimes in terms of personal, familial, or—in some cases—cultural group terms rather than as significant *national* events.[67] In a concrete illustration of this idea, Gable and Handler learned that visitors to Colonial Williamsburg engaged in memory practices that connected their experiences at the site to current family memories and/or to ancestors instead of to the historical information provided within the site.[68]

We also bring expectations with us, not the least of which is the anticipation of visiting someplace "special" and out of the ordinary. Such a touristic frame of reference, Blair, Dickinson, and Ott pointed out, "almost certainly predisposes to visitors" to frame the site "as worthy of attention, investment, and effort."[69] Of course, those expectations are no guarantee that our initial reaction to the site will be one of awe and/or reverence. As we approach, enter, and/or experience a site, we make what McGee called, in a reference to discourse in general, "snap judgments" about what we have encountered, beginning with an assessment of its relevance to our interests.[70]

Not all our reactions, however, are cognitive. While our minds work to *make sense* of memory places, our bodies primally *sense* and emotionally respond to the aesthetics and stories of the site. In fact, Kirk Savage pointed out, "national memorials are now expected to be spaces of experience, journeys of emotional discovery."[71] Blair's reflections about her visits to sites of memory, for example, vividly illustrated how the bodily experiences of being in, and moving through, these sites generated powerful emotional responses. She described her experience at the U.S. Holocaust Memorial Museum: "I felt exhausted, overwhelmed, resentful, and nearly frantic for some respite. . . .

The Museum is an ordeal, not just because of its collection or the story it tells (although, of course, those are devastating), but because of the dehumanizing force of its interior space on the body."[72]

Indeed, many newer memory sites, especially those that address events involving a traumatic experience of some sort, actively seek to generate profound emotional experiences. As the architect of the Flight 93 Memorial outside Shanksville, Pennsylvania, pronounced, "The Memorial should be quiet in reverence, yet powerful in form, a place both solemn and uplifting."[73] The Oklahoma City National Memorial and Museum's website proclaims: "We come here to remember those who were killed, those who survived and those changed forever. May all who leave here know the impact of violence. May this memorial offer comfort, strength, peace, hope and serenity."[74]

Visitors to memory sites such as these may also, of course, respond emotionally to the stories recognized at the site. Many of the visitors to Gettysburg National Military Park, for instance, "are profoundly aware of and disturbed by the carnage of the July campaign, and they respond to the site with emotion."[75] In fact, some people deliberately seek to visit sites that offer powerful emotional stories. Catherine Cameron and John Gatewood discovered that roughly one-fourth of the people they talked with at historical sites sought experiences that encouraged deep engagement, empathy for those acknowledged at the site, and awe or reverence.[76] To a large degree, such visitors use the place of memory as a portal to move imaginatively to the place in time remembered in the site.[77] In these cases, "space envelops the body, lifts it, and *moves* it," argued Savage. "The experience is not exactly in the realm of imagination or reason, but grounded in the felt connection of individual to collective body."[78] Savage's language reaffirms the emotional and embodied dimensions of memory sites, experiences that we encounter as individuals, yet his last phrase points to the fact that we also experience and make memory places *together*.

Individuals Experiencing Memory Places Together

Our individual experiences are, of course, intertwined with the experiences of others. Our cognitive maps contain memories of our interactions with others, our expectations about what the site will offer are embedded in our cultural understandings of what a memory site should be, and our physical experiences at the site are almost always in the company of others.[79] In addition, we bring established conceptions of our group identities with us; we share the site with others who may not be present but who share our outlooks and backgrounds. Or, as Blair, Dickinson, and Ott noted, we share *affiliations* with others;

each affiliation "produces, mediates, and sustains emotional connection[s]" with others and with the sites in which we envision ourselves together.[80] The rancher and anthropologist Keith Basso offered an exceptionally rich and thoughtful illustration of this process in his book *Wisdom Sits in Places*. Basso's examination of Western Apache memory places—which, unlike Anglo memory sites, are typically carved by Mother Nature rather than by human hands—revealed that the Western Apache tell stories about historical events that occurred near natural landmarks as a means of remembering how tribe members should act in contemporary times. "Such locations, charged as they are with personal and social significance, work in important ways to shape the images that Apaches have—or should have—of themselves."[81]

Basso's work not only underscores how memory sites provide the social glue that bonds cultural groups over time and across space; it also illustrates that a profound place of public memory for one group of individuals may mean much less—if anything at all—to another group of individuals (memory places are, of course, partial).[82] In the final chapter of his book, Basso related how an old cottonwood tree—which might be noticed, but certainly wouldn't be considered remarkable, by someone not affiliated with the tribe—is a crucial part of a Western Apache story about wisdom. Similarly, other, more formal, memory sites may be evaluated differently by individuals who hold dissimilar cultural affiliations. Tamar Katriel pointed out how Arab visitors to Israeli settlement museums took issue with the way in which stories about historical objects from the area were presented, while Bryan Hubbard and Marouf A. Hasian, Jr., documented how World War II veterans and historians clashed over the interpretation proposed for a display of the *Enola Gay* aircraft (which dropped the atomic bomb on Hiroshima) at the National Air and Space Museum.[83]

These examples, while illustrative, may also be misleading, for they can be taken to suggest, first, that the cultural groups existed *entirely* in that form before their members encountered the memory site, and second, that everyone within that group would possess the same perspective—in other words, that we can conceptualize groups solely in demographic terms. "Sociodemographics are largely irrelevant in the understanding of tourist experiences, at least at the park studied," asserted Richard Prentice, Stephen Witt, and Claire Hamer following their investigation of how visitors defined their experiences at a coal mining heritage park in northern England."[84] This discovery, I believe, is not unique to that single site, for any demographic group will contain individuals who see the world differently than some of their peers.

Although we imagine affiliations with different groups of others, and many of those others undoubtedly share demographic similarities with us, I find compelling Michael Warner's suggestion that we think of *publics* as entities addressed by discourse. "Publics differ from nations, races, professions, or any other groups that, though not requiring copresence, saturate identity," he asserted. "Publics do not exist apart from the discourse that addresses them."[85] In addition, and I take this idea up more fully in Chapter 5, I believe we may benefit from dividing those paying attention into multiple publics, depending on how they evaluate and interpret the discourse addressed to them.[86] Warner explained, in fact, that publics are organized not simply by attention to discourse but also by "preexisting forms and channels of circulation."[87]

The difference is perhaps best explained in terms of noun (*affiliation*) and verb (*affiliating*). Rather than think of my *affiliations* as Caucasian, male, white-collar, professor, rural, and so forth, I find myself *affiliating* with others on the basis of how we respond to the words, ideas, practices, and places we encounter. To return to Basso's example, not every Western Apache knew of the story associated with the cottonwood tree; despite their demographic similarity, they would not be part of the same public as those who embraced the story of wisdom in which the tree served an integral role, or even those who were aware of the story yet found it inapplicable to contemporary times. Similarly, Erika Doss outlined the variety of responses, many of them negative, among Native Americans to the Indian Memorial at what is now Little Bighorn Battlefield National Monument.[88]

Because places of public memory are inherently partial, the meaning of a memory site is far from consistent—either across time or across social space. In fact, the phrase "the meaning" is misleading, for memory sites will generate a number of meanings as we engage and experience their terrain; we bring different experiences, motivations, and perspectives to the site, each of which contributes to how we assign meaning to the site. In short, "a heritage site experience is not monolithic."[89] I would thus amend Paul Shackel's assertion—"Frequently there is not one agreed-on interpretation for the historical landscapes and monuments of America"[90]—by striking the word "frequently." As the historical landscape evolves over time, we gather new sets of stories about the past to draw on as we experience places of public memory. We thus "graft different historical narratives onto the memorial landscape over time."[91]

Even at the same moment in time, however, we can identify distinct publics through their expressed reactions to places of public memory. Although such evidence is typically collected from critics or news accounts to illustrate, rather than analyze, the contestability of a memory site's meaning, the backstage dramas involved in the development of the Vietnam Veterans Memorial highlight how one public's somber tribute to fallen soldiers may be another public's "gash of shame and sorrow."[92] More recently, in their revealing illustration of film critics' reactions to *The Green Mile,* A. Susan Owen and Peter Ehrenhaus identified three "communities of memory," each of which relied on different memories of race relations to interpret the historical fiction of the movie's narrative.[93] And, in his engaging analysis of community responses to a proposed slavery museum in Fredericksburg, Virginia, Stephen P. Hanna identified how different factions—some overtly focused on race, some not—emerged during the controversy.[94]

How might one identify communities of memory as their members experience places of public memory? Ideally, as Warner's ideas suggest, by their discourse; that is, what do people tell us about the memory site? These tellings can be noticed by means as subtle as Blair and Michel's observation of the apparel and actions of visitors to the Space Mirror or as direct as approaching visitors to ask for an interview. Thus, visitors who experience places of memory can tell us about their experience through their actions, words, or completion of surveys,[95] their sharing of stories,[96] and/or even their images of the place.[97] For example, Sather-Wagstaff investigated how visitors to the Twin Towers site in lower Manhattan remembered 9/11 by snapping pictures of the site, then talking to other visitors who were also taking photographs, and—in some cases—later conversing with them by e-mail.[98]

Undoubtedly, the nature of the memory place and the types of experience it offers will guide how one should most appropriately and respectfully collect visitor accounts. For example, those who visit the reconstructed site Colonial Williamsburg are not typically as emotionally invested as many of those who visit the Vietnam Veterans Memorial.[99] When visitors to a site are manifestly moved by their experience, one would not immediately approach them to request an interview. Instead, other means of noticing experiences and/or asking for feedback should be considered. No matter the situation, however, if we are to assert that places of public memory matter to those who visit them, we must seek ways of ascertaining how and why the place matters.[100] To that end, let me now turn to a brief description of how I approached my investigation of the President's House as a site of re-collection.

Re-collection at the President's House

The story of the President's House is firmly planted within the national commemorative landscape of the United States and its specific manifestation within INHP. We cannot identify the meanings of the President's House without knowing how the site fits (and does not fit) within those landscapes. Each of the chapters that follow, then, relies on—and occasionally revisits—

these two landscapes. In addition, because the meanings of the President's House are found among those who engaged its symbolic—and then physical—terrains, the remaining chapters in this book are built on the words and actions of those who felt compelled to speak about and/or encounter the installation. My approach was to draw on those words and actions, consider them within the landscapes that encroach on the site, and make sense of the communities of memory that are revealed by those words and actions.

More specifically, as shown in the next chapter, I listened to how those who worked within INHP described their mission, especially the task of interpreting the history embedded within the park's landscape. INHP's mission has changed over the years, as both the park's leadership and the NPS itself have changed, yet—as anyone associated with the park would acknowledge—INHP is like any commemorative site in that it does not have the space, financial resources, and personnel to tell every story connected to the park. At the same time, as the second half of the chapter illustrates, African American stories have long been excluded from both INHP and the U.S. commemorative landscape. Given this context, the President's House provided an opportunity to reassess how the story of the liberty in the United States was told.

3

Displacing the Inconvenient

The Incomplete Story of Liberty

That Lawler's work placed slavery on the threshold of the Liberty Bell's home seemed only fitting, for the bell's story serves as an apt metaphor for the nation's expedient embrace of slavery while proclaiming the idea of freedom. From the beginning, both the bell and the country contained a flaw that their makers toiled diligently to address; yet, in both cases, their efforts could not ultimately repair that which was undeniably present at their origins.

In 1751, Isaac Norris, the speaker of the Pennsylvania legislature, placed an order in England for a new bell for the steeple of the State House in Philadelphia. Unfortunately, when the iron bell arrived nearly a year later, it cracked during its first ringing. Today, returning flawed merchandise is a much easier task than it was in eighteenth-century Pennsylvania, especially when our products weigh a good deal less than one ton and do not have to be returned over three thousand miles by sea. In stepped two local foundry workers, John Stow and John Pass, who melted and then recast the bell, adding a bit of copper for (they hoped) additional strength. Unfortunately, their first attempt was also flawed. As Philadelphians gathered to hear the recast bell ring, "the hoped-for melodious sound that everyone anticipated instead registered as a discouraging thud."[1] Their second effort produced a better sound, and the bell served its purpose for many years, including ringing to announce the reading of the Declaration of Independence on July 8, 1776— at which time it most certainly did *not* crack.

While stories of the crack's origin abound, "the most reputable account is that the bell cracked [when it was rung] on Washington's birthday in 1843."[2] Three years later, the crack grew irreparably large while again being rung on Washington's birthday. Fittingly, the bell's last public ringing marked the birth of the man whose actions in the executive mansion delivered the story of slavery to the doorstep of the cradle of liberty more than two hundred years later. And also fittingly, in the decade before its cracking, the bell had become the symbol of the nation's abolitionists, who embraced the inscription ordered by Norris, "Proclaim Liberty throughout all the Land unto all the Inhabitants thereof," as well as the unstated remainder of the verse from Leviticus 25:10: "Ye shall return every man unto his possession, and ye shall return every man unto his family." That the nation could not enact this admonition was already apparent; when the bell split in the 1840s, it foreshadowed the nation's split shortly thereafter.

The full story of the Liberty Bell, which is now—along with Independence Hall—one of the two chief visitor attractions in INHP, would seem to fit well with the stories that Lawler unearthed about the President's House. Indeed, as the next chapter illustrates, historians were practically giddy about the prospect of telling these entwined stories at INHP. Yet, since its inception as a historic site in 1948, the park has told a much more selective and celebratory story about the bell, the idea of liberty, and their role in the nation's history. As this story has echoed throughout the park, textbooks, and the national consciousness, the stories of the roles played by enslaved Africans and their descendants have been nearly muted. To understand fully the conflict that emerged in INHP, one must know both the relatively short history of the park and the longer history of how African Americans have been excluded from public spaces in the United States generally and the U.S. commemorative landscape in particular.

The Story of Independence National Historical Park

The idea for what we now know as Independence National Historical Park was first proposed in 1928 by, of all people, a professor of hygiene at the University of Pennsylvania named Seneca Egbert. Although a number of civic groups had crafted, and would continue to craft, grand plans for developing the area around Independence Hall, the National Park Service acknowledges that Egbert seems to be the first person to have proposed the idea of a three-block mall stretching north of the hall. Twenty years and countless plans later, INHP was created through an act of Congress. At that time, INHP did not include the land area now covered by Independence Mall; instead, those three blocks (which included the site of the President's House) were developed by the city of Philadelphia and Commonwealth of Pennsylvania as Independence Mall State Park. Due to business, neighborhood, and political concerns, the construction of the mall proceeded slowly; another twenty years passed before the mall was completed in 1969. In 1974, administration of Independence Mall State Park was transferred from the Commonwealth of Pennsylvania to the NPS, and the land was integrated into INHP. In 1998, after construction bonds issued to fund the development of the mall were retired, the NPS purchased the land for one dollar.[3]

The change in ownership allowed the park to redesign the three blocks of the mall. Today, following that extensive makeover—which included the construction of a new home for the Liberty Bell, the new Independence Visitor Center, and the National Constitution Center (NCC), a park-affiliated, nonprofit entity—INHP is a sprawling fifty-five-acre set of twenty-one individual sites and four other NPS-affiliated sites, mostly concentrated in an L-shaped area in downtown Philadelphia. Independence Mall marks the vertical, or north/south, line of the L. The first block contains the Liberty Bell Center and the President's House site; the second block is home to the Visitor Center; and the third block houses the NCC. The park's prominent original structures, which, in addition to Independence Hall, include Congress Hall, Old City Hall, and the First and Second Banks of the United States, are largely located along the horizontal, or east/west, leg of the L (see Figure 3.1).

Without a doubt, most visitors to the park are drawn to Independence Hall, the Liberty Bell, and the National Constitution Center. While the new Visitor Center is understandably the most popular stop in the park, the LBC and Independence Hall attract by far the most visitors among the historic sites. During 2012, for example, 2 million of the 3.6 million people who visited the park during the year entered the Liberty Bell Center. Another 687,000 visitors took the appointment-only tour of Independence Hall, and 778,000 visitors paid the admission fee to the contemporary NCC. The fourth-most popular site at the park in 2012 was Congress Hall, located next door to Independence Hall, with 246,000 visitors. By comparison, the Deshler-Morris House—also called the Germantown White House because Washington used the home as a refuge during the 1793 yellow fever epidemic and then, a year later, as a retreat—attracted only 1,207 visitors during 2012, largely because of its location nine miles from the mall.[4]

That Independence Hall and the LBC—along with the NCC—draw the lion's share of visitors to the park is not simply a matter of their convenience in relation to the Visitor Center or their location in the heart of the park. Before these changes to the park occurred, both Independence Hall and the old

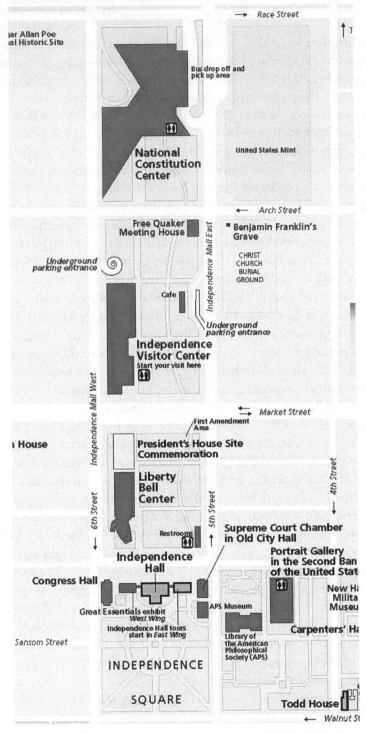

Figure 3.1. Map of the primary sites on Independence Mall. (Courtesy of Independence National Historical Park.)

Liberty Bell Pavilion (a much smaller structure built to house the bell after it was moved from Independence Hall during the Bicentennial celebration) still served as the main draws of the park. In both 1989 and 1990, for example, nearly 1.5 million people visited the bell pavilion and another three-quarters of a million people toured Independence Hall. Discounting attendance at the old Visitor Center, which drew about the same number of visitors as Independence Hall, these two sites remained a clear one-two in popularity throughout the 1990s; Congress Hall and Franklin Court (the location of sites that interpret the life and legacies of Benjamin Franklin) typically ranked third and fourth, with roughly one-third as many visitors as Independence Hall.[5] In the summer of 1986, a study by the Cooperative Park Studies Unit of the University of Idaho—which continues to provide survey and ethnographic data to the NPS—discovered that that 86 percent of the park's visitors reported seeing the Liberty Bell and 83 percent said they visited Independence Hall. In fact, more people admitted they made the Liberty Bell, rather than the Visitor Center, their first stop (36 percent to 31 percent).[6]

The long-standing lure of the bell and the hall are undoubtedly rooted in their roles as the symbolic core of the park. As Charlene Mires explained in her compelling history of Independence Hall, the structure contains "a powerful array of memories" associated with the nation's founding.[7] The park's 1948 enabling legislation (Public Law 795, H.R. 5053), while written in broad strokes, leaves little doubt that these two symbols of U.S. history— a structure and a property—served as the motivation for creating the park. The park's purpose, according the legislation, is to preserve "certain historical structures and properties of outstanding national significance . . . associated with the American Revolution and the founding and growth of the United States." The language of this legislation has guided the park's mission over the intervening years, and its spirit has permeated the interpretive resources offered throughout the park. In fact, the park's 1995 Draft General Management Plan (GMP) echoes this language while amplifying its implied intent: to celebrate the birth and growth of the United States. "The purpose of Independence National Historical Park is to preserve its stories, buildings and artifacts as *a source of inspiration* for visitors to learn more about the ideas and ideals that led to the American Revolution and the founding and growth of the United States."[8]

In particular, the sounds of American exceptionalism reverberate throughout the park's sites. This story defines the founders of the United States as devoted to the causes of liberty, freedom, and democracy, and the nation as an exceptional example created as a model for other nations to emulate. "[This] history was simple but powerful," wrote the distinguished

African American studies historian Nathan Irvin Huggins, and grounded in the influential, ten-volume story told by nineteenth-century historian George Bancroft, whose work led Huggins to call him "the American Homer." Bancroft's history

> told of a people (mainly English) who fled from social and economic restrictions of the old world—religious intolerance, class discrimination, the decadence and corruption of inherited privilege. They came to the new world—held virtually empty awaiting their coming—and struggled against the wilderness (of which the Indians were a part) to establish societies which were open and free even before the Revolution made a nation so. . . . It was a free land for free men, uninhibited by outmoded laws and customs based on rank and privilege of birth. . . . Nor was that all. It was providential. God was the prime mover.[9]

Although the founders were generally men of the Christian faith, Robert Bellah emphasized that the civil religion they espoused was not distinctly Christian. Instead, although their enactment in word and deed of an American civil religion was not incompatible with Christianity, it reflected their beliefs that religion and government should be practiced distinctly. And, as Bellah explained, governmental leaders invariably embraced the idea of a civil religion ever since; every president, for example, has referred to God in his inaugural address.[10]

More to the point, the ongoing interpretation of the sites of INHP has reflected the nation's enduring symbolic commitment to, in the words of Michael Chornesky, "glorifying" the idea of American civil religion.[11] A 1979 park brochure, for instance, speaks of "the hallowed ground of Independence National Historical Park" and quotes from Washington's first inaugural (delivered in New York City) to assert the United States' "special role as a symbol of the democratic way of life both at home and abroad."[12] A 1984 visitor's schedule and map refers to "the great beginnings" of the nation as represented in the park, and an undated pamphlet promoting the park's Independence Park Institute describes INHP as "the premier historic park in the country."[13]

As these excerpts suggest, the park has defined its mission as sharing the gospel of this civil religion. The park's 1997 GMP illustrates this mission vividly. Under the heading "Vision," the GMP describes INHP as "a place that embodies the courage and idealism of a remarkable group of citizens who came together to debate and then create a new government that became a model for modern democracies," a place where park staffers will share stories that "will foster the spirit of reverence that people bring to this national shrine." Noting that "the park has special meaning as a place of freedom and liberty," the GMP claims that "the bells of freedom rang for the end of tyranny and oppression and the American potential. People in other places, including Europe and South America, shared these dreams."[14]

This spirit of a special, even blessed, nation resonates most powerfully, of course, within the corridors of Independence Hall and the symbolism of the Liberty Bell. A 1965 park brochure points out that both the Declaration of Independence and the Constitution were worked out in one room in Independence Hall: "No other room in America has ever been the scene of such political courage and wisdom." The same brochure describes the Liberty Bell as "the most venerated symbol of patriotism in America, and its reputation as an emblem of liberty is worldwide."[15] The audio tour of the park notes that "although we can no longer hear the Liberty Bell ring, for more than 200 years people have felt the bell's message. . . . Silent, it's still reminding us of liberty's magnificence." Listeners also learn that Independence Hall is "the place where modern democracy was born. . . . Here, the inspiring words of the Declaration of Independence were conceived." Similarly, the NCC features the primary interpretive theme "We the People": "The Constitution boldly expressed a new ideal of popular sovereignty: the idea that government belongs not to monarchs and tyrants, but to 'We the People,' thus beginning an extraordinary experiment in self-government that has endured for more than two centuries."[16]

While this type of language has long been a part of the INHP's stories, it was formalized in the 1960s with the park's first systematic interpretive efforts and then, in 1971, while the state operated the park, with the development of the park's first GMP. This plan was, in some ways, a mere formalizing of interpretive practices that had been developed in the preceding decade. In fact, the three themes outlined in the 1971 GMP (the American Revolution; Benjamin Franklin—Man of Ideas; and Philadelphia—Capital City) had already been identified as early as 1968.[17] As the park developed interpretive material around these three themes during the 1960s–1990s, it focused on stories that occurred largely between 1774 and 1789. For example, in 1991, the park listed the primary interpretive objective of the American Revolution theme as explaining "what major Revolutionary political and constitutional events occurred in Philadelphia beginning with the First Continental Congress and culminating in the adoption of the Bill of Rights." Similarly, although "the Franklin story could be approached from hundreds of different directions," the park chose to focus on Franklin's "life and accomplishments as a Philadelphian and as an actor on the stage of national politics in Independence Hall." Strangely, but not surprisingly, even the final theme, Philadelphia—Capital City, was positioned as beginning before the city's designation as the national capital in 1790 because Philadelphia "certainly served as the center of activity for the national government for most of the period beginning in 1774 with the convening of the First Continental Congress."[18]

The 1971 GMP also provided a foundation for the park's preparations to celebrate the bicentennial of the Declaration of Independence in 1976. From this point until 1991, the park moved into a new means of celebrating the story of American exceptionalism: creating special events and programs to honor two hundred years of great American deeds, including the beginning of the Revolution, the work of the First and Second Continental Congresses, the death of Ben Franklin, the crafting of the U.S. Constitution, and, in 1991, the ratification of the Bill of Rights.[19] As retired INHP interpretive specialist Mary Jenkins told me, "We were focused on celebrations. . . . We did celebrations of special anniversaries [involving] events and famous people." Throughout the nearly two decades of celebration, Jenkins noted, "We didn't use this word but it was America's exceptionalism, that we were the first modern republic." This theme, Jenkins continued, was also embedded in the park rangers' talks at sites throughout INHP.[20]

After the spate of bicentennial celebrations had concluded, the park's interpretive efforts began to move in a slightly different direction. With changes in the NPS orientation to interpretation and in leadership in INHP, the park began a lengthy process to develop a new GMP. This process was designed to identify "what major stories we want to concentrate on" through interpretation and how the park's design might be modified in conjunction with those stories.[21] After fourteen public meetings to gather input and ideas, the park revealed a preferred plan for redesign in 1995—followed by another round of public feedback. The plan for interpretation that emerged in 1997 identified five themes:

> Independence Hall and related structures . . . are physical reminders of the epic struggle for freedom and self-government not only as they relate to the founding of the United States, but to the birthplace of modern democratic governments world-wide.

> The evolution of the American idea of democratic or representative government articulated in the Declaration of Independence, Articles of Confederation, the U.S. Constitution, and the Bill of Rights took place during a period of world change.

Benjamin Franklin was a self-made and self-educated intellectual co-
lossus . . . [and] a towering figure in Philadelphia and in the founding
of this nation.

Eighteenth century Philadelphia was the political, economic, and cultural center of colonial America.

The Liberty Bell, an international icon and one of the most venerated
objects in the park, became a symbol because of its association with
various struggles for freedom and not solely because of its association
with the events of 1776–1787. It is irreparably damaged, it is fragile
and imperfect, but (like the republic it symbolizes) it has weathered
threats and has endured.[22]

As the wording of these five themes makes clear, INHP's new emphasis
on ideas still pivoted around the central concept of the exceptional character of the United States. In addition, three of the five themes ensured that
the Liberty Bell—housed in a pavilion since the 1976 bicentennial celebrations—and Independence Hall would continue to serve as the core sites of
the park. Indeed, a 1996 overview of the plan asserted that "interpretive
rangers will use the park's historic core . . . as the places where the stories are
told."[23]

Visitors to the park recognize, and embrace, the fact INHP is still known
as the place to explore the key sites of the nation's founding. The first few pages of comments on the park's Yahoo! Trip Advisor site, for example, reflect the
park's story. Traveler reviews use self-generated headlines such as "Birthplace
of the American Experiment," "America's Foundation," and "Instant Patriotic
Pride." One reviewer promises that "a visit to Independence National Historical Park will lift your American Spirit," while another gushes, "Literally just
amazing. All of our history starts here."[24]

Two elements of our history, however, have been largely absent from
the park's stories about the birthplace of the American experiment. First,
despite the fact that Washington and Adams were exploring the powers
of the presidency on the fly—which included the uneventful yet remarkable transfer of power following Washington's second term—the park's interpretive resources were funneled into its most popular sites, which had
little to do with the executive branch. Second, the stories told within these
sites generally steered clear of the founders' moral compromises regarding
slavery.

Incomplete Stories in Independence National Historical Park

"It was never that we didn't know the [president's] house was there," observed retired INHP interpretive specialist Jenkins. She pointed out that a bronze plaque marked the site of the house beginning in the 1950s; in 1986, a colorful wayside marker was erected at the site. Instead, Jenkins continued, the park's managers recognized that (1) historic sites dedicated to both Washington and Adams existed outside the park and (2) the park's resources were poured into interpreting its existing structures. A one-time plan to interpret the executive branch in the First Bank of the United States building, for example, was so low on the priority list that funds ran out before the work could begin.[25]

Before Lawler's discoveries, then, INHP's focus on the executive branch had been limited to relatively meager efforts such as a passing mention of the presidencies of Adams and Washington in a printed tour guide about the park, the installation of the wayside marker at the President's House site, and an interpretive foot tour called the Washington Walk (a forty-five-minute walking tour about Washington's presidency, initiated in 1992).

Similarly, the park's focus on celebrating the new nation's embrace of liberty was so single-minded during this time period that recognition of its incomplete enactment could not be shoehorned into the story. So even though the National Park Service staff who took over the park from the Commonwealth of Pennsylvania in 1974 knew that Washington kept slaves within the park, this story of liberty denied was incongruous with the park's celebratory version of the story. "No one spoke of the slaves—not out of any deliberate conspiracy of silence," wrote former park employee Ogline, "but because Washington's labor arrangements lay outside the park's field of vision."[26] Even interpretation of the Liberty Bell emphasized its symbolic power as a general icon of liberty while downplaying (and occasionally ignoring) the fact that its name emerged through its association with efforts to abolish slavery. Ranger talks in Independence Hall told tales about how the Declaration and Constitution were developed within the building but typically omitted the facts that both documents directly dodged the issue of slavery and that all but two of the non–New England signers of the Declaration enslaved Africans during their lifetimes.[27]

The park made some uneven efforts to tell the stories of African Americans who lived and worked in the park's area during the nation's early years and, less occasionally, to broach the topic of slavery. For example, a 1979 park pamphlet overtly references Franklin's efforts to abolish slavery and directly mentions "the deletion by Congress of the condemnation of slavery and the slave trade" in its work on the Declaration of Independence.[28] In addition, early in its lengthy 1979–1980 Interpretive Statement, the park notes several programs devoted to sharing such stories, including a film about the efforts of Philadelphia's African American community to fight an outbreak of yellow fever in 1793, a celebration of the two hundredth anniversary of Pennsylvania's Gradual Abolition Act of 1780 (freeing the state's enslaved over a period of years), a discussion of the role of black soldiers in the revolutionary armies within a larger interpretive program, and interpretation in a museum devoted to artist Charles Willson Peale about his African American assistant Moses Williams, who operated a physiognotrace machine to make silhouettes.[29]

Yet, just over a decade later, the park seemingly offered fewer, and more compartmentalized, stories about the new nation's African Americans. Its 1991 Statement for Interpretation lists the following items under the heading of "Minority/Cultural Information" on page 55 of the sixty-seven-page report: "Special topic tours of the Todd and Bishop White Houses periodically discuss the role played by Blacks, women, and children in the 18th century"; "The Park sponsors several events during Black History Month"; "Physiognotrace demonstrations interpret the life and contributions of Moses Williams, black assistant to Charles Willson Peale in his museum"; "Close Encounters vignettes interpret the role of both women and Blacks in Philadelphia in the 1790's." Interestingly, the same Statement for Interpretation outlines one primary and seven occasional interpretive objectives for the Liberty Bell—and not one mentions the bell's historic connection with the abolition movement.[30]

Only a few years later, the park was making a more concerted effort to recognize the role of African Americans in Philadelphia and the United States in the late 1700s. Steve Sitarski, retired INHP chief of interpretation and education, noted that in the 1990s he promoted "a series of programs" designed to diversify the park's storytelling but acknowledged that these programs were "scattered throughout the park . . . [and] within the tier of interpretation, most people, including myself, would have viewed them as secondary."[31] In 1993, for example, the park observed the bicentennial of the yellow fever outbreak with a variety of programs designed to recognize how "Philadelphia's African American community played a vital role" in responding to the epidemic.[32] Two years later, INHP offered a walking tour of African American neighborhoods in eighteenth-century Philadelphia and a one-woman show about "slavery, freedom's promise and the message of the Liberty Bell."[33]

By 1997, INHP formally recognized that its interpretive efforts still had room to improve. That year's GMP, long in the making and long overdue, asserted that "the park will interpret the stories of diverse people and populations who affected and have been affected by the founding of the nation and the evolution of American freedoms."[34] The oblique wording of this assertion, however, underscored what seemed to be continuing discomfort about *how* to tell those stories when, as we saw above, the park's purpose statement on the first page of the GMP "is to preserve its stories, buildings, and artifacts as *a source of inspiration* for visitors to learn more about the ideas and ideals that led to the American Revolution and the founding and growth of the United States."

Before Lawler's discovery, then, did park officials *maliciously* make these choices to minimize stories of the executive branch and the founders' moral failures in their decisions about slavery? The answer, of course, is complicated. Even the most reflective park employees would likely answer in the negative, while many members of Michael Coard's ATAC organization would no doubt vehemently disagree. Many reasons explain such disparate responses. To begin, the dominance of the nation's foundation myth—the story of American exceptionalism—is so powerful that it may prompt the most well-intentioned among us to overlook how strongly it eclipses other stories. *Every* nation wants, perhaps *needs*, to believe that its formation is in some way special rather than tainted by political expediency, historical accident, moral compromise, or any of a number of other less pure considerations. In the case of INHP, in particular, four additional factors have contributed to the way in which it told its story in the years before Lawler's discoveries.

Independence Hall as a Place of Authenticity

First, the park was built around existing, original structures—Independence Hall in particular. Surprisingly, this centerpiece of the park was almost demolished after both the state and federal governments moved from Philadelphia in 1800. After the state government voted to tear down the structure, still known as the State House, and sell the land to pay for the new capitol in Harrisburg, the city of Philadelphia purchased the building and, with intermittent levels of support and interest, continued to maintain it. The transformation of the building from the State House to Independence Hall began in 1824 when the Revolutionary War hero Marquis de Lafayette returned to the United States and visited Philadelphia. After his inspiring speech at the structure, during which he praised the nation's quest for independence, it became known as Independence Hall.[35]

Later that century, as the nation celebrated the 1876 centennial of the American Revolution with an exposition in Philadelphia, both the building and the adjacent Independence Square received a makeover. In the ensuing decades, as the cause of historical preservation in general grew in popularity, the Philadelphia chapter of the American Institute of Architects took a particular interest in renovating Independence Hall and restoring Independence Square. As the first half of the 1900s unfolded, citizen groups, urban planners, and architects offered a number of plans to clear and then redevelop the land north of Independence Hall, the area now known as Independence Mall. In each of these plans, the venerable structure served as the anchor.[36]

Not surprisingly, when plans to develop the area into a state historical park came to fruition in the 1940s, Independence Hall stood tall at the center of those plans—and the stories told about the hall's place in American history featured the heroic drafting of the Declaration of Independence (while overlooking the deletion of the condemnation of slavery in the document) and the historic adoption of the U.S. Constitution (while downplaying the compromises regarding slavery embedded within it). As a result, Independence Hall has come to be known as the site where great men made great decisions; it is a living monument to the courage that gave birth to the United States. No wonder, then, that a 2007 survey of park visitors discovered that 49 percent of those surveyed answered Independence Hall when asked, "Which one site was the most important to your visit to Independence NHP?" Additionally, "birthplace/founding of the United States" was by far the most popular response to the question "What is the national significance of the park?"[37]

Visits to Independence Hall thus function as ongoing commemorations of a collective *we* in the place where *we* began. "Commemorating, by its very structure," observed Edward Casey, "encourages and enhances participation on the part of those who engage in it."[38] When visitors gather for a tour of Independence Hall, and join to enter the place where the Declaration and Constitution were born, they also symbolically join the founders to celebrate the uniqueness of the United States. In fact, in their extensive exploration of Americans' feelings about the past, Roy Rosenzweig and David Thelen discovered that individuals' encounters with authentic places from the past made them "feel that they were experiencing a moment from the past almost as it had originally been experienced."[39]

Not surprisingly, three of the top five responses to a 1987 survey that asked INHP visitors what they liked most about the park were historic information; historic atmosphere or sense of history; and seeing historic areas, features, or artifacts.[40] As tangible evidence of the nation's creation, Independence Hall draws visitors who, understandably, want to see and touch the place where the nation began. And, as an intact structure, it offers a far more compelling visitor experience than a wayside marker, walking tour, or occasional dramatic program. Walking through the doors of Independence Hall and seeing the room where the nation's founders debated the principles that the United States would embody can hardly compare with indirect, incomplete, mediated, and/or contemporary presentations of the past. Had the park not embraced Independence Hall and its sister structures as its symbolic foundation, one has to wonder how the park could have even existed.

Independence National Historical Park as a Place of Tourism

The park has also long served as a tourist attraction for the city of Philadelphia. As with most historic attractions, the primary intention of honoring and remembering the past in Philadelphia has been supplemented by a motivation to attract tourism dollars. When Philadelphia civic leaders and elected officials began mulling the possibilities for developing the area around Independence Hall in the early part of the twentieth century, their desire to make the city center an attractive place to visit drove much of their thinking. In this respect, INHP's development is like that of many other NPS historic sites. In his account of how the NPS has handled historic sites, John Bodnar noted, "Many of the places ultimately selected by the NPS as historic sites certainly reflected themes of national significance but were also promoted by local groups out of pride or out of a desire for stimulating local economic growth."[41] Noting that the declining state of the buildings bordering Independence Square reduced both the aesthetic appeal of the area and the city's property tax revenues, proponents of the mall/park pointed to the economic benefits for the city of Philadelphia while embracing the rhetoric of preserving the nation's heritage. These messages converged in the recognition that, in the words of the park supporter Isidor Ostroff, the new area would create "a center of interest so noteworthy that it will attract visitors from all over the world."[42]

This prophetic proclamation has indeed come to pass, and the city of Philadelphia's continued ownership of the buildings in the Independence Square area means that NPS and INHP decisions about the park's stories and design require buy-in from local officials and citizens as well.[43] As a result, the park's development of the 1997 GMP, which laid out the vision for the extensive redevelopment of the park at the turn of the century, was very much a collaborative effort: multiple public meetings, public presentation of design plans, and public commentary on those plans all contributed to the final shaping of the new Independence Mall. Of primary importance in this process was the construction of the Independence Visitor Center in the middle of the mall. Traffic patterns before the redevelopment brought most park visitors directly to the site of the Liberty Bell and Independence

Hall; the old Visitor Center was a couple of blocks away. So, after seeing the two centerpieces of the park, visitors would often depart (visitor surveys have found that about 70 percent of park patrons stay for half a day or less)[44]—and take their vacation money with them.

The new plans, however, not only made the Visitor Center the central physical element of the mall; they also ensured that the Visitor Center would contribute to the tourism industry in greater Philadelphia as well. In fact, in addition to being the most visited site in the park, the Visitor Center is a co-operated venture in which both the park and greater Philadelphia area are promoted. As the park's public affairs officer noted in introducing the final plan, the Visitor Center's new location "better integrates [it] with the fabric of the city, situating it on a major street to link it with all the city and region have to offer."[45] The plan itself notes on its second page that "the proposed action would provide the most effective and feasible means to meet the goals of the park and community to protect cultural resources, enrich interpretive and educational opportunities, improve visitor orientation and services, and *enhance heritage tourism.*"[46]

The city's long-standing interest in the park, in terms of both its property holdings and the park's impact on the city's economy, means that any decision made by the park is far from a decision made by *only* the park. Indeed, the park's interpretive foundation was built by Philadelphians who saw the civic and economic advantages of framing the area as the birthplace of both the United States and contemporary democracy. Philadelphia and the surrounding area, which includes Valley Forge, have benefited tremendously from the park's storytelling efforts, and the city—despite occasional and understandable moments of tension that arise when the federal government controls the operation of a vast swath of a major city's center—has tacitly and explicitly signed off on the park's tradition of celebratory interpretation so that visitors may spend more time and money while visiting the historic sites.

Independence National Historical Park and Organizational Dynamics

In addition, the organizational dynamics of the NPS and INHP have fostered approaches to interpretation that have encouraged both parks and their employees to tell celebratory stories. From the beginning, the NPS chose to present stories at its sites that featured the greatness of America. As Bodnar explained, the proliferation of historic sites in the 1930s required the NPS to develop a strategy for interpretation at those sites. NPS's approach, Bodnar noted, recognized that "the public could comprehend neither all the historical detail given at a site nor the entire mass of American history." So the NPS identified an interpretive strategy designed to educate and inspire. Its first chief historian, Verne Chatelain, "felt deeply that these objectives could best be accomplished by the creation of patriotic sentiments."[47] This interpretive mission is rooted in the nation's foundational myth and was, of course, integrated into the storytelling found at NPS sites such as INHP. Nearly seventy-five years later, former INHP employee Ogline pointed out that the park "has long viewed itself as a site of celebration, a site at which the divisions that fracture American life can be subsumed in a triumphant and unifying national narrative of self-determination, equality, and self-sacrifice."[48]

Beginning in the 1990s, however, the NPS pushed for a more complicated portrayal of the past at its historic sites. Dwight Pitcaithley, former NPS chief historian, has outlined how congressional action in the 1990s generated new interpretive efforts, new parks, and newly named sites throughout the NPS. "Congress sent a message," he declared, "not only to the National Park Service but also to the American public that a useful history must include both painful as well as prideful aspects of the past."[49] In particular, Pitcaithley noted, administrators of Civil War sites were directed to acknowledge that slavery was the root cause of the war—a topic to which we return shortly.

The resistance fostered by these directives pointed to another complicated aspect of the NPS organizational culture: "Within the NPS, most decisions regarding a site's planning and interpretation are usually made on a local level."[50] At INHP, the park superintendent has asserted a general tone for the park's approach, while ground-level interpreters have been given freedom to tell their own stories within that general framework. For example, beginning with the 1976 bicentennial and continuing to 1990, INHP superintendent Hobie Cawood devoted his energies to framing the park as a site of celebrations. "He loved celebrations because he loved to bring big crowds to the park," noted retired interpretive specialist Jenkins. Cawood's successor, Martha Aikens—who was appointed in 1990—embraced an approach more consistent with what the NPS was beginning to enact at the time. She was more "interested in ideas and ideals and in populations that we generally didn't talk about," said Jenkins, and she initiated the development of the 1997 GMP.[51] When Aikens ascended to the top spot at INHP, the interpretive focus of the park also changed. Sitarski, for instance, began pushing for diversified stories within the park's interpretation and, he said, "looking at history from multiple perspectives."[52]

Yet the park's generally decentralized organizational culture also meant that not every person employed in INHP eagerly embraced, let alone enacted, this more diverse approach to interpretation. Jenkins indicated, for example, that some people working in INHP still resist integrating outside perspectives, such as those of historians or community members, into their work. Even as recently as 2005, a team of four outside historians from the Organization of American Historians (OAH) who, at the park's invitation, reviewed INHP's interpretive efforts during the preceding year, concluded, in a summary written by Sitarski and Doris Fanelli, chief of the INHP Division of Cultural Resources Management, that "the park is bound by the 'inertia of tradition.' . . . Interpretation at the park core is inflexible."[53] As part of that report, the historian Gary Nash noted that "key members of the INHP leadership team distanced themselves" from the mid-1990s NPS efforts to diversify and complicate interpretation throughout the park service.[54]

With dissonant messages emanating from the top levels of the INHP organizational structure, other park employees may have felt comfortable clinging to the park's traditional narrative strategies. The park's varying levels of commitment to embracing NPS directives, of course, reflected the continuing nationwide uncertainty about how to address difficult elements of American history—especially at sites developed to honor the past. As Nash continued in his report, "There is still a reservoir of public opinion holding that rangers should tell simply the heroic political story of achieving independence and writing the constitution as they guide visitors through Independence Hall and Congress Hall."[55]

The park's organizational culture allowed employees reluctant to enact NPS directives the latitude to treat these instructions with indifference if they wished. Jenkins commented that employees who are in direct contact with visitors to the park receive a great deal of leeway in how they craft their talks to tourists. Although all interpretive employees who interact with the public are required to identify how they propose to connect their talk or program to one of the park's interpretive themes, "everybody writes their own program," Jenkins said.[56] As a result, OAH reviewer J. Ritchie Garrison observed in 2005, "park rangers deliver essentially the same interpretive script that I remember from the mid 1970s when I was a graduate student at the University of Pennsylvania."[57] The ranger who led my group's tour of Independence Hall in 2011, for example, named and encouraged us to visit other sites within the park— and added a pitch to check out Valley Forge—but neglected to mention the President's House site one block away. Over a decade earlier, James Loewen also observed that the park "relies on its staff to tell visitors the history that makes [Independence Hall] so important." And, Loewen continued, "the strategy doesn't work—the history doesn't get told. . . . Instead of revealing *what* happened here . . . they tell mildly amusing anecdotes about *how* it happened."[58]

Although the stories told by INHP had become more diverse before Lawler's discovery, the complex mesh of NPS and INHP organizational cultures produced a situation in which some park employees knew that a revised history needed to be told and others were reluctant to tarnish INHP with a story about freedom denied, especially at the front door of the LBC. Indeed, even Aikens—an African American woman who had encountered her share of prejudice in working her way up the NPS ranks—resisted integrating Lawler's findings. She, as the administrator of the park, recognized that no funds were available, and, perhaps just as important, she was intent on avoiding an intrusion on the new LBC, which she had personally championed as a quiet site of contemplation and reflection.[59]

Independence National Historical Park and the Partiality of Remembering

Finally, and more generally, the park has been susceptible to the same sorts of influences that affect the practices of remembering at other public memory sites. In particular, places of public memory reflect the needs of the present more than a desire to recognize the past, and those present needs guarantee that any public memory will be told in a story that is partial.[60] The story told in INHP since its inception has been overtly patriotic because, at key moments in the park's history, the United States has required reassurance that its self-identity as a beacon of freedom and liberty is vital not just to itself but to the world. Although ideas for developing the area around Independence Hall had been gathering interest in the first part of the 1900s, the park came to fruition during World War II—a time when the United States emerged as the world's foremost defender of freedom across the globe.[61] As the final push for the park commenced, for instance, park advocate Judge Edwin Lewis told Pennsylvania's governor that he should frame state legislation for the site "as a State Memorial to our war heroes."[62] Immediately following the war, of course, the Cold War began in earnest; it rhetorically wound down as INHP and the nation celebrated the spate of bicentennial anniversaries throughout the 1970s and 1980s.

Surely the park could have featured other stories during these four-plus decades that also served the needs of the present. The civil rights movement of the 1950s and 1960s, for example, embraced the causes of freedom and equality embedded in the park's foundations. During those decades, INHP could have just as easily expanded its narrative of freedom to reflect the goals of the movement by emphasizing how the nation's enactment of liberty had been historically, and contemporaneously, incomplete. In fact, historian Charlene Mires catalogued how the notions of freedom and enfranchisement symbolized by Independence Hall have been utilized over the past 150 years by groups protesting the incomplete enactment of those ideals: "People have injected an interpretation of Independence Hall as a place associated with exclusion . . . [noting] that liberty has not been shared by all the inhabitants of the land."[63] The park's relative silence on these matters signifies that public memory is also partial, in the sense both that it is always incompletely presented and that its presentation reflects a partisan point of view—a notion that reappears throughout this book.

Given these four contributing factors—Independence Hall as the park's physical anchor, the city of Philadelphia's interest is marketing the park as a tourist attraction, the organizational culture of INHP and the NPS, and the nature of public memory in general—the park's overall neglect of both the executive branch and African American history is understandable. Given the power of a dominant historical narrative to eclipse those stories, INHP's generally celebratory telling of history within its borders is not surprising. It is also wholly consistent with stories told throughout the U.S. commemorative landscape.

Commemoration and Segregation

Equally unsurprising, then, is the fact that African Americans, before the publication of Lawler's research, had little to no interest in visiting INHP. The park has told a white story of American history, so its visitors have largely been white. A 2007 park study revealed that only 3 percent of INHP's visitors were African American, and only 11 percent of the park's visitors were from the Philadelphia metropolitan area.[64] Michael Coard, for example, pointed out that the park was not a point of interest for him and his black friends as they grew up. He recalled a visit to the park as an elementary school student; the white kids in his class were ecstatic when they saw the Liberty Bell, "but for me and the few other African American kids, we didn't get it. We didn't understand—'What's the big deal? It's a cracked bell.'"[65]

Coard's reaction does not mark him as someone who never learned history as a child or who is in some way anti-American. Instead, his response reflects the fact that "[public] memory narrates shared identities, constructing senses of communal belonging," and when those shared identities exclude you, you feel as if you don't belong.[66] The symbolic and literal exclusion of African Americans from the "cradle of liberty" occurred well before the park's establishment. Nash reported that the white Americans began crafting an exclusive image of communal belonging shortly after the Revolutionary War. In Philadelphia, that meant beginning to "exclud[e] black citizens from public celebrations."[67] In the 1830s and 1840s, Mires reported, "black Philadelphians were targeted repeatedly by white rioters who attacked people in the streets and invaded homes and churches," and in 1838 the Pennsylvania legislature revoked the right of free African Americans to vote in the commonwealth.[68] In addition, Mires pointed out that Independence Hall "represented the antithesis of freedom" for nineteenth-century African Americans because it contained the federal courtrooms in which "fugitive slaves faced the prospect of losing their freedom."[69] The contrast between liberty espoused and liberty denied drew Frederick Douglass to speak at Independence Hall in 1844, an experience that, Mires argued, contributed to his famous "What to the Slave Is the Fourth of July?" address eight years later.[70] Then, in the second half of the twentieth century, the city of Philadelphia literally removed African Americans from a neighborhood bordering the park as part of an urban renewal project. "In the process, the remaining African American residents were essentially forced from their homes, which were then acquired and sold to wealthier people who could afford the stipulated restorations."[71]

The informal and formal exclusion of African Americans from the nation's historic sites is not limited to INHP; by and large, these sites—including national parks—are destinations for white Americans. In their book encouraging African Americans to visit NPS sites, Audrey and Frank Peterman wrote: "By some unwritten, unspoken rule, the most beautiful and inspiring public places in our country remain the playgrounds of white people, almost as if there is an invisible barrier separating them from Americans of other races."[72] The Petermans, who visited fourteen national and state parks during a trip across the country, saw "less than a handful of black people, Latinos, Asians or Native Americans among the hundreds of thousands of white visitors enjoying the national treasures."[73] Perhaps, as the Petermans noted, many persons of color feel as out of place in NPS sites as many white Americans do in neighborhoods largely populated by people of color: "There are large swaths of the country where we feel unwelcome, or which we mentally write off as the domain of white people."[74]

This feeling was reinforced when the Petermans reported reading letters to the editor of *National Parks* magazine. The periodical, published by the National Parks Conservation Association, outlined NPS efforts to attract a more diverse set of visitors to its properties. Some readers of the magazine were less than thrilled by the prospect. "Many of us look to the parks as an escape from the problems ethnic minorities create," wrote one. "Bringing in blacks and Latinos from the ghettos will only contribute disproportionately to vandalism and other criminal activities, including robbery, murder, drug trafficking, and gang activity," worried another. A third reader, who chose less stereotypical language, nonetheless reflected a lack of awareness that a white bias has long been embedded in NPS sites: "The visitors who do frequent the parks are there by personal choice, not by some undefined social bias that has been built into the park system."[75]

This "undefined social bias," or the "unwritten, unspoken rule" of which the Petermans wrote, is the phenomenon of whiteness. First coined by Peggy McIntosh, the idea of whiteness is that those ideas, practices, values, narratives, and the like that are familiar to white Americans are taken as natural for all of society. For example, McIntosh listed the following among her twenty-five indicators of whiteness:

> I can easily buy posters, postcards, picture books, greeting cards, dolls, toys, and children's magazines featuring people of my race.

> I can choose blemish cover or bandages in "flesh" color that more or less match my skin.

> I am never asked to speak for all the people of my racial group.

> I can take a job with an affirmative action employer without having coworkers on the job suspect that I got it because of race.

> When I am told about our national heritage or about "civilization," I am shown that people of my color made it what it is.

Just these few items illustrate the extent to which whiteness functions as what McIntosh called "an invisible knapsack of privilege"—something that white people unknowingly carry with them in their everyday interactions.[76] Persons of color, on the other hand, are well aware of this privilege because they are frequently reminded that when they enter landscapes of whiteness—whether those places are sites of education, work, or leisure—they are noticed as different.

Not surprisingly, persons of color have historically not been noticed as the subjects of public memory—to a large extent because the history of the United States, especially as it has been presented within the commemorative landscape, "has effectively conflate[d] American heritage and identity with whiteness."[77] This characteristic of public memory both reflects the longer history of racial exclusion in the United States (which encompasses everything from the familiar institutions of slavery and Jim Crow laws to the less familiar institutions of sundown towns)[78] and refracts the key roles played by African Americans in the building of the United States. A thorough accounting of these historical practices is impractical here, so I instead offer a brief illustration of how "whiteness [has been] the invisible hand of official [U.S.] public memory."[79]

In short, public memory in the United States "commemorates white innocence and self interest."[80] The nation's foundation narrative, historically embedded within the nation's commemorative landscape, "persists because it feeds and satisfies our most profound sense of identity."[81] It also keeps us from looking at what the historian Nathan Irvin Huggins called "the deforming mirror of truth," namely that "a free nation, inspired by the Rights of Man, [had] to rest on slavery."[82] The best way to avoid looking in that mirror is to forget, officially at least, that it exists. In his exposition of the types of forgetting in which societies engage, Paul Connerton identified "forgetting as humiliated silence," the product of a "collective shame" about something perpetrated by the society.[83] Others have referred to the United States' forgetting of the history of African Americans, especially the practice of enslaving them, as a type of willful amnesia.[84]

The forgetting, Huggins observed, began when the nation's founders wrote documents in which discussions of black persons were consciously evaded: "In no official document of their creation did they address, frankly and openly, the conspicuous fact of racial slavery."[85] We have continued to dodge that conspicuous fact by avoiding the issue of race in the commemorative landscape. Although the United States did not fully embrace the commemorative urge until after the Civil War, a survey of the nation's monuments and memorials between the nation's birth and its temporary split reveals an absence of black Americans.

To begin, the memory of perhaps the most famous black revolutionary, Crispus Attucks, was—like those of his fellow Boston Massacre victims—erased and replaced with a more general accounting of the massacre as a moment when the nation began to form. In the thirteen orations delivered between 1771 and 1783 to mark the anniversary of the March 5 event, only one mentioned the names of those who lost their lives. "Rhetorically speaking," argued Stephen H. Browne, "there was no Crispus Attucks in late eighteenth-century America because, from the [anniversary] celebrant's point of view, there was no need for him beyond his status as a body in the street, a unit of proof in the colonial case against British depredations. Racially he was invisible."[86] In fact, Margot Minardi noted, black Americans who fought in the Revolutionary War were invisible throughout the Massachusetts commemorative landscape. Joseph Warren, however, was very visible in the Boston commemorative landscape. The white physician, who perished in the Battle of Bunker Hill, "proved to be a far more appealing patriotic martyr than Crispus Attucks could ever be."[87]

As the nation invented itself, both institutionally and symbolically, in the years between the Revolutionary and Civil Wars, the stories told and the deeds commemorated invariably featured white heroes such as Warren and, especially, George Washington.[88] Undoubtedly, Washington, Warren, and other notable white revolutionary figures engaged in actions worthy of being honored; without their efforts, the American experiment may well have failed. In the beginning, these early American leaders rhetorically worked to define their nation as distinct from the British; every definition, after all, requires an antipode, a "not" to partner with an "is."[89] After the revolution, however, the "not" came to be black residents of the new nation. "Slavery," noted Eric Foner, "helped to shape the identity, the sense of self, of all Americans, giving nationhood from the outset a powerful exclusionary dimension."[90]

At the same time, this exclusion of one group of people meant that the nation's autobiography must remain silent on the issue of slavery; black Americans remained largely invisible in the commemorative landscape because their presence would testify to the incompatibility of the nation's foundation myth with its institutionalized practices. To give African Americans a presence within the commemorative landscape would have suggested that they also played a role in the nation's birth and growth. While such a role is factually undeniable—the enslaved, as Coard pointed out, contributed labor that produced both economic and political benefits (slave labor provided the founding fathers with time to think, write, and organize); "had it not been for slavery, America wouldn't be what it is today," he argued—it was symbolically untenable to recognize this role at the time.[91] "Public monuments were meant to . . . be a chronicle of heroic accomplishments, not a series of messy disputes with unresolved outcomes," noted Kirk Savage in his survey of U.S. public commemorations before the Civil War. So, until 1860, Savage observed, no bronze or marble statues of black people existed in the United States because African Americans "could hardly ever be acknowledged in public space without exploding the myth of a democratically unified people."[92]

The cannon fire at Fort Sumter, S.C., on April 12, 1861, began to explode this myth. After the carnage of the Civil War, and Abraham Lincoln's issuance of the Emancipation Proclamation, the United States had an opportunity to redefine itself as a nation in which all persons were considered equals. Instead, in an attempt to accelerate reconciliation between the South and North, monuments and memorials honored the common soldier, a figure that people on both sides could identify with and honor.[93] Only one of the hundreds of these sites featured an African American soldier in uniform.[94] Reconciliation through commemoration may have been motivated by a desire to heal national divisions between North and South following the war, but this effort merely papered over the divisions. The results endured for generations.

The focus on reconciliation meant that the root cause of the war—slavery—was swept to the side. In his extensive study of how the nation's commemorative landscape was shaped after the war, David Blight described these efforts as "the attempted erasure of emancipation from the national narrative of what the war had been about."[95] With the shoving of slavery to the periphery, those directly affected by slavery—the now free enslaved Africans and their descendants—could continue to be cast as outsiders to America and their stories either ignored or integrated into the more general foundation narrative of the nation. Crispus Attucks, for example, had begun to be embraced by African Americans in the 1850s as a symbol of both resistance to tyranny and a desire for independence. Specific acts of commemoration among African Americans, Browne revealed, did not directly challenge the foundation myth of the United States but instead sought to integrate black Americans as part of the story. Yet, in the years following the Civil War, this memory of Attucks was eventually replaced by one in which he was officially remembered, through a memorial on Boston Common, as an exemplary American: "The revolutionary hero was transferred from the halls of dissent onto the grounds of racial accommodation."[96]

This lost opportunity to confront the nation's contradiction between its stated ideals and its historical practices also planted the seed for an alternative history of the Civil War to germinate and grow: the myth of the Lost Cause. In this telling of history, which began in the late 1800s and continued into the twentieth century, the Confederacy's goal was to preserve states' rights rather than to perpetuate the practice of slavery. As a result, some Confederate memorials labeled the conflict the "War of Northern Aggression."[97] This story, wrote Steven Hoelscher, was grounded in not only a defeated Confederacy's search for dignity but also the South's quest to define itself in the midst of political and economic changes occurring throughout the United States; in short, the South—like many regions of the country—sought "new foundations for identity." Southern states turned back in time to do so, developing what Hoelscher called a "white-pillared past" in which plantations were represented in cultural and public memory as locations of gentility and grace.[98] In this story, "the memory of slavery was recast as benign and civilizing,"[99] and "enslaved African American men and women lived contented lives under the benevolent care of the white plantation master."[100]

Oddly, given the commemorative traditions of ignoring race, slavery, and emancipation immediately after the Civil War, some of the monuments and memorials that emerged in the South during the heyday of the Lost Cause directly and specifically acknowledged the role of enslaved Africans during the war. Not so oddly, Loewen illustrated, these memory sites praised slaves for their dedication to the cause: "Across the former Confederacy from the 1890s on, whites put up markers and monuments honoring slaves who served the Confederacy and their owners loyally throughout the Civil War. Sometimes it seems that neo-Confederates want to remember by name each and every African American who fought, dug ditches, cooked, or otherwise aided the Confederacy." In reality, Loewen continued, enslaved Africans spied for the Union, engaged in mass escapes, enlisted in the Union army and navy, and either refused to work or slowed their work if their owners were off fighting.[101]

Yet, even well into the 1900s, memorials praising the benevolence of enslaved Africans continued to grow across the South. The Mammy memorial movement, for example, led to the installation of countless statues featuring "the benevolent mythic image of the Mammy, ostensibly the source of unconditional love and support for her white charges." The strength of this trend was so strong that, in 1923, U.S. senator John Sharp Williams of Mississippi sought to create a monument to the "Negro Mammy" in Washington, D.C.[102] Similarly, a statue of an older African American male, slightly stooped, was installed in Natchitoches, Louisiana, with a plaque offering "grateful recognition of the arduous and faithful services of the good darkies of Louisiana." This particular memorial was eventually moved and now stands outside Louisiana State University's Rural Life Museum (although the inscription is no longer visible).[103]

More recently, Bruce Levine noted, a spate of academic-sounding books have appeared in which authors have asserted that tens of thousands of blacks fought for the Confederacy during the Civil War. Sporting titles such as *Black Southerners in Gray, Black Confederates,* and *The South Was Right!,* these books both "hotly deny that the South fought for slavery" and insist that the enslaved embraced their servitude "because masters were loyal to them, affording them security, social welfare, dignity, and affection."[104] As Levine observed, these and other efforts at Civil War revisionism exist not simply to preserve a memory of slavery as benign; they also serve contemporary purposes: if slavery wasn't so bad, any current problems with race relations cannot be tied to the peculiar institution.

Undoubtedly, for the states of the Confederacy, the story of the Lost Cause has been hard to put down: "Until the 1980s, the memorial landscape in most southern cities and towns was dominated by monuments and markers devoted to Confederate military heroes and the grand 'Lost Cause' for which they fought and died."[105] Although the commemorative landscape may not be dominated by such markers today, the legacies of reconciliation and the Lost Cause still linger throughout the nation's sites of memory. For example, Nathan Bedford Forrest—a Confederate general, slave trader, and, following the war, the founder of the Ku Klux Klan—recently has been embraced by working-class white people as a more contemporary, and "overtly racialized," symbol of the Lost Cause through the explicit recognition of his service as a general and an implicit acknowledgment of his pre- and postwar exploits. According to Owen Dwyer, Forrest's popularity among working-class white Americans is evident in "new memorials, biographies, and most ubiquitously, T-shirt sales."[106] In addition, tours of southern plantations routinely downplay, if they mention, the institution of slavery and instead laud the cultural, economic, and social contributions of southern agrarianism. For instance, a one-time tour guide at Arlington House, an NPS site near Washington, D.C., that was home to Robert E. Lee before the Civil War, told the historian James Oliver Horton that "white visitors often bristle at the mention of Lee as the owner of slaves . . . [while] some white interpreters at the site used the less emotionally charged term *servants* instead of *slaves* to describe the plantation laborers."[107] This pattern of effacement is widespread among tours of former southern plantations. In their 2002 study of 122 southern plantation museum tours, most of which were operated privately, Jennifer L. Eichstedt and Stephen Small reported that "overwhelmingly, the enslavement of millions of human beings is not discussed. Instead, there is a ringing, terrible silence; where silence doesn't reign, stories of Black loyalty and white benevolence are whispered."[108]

This emptiness, which Eichstedt and Small term *symbolic annihilation*, can be found throughout the nation's commemorative landscape. Dwight Pitcaithley, former chief historian at the NPS, who led the battle within his agency to integrate the topic of slavery within relevant park sites, observed that "the NPS avoided all mention of the causes of the war in its exhibits, films, and publications" until 1998.[109] At that time, the NPS convened a meeting of the managers of Civil War battlefield sites to discuss the needed updating of their interpretive strategies. Even though the report from that conference did not use the word *slavery* a single time and used the word *slaves* only once,[110] perhaps to avoid the inevitable response that followed, Pitcaithley reported that the Park Service "was inundated with approximately 2,400 cards and letters from the Sons of Confederate Veterans, members of Civil War Roundtables, and the general public" who were responding to "incendiary articles" suggesting that the federal agency was about to smear the South in its retelling of the history of the war.[111] In one of those responses, the voices of reconciliation from over a century earlier echoed: "I am completely disgusted with the National Park Service's new policy to post South-bashing propaganda about slavery at National 'Civil War' Battlefield Parks. This mindless South-bashing has to stop if this nation is to continue being united."[112]

That the Lost Cause, according to Pitcaithley, "retains much of its power among a large portion of the American public" is evident in many places.[113]

In the past few years, for example, the governors of Virginia, Georgia, and Mississippi have declared Confederate History/Heritage Months—without mentioning slavery in their official proclamations.[114] When African American history *is* integrated into the commemorative landscape, those comfortable with colorless stories of American history have worked to minimize or trivialize threats to traditional narratives. Interpreters at Colonial Williamsburg, for instance, responded to administrative efforts to diversify the site's interpretation in the early 1990s by presenting information about white colonials as *facts* and information about African Americans of the time as *conjecture,* even though a wealth of evidence and artifacts about early black Americans exists throughout the site.[115]

Despite the long-standing and significant resistance to including the stories of slavery and African American experiences at commemorative sites, the last two decades have marked what Derek Alderman called "a new geography of African American memory, a direct challenge to the control that whites have historically wielded over the visibility of black-led commemoration and the tradition of symbolically annihilating the histories and identities of the enslaved."[116] Monuments have been erected to black victims of lynching, memorials have been built to acknowledge sites of the slave trade, and museum exhibits have depicted the horrors of slavery.[117] In 2015, the National Museum of African American History and Culture, a new branch of the Smithsonian, is scheduled to open on the Washington Mall.

The NPS has also encouraged its employees to diversify the stories told within its sites. In 1994, the NPS partnered with the Organization of American Historians in an effort to update the ways in which history was presented at NPS sites. One result of this agreement was the visit, mentioned earlier, of OAH members to INHP in 2005. INHP has also attempted to re-envision itself, thanks to the collective forces of NPS encouragement, OAH suggestions, and President's House advocacy. In 2007, INHP rolled out a new long-range interpretive plan in which the park outlined new themes for interpretation, including one called "Liberty: The Promises and Paradoxes," which pledges to explore "the theory and reality of attaining liberty and ensuring equality," and another called "E Pluribus Unum: Out of Many, One," which "looks at the many forms of diversity in the United States."[118]

Americans will no doubt continue to struggle with what Erika Doss has identified as the shame involved in the nation's past. "Recalling shameful episodes and histories is fraught with struggles over their very admission in the national narrative," she observed. "To acknowledge shame, after all, is to admit that there is something to be ashamed about."[119] This difficulty is not limited to proponents of the Lost Cause or even to white Americans generally.

African Americans have long grappled with how to remember slavery in contemporary contexts. David Blight, for example, pointed to a late nineteenth-century public debate between Alexander Crummell and Frederick Douglass regarding the extent to which black Americans should incorporate memories of slavery into their identity. Their dispute, Blight reported, marked what came to be a division among African Americans: "Both sought racial uplift, but one [represented by Douglass] would take the risk of sustaining a sense of historic grievance against America as the means of making a nation fulfill its promises, while the other [represented by Crummell] would look back only with caution and focus on group moral and economic regeneration."[120] Taking a slightly different tack, Ira Berlin suggested that both black and white Americans struggle with the memory of slavery for two equally accurate and compelling reasons: slavery was an abomination yet those enslaved grew strong because of it. "One says slavery is our great nightmare," Berlin pointed out, and "the other says slavery left a valuable legacy."[121]

In short, "African Americans are ambivalent and divided in their thinking about slavery."[122] At minimum, black Americans tell at least three types of stories about their history in the United States, according to Rosenzweig and Thelen's extensive survey project. The first story recalled "oppression, discrimination, and racism; slavery obviously plays a central role in such narratives, but so do later episodes of racial violence and discrimination." A second story focused on individual African Americans, heroes of some sort, who "overcame oppression and made important contributions to crafts, agriculture, or science." A third story, which Rosenzweig and Thelen reported was the most frequent narrative mentioned, "combines the first two by describing group struggle to overcome the racism and oppression of white society."[123]

John Michael Vlach discovered firsthand the difficulty of commemorating the experience and practice of slavery. Vlach's "Back of the Big House: The Cultural Landscape of the Plantation" was exhibited for only half a day at the Library of Congress because of "cries of protest by a number of the library's African American employees." Vlach concluded, "Many African Americans find that the best way to deal with their anger and disappointment is just not to talk about it in public."[124] As a result of these tensions, commemorative responses tend to circle around the nation's embrace of slavery rather than directly address its practices and effects.[125]

That is not to say, however, that African Americans do not generally share a collective awareness of their overall absence in the U.S. commemorative landscape. Even though Rosenzweig and Thelen discovered that only about one-fourth of African Americans said ethnic or racial history was the most important element of the past in their lives (compared with the other options of family, nation, or community), this percentage was "almost seven times greater than among white Americans." As a result, they continued, black Americans "tended to blur the 'I' and the 'we'" as they spoke about the past; the "we," moreover, frequently referred not to family—as it did among white Americans who were interviewed—but to a racial collective. "We all come from the same place. Our roots are all the same," explained an African American woman interviewed for Rosenzweig and Thelen's research.[126] Moreover, African Americans share a general collective memory full of stories of discrimination and oppression, both on a national scale and in everyday local occurrences. Reuben A. Buford May, in his study of how African American men created local collective memories through storytelling, pointed out, "This collective memory intensifies individuals' awareness of racism and discrimination."[127]

To be sure, every group and every story has its absences; no memory can wholly reveal a past. Yet some absences matter more than others. Kristin Hoerl underscored this point when she wrote of "the importance of distinguishing between absence that is inevitable in any commemoration of the past and absence that negates our deep histories of social injustice."[128] The stories of African Americans have been absent from these places, but they have always been present in U.S. history. "Black people told their own stories again and again during their time in America . . . in oral testimony, in written petitions to the government, in autobiographical narratives, in poetry and song, in dance and religious ceremonies."[129]

That some of these stories had been buried within the archives of INHP infuriated African Americans who had long seen their stories erased from official history and excluded from places of public memory. "I was outraged that nobody told this story," Coard exclaimed, "because had I known then back as a kid what I know now, I would have been, and so would all the other African American students, as ecstatic as the white boys were and the white girls were. We would have seen ourselves as a part of the greatness that is America. And I felt cheated. I felt lied to." Yet the emergence of the President's House also provided an opportunity to place those stories within the symbolic birthplace of the United States, and to polish those stories with the sheen of equality in so doing. Coard continued:

> I was literally on a cultural mission to make sure that in the future little black boys and little black girls would know that their ancestors contributed to the greatness of America as much as—actually, even more than—the founding fathers because had it not been for slavery, America wouldn't be what it is today. . . . This site, the President's

House/Slave Memorial, is so important to me not only because it tells of the contributions of Africans and African descendants in a way that's never been told before, and it instills pride in those black boys and little black girls. But maybe most important it finally allows for white America to look at African Americans as legitimate contributors to the greatness of America.[130]

As Coard's words illustrate, the importance of placing the stories of early African Americans in the commemorative landscape extends beyond the borders of the park, and even past the reaches of U.S. history in general. A large part of the reason black Americans treasure these historical memories is that their history has been displaced. When the nation's first black slaves were ripped from their homes in Africa, their history and stories were largely left behind. When their histories in the United States were systematically omitted from the commemorative landscape and left out of history textbooks, their progeny had no place to ground their identity. Any group, explained Christine Chivallon in her analysis of giving slavery presence in the commemorative landscape, may struggle to define itself in the present if its members are not integrated through "a narrative of common origin."[131] Coard described this absence more poignantly when he described how one of his childhood friends knew so much about his Italian heritage. But, Coard said, "for me and for most African Americans we start sometime maybe early 1900s, maybe middle 1800s, but beyond that we don't know anything. We know Mississippi. We know Georgia. We know Virginia. But we know nothing about the west coast of Africa, the interior of Africa, what language we spoke, what religion we practiced."[132]

Black Americans have thus long worked to make their own places in a nation that formally and informally excluded them from large swaths of public space. These efforts—which could fill volumes—include everything from reappropriating white spaces such as lunch counters and even, as Frederick Douglass did, the steps of Independence Hall, to celebrating alternative holidays such as Juneteenth and National Freedom Day (which, respectively, recognize the abolition of slavery in Texas in 1865 and Abraham Lincoln's signing of the Thirteenth Amendment). The President's House provided another opportunity: the chance to place the first memorial to enslaved Africans on federal land.

4

Honoring the Ancestors

The Quest for Acknowledgment

The publication of Lawler's first article in the *Pennsylvania Magazine of History and Biography* could hardly have come at a worse time for the staff at INHP. The groundbreaking for the new Liberty Bell Center (LBC), a pet project of INHP superintendent Martha Aikens, was only two months away, and—as in many public history projects of this sort—park officials and private consultants had gone through numerous revisions of the interpretive material that would be displayed within the LBC. From the perspective of park officials, the design and content of the LBC were finished.

Not that park officials should have been surprised by Lawler's 2002 article; it was not the first time the park had heard from him on the subject of the President's House. In 1996, as the park was holding public meetings on plans to redesign the mall, Lawler and others had urged INHP during one of those meetings to consider reconstructing the President's House. "The answer," Lawler noted in a letter to the editor, "was that they didn't want to confuse the public by mixing the real and the unreal" within the confines of the park.[1] In her letter to advocates for reconstruction of other colonial dwellings as part of the mall makeover, Aikens noted that NPS policy frowned on reconstructions "except in special circumstances, including the availability of detailed and incontrovertible documentation of a lost building, remarkable significance, and exceptional interpretive value."[2]

Lawler provided just that information to the park in early 2001, nearly a year before his research was published, in the hope that the park might be willing to consider doing something more than erecting a wayside marker.[3] Yet, even with the support of an assistant to the NPS regional director for the mid-Atlantic states, Lawler had to wait more than five weeks before INHP's then chief of interpretation, Chris Schillizzi, would meet with him and the regional director's assistant. When the meeting finally occurred, Lawler described Schillizzi's reaction as "skeptical, bordering on hostile, and, in my opinion, disingenuous throughout." Schillizzi told the pair to communicate with only him; he then, Lawler noted, "cut off communication for seven months."[4] In the fall of 2001, park officials again demonstrated their lack of interest in the site by digging a utility trench through the footprint of the President's House without, initially, the knowledge or presence of an archaeologist from the historical and cultural preservation firm contracted to oversee excavations on the mall.

Not surprisingly, after Lawler's research became public knowledge in 2002, INHP officials continued to downplay the significance of the site. Setting the tone from the top of the park hierarchy, Superintendent Aikens generally refused to use the name *President's House* in her public pronouncements, preferring instead to say "the Robert Morris mansion site" or "the Morris mansion," or "the former 190 High Street."[5] Over the next few years, the park at times continued to resist, downplay, and/or reframe the President's House site, its inhabitants, and the symbolic power of their activities within the house.

The park's stonewalling, which seems shortsighted in retrospect, can likely be explained in three ways. First, advocates seeking to integrate Lawler's research into the park's offerings initially presented a set of mixed demands, ranging from recognizing the executive branch within the park, to changes in the interpretation inside the LBC, to telling the story of slavery in an installation parked in front of the LBC. Initially, the Independence Hall Association (IHA) urged the park to recognize the President's House site so that INHP could tell the stories of all three branches of government. The executive branch, as noted earlier, had historically been given short shrift in the park's interpretation, so Lawler's research provided a rich historical basis for integrating the house into the park's storytelling. Specifically, the IHA urged the park to mark the site of the home in the pavement in front of the LBC. In her August 15, 2001, letter to Aikens, IHA chair Nancy Gilboy argued that marking the outline of the President's House would "create a complete and balanced picture of our government by including all three branches."[6] Eight months later, Gilboy again returned to the theme of representing the executive branch within the park. She wrote, "At present, the park that's dedicated to American history interprets only two branches of government in the city where three were created for checks and balances."[7]

At the same time, the explosive revelation that Washington had skirted Pennsylvania law to deny freedom to the nine enslaved Africans in the home generated calls either to revise the interpretation planned for the interior of the LBC or to construct a physical installation on the site of the President's House. Both Philadelphia elected officials and local advocates asserted that the story of the enslaved must be told at the site. "The city is not about to let this slide by," asserted a spokesperson for Philadelphia mayor John F. Street.[8] The Ad Hoc Historians organization repeatedly asked INHP officials for a copy of the interpretation planned for the LBC (and were repeatedly rebuffed) so that they could propose modifications designed to reflect the fact that, as Gary Nash argued, "millions of visitors are going to go into the Liberty Bell [Center] not knowing they are walking over the site of Washington's executive mansion, indeed walking over the slave quarters he built at the rear of the house."[9] Lawler's revelation that the slave quarters existed only a few feet away from the front door of the LBC prompted local African American leaders to push for an even stronger, and more permanent, reminder of the enslaved. Charles Blockson, curator of an eponymous Afro-American Collection at Temple University, proclaimed: "We need a memorial there. . . . A memorial to enslaved ancestors means more to me than the Liberty Bell." Similarly, Michael Coard declared: "We want a monument, a memorial, a bold, serious structure that people can see and touch, just like they touch the Liberty Bell."[10]

Second, these mixed demands for revision gave INHP officials political space to maneuver because, simply put, they did not want to reconsider designs for the mall and the LBC that had been developed over nearly five years and eighteen public meetings, nor did they have the funds to do so. Beginning in the mid-1990s, INHP staff held a series of public meetings intended to gather information that would lead to the $314 million makeover of the mall. As part of this process, park officials eventually presented five proposed designs for redeveloping the mall, pointing to one as its preferred alternative. After such an extensive and public process of information gathering and sharing, INHP officials were not keen to make last-minute changes, especially when those changes affected the crown jewel of the mall makeover.

Aikens, for example, dismissed the IHA proposal to mark the house's location in the pavement between the two new structures by arguing that "the entire landscape from Market Street to the LBC would require redesign," which would "create a design dissonance" that would ultimately "be more confusing rather than revelatory."[11] Instead, she argued, the executive branch would be interpreted at the Deshler-Morris House, the home in suburban Germantown where Washington occasionally stayed as a retreat. Not surprisingly, the park also began work to rename this site the Germantown White House, a move perhaps also motivated by a desire to increase attendance at one of the park's least popular attractions, given its distance from the mall. Perhaps more to the point, Schillizzi said that the park was "out of time and out of money. 'The train has left the station,'" he told Nash.[12] This theme was emphasized in public pronouncements as well. Park spokesperson Phil Sheridan proclaimed, "We don't have the money. . . . There's no money to get people together. No money to go through conceptual designs and bring them to fruition. . . . To do any type of design is not possible without funding."[13]

Third, the lack of funds and time allowed park officials another way to avoid building anything in front of the LBC or telling a story inside the new pavilion, neither of which would mesh with the traditional hagiography associated with the Liberty Bell or Aikens's envisioned inspirational journey that visitors would take through the (incomplete) story of liberty and freedom in the United States. INHP officials not only rebuffed all calls to change anything about the park's redesign; they also worked diligently to avoid placing the story of slavery on the front porch of or inside the LBC. At first, they sought to deflect efforts to highlight slavery either within or outside the LBC by noting that slavery was *already* discussed within the confines of the park *and* that additional plans to interpret those enslaved by Washington were under way at the Deshler-Morris House. "The story of slavery in our nation is a story told throughout the park," Aikens asserted in her *Inquirer* editorial.[14]

Then INHP staff engaged in linguistic evasion by using the word *servant* to refer to *all* those who labored in the President's House. When INHP staff posted preliminary text for the revised LBC interpretation on its website in October 2002, it referred to the slaves' quarters as "servants' quarters" because indentured servants may have resided in the repurposed smokehouse as well.[15] In responding to the predictable uproar, INHP officials claimed that no evidence conclusively demonstrated that the structure housed *only* the enslaved.[16] "Do you believe there were no slave quarters?" asked Lawler at the time. "It's almost absurd to think that."[17]

Even a year later, INHP staff, ostensibly engaged in a goodwill effort to integrate the perspectives of historians both among park staff and outside the park, proposed that a roundtable gathering consider—among others—the two following questions: "Was the smokehouse a slave quarters? Does 'slave quarters' apply to the President's House consistently?" The staff pointed out that a white indentured servant was also quartered in the smokehouse and "President Adams had no slaves and thus marking a slave quarters site would misrepresent the property under his presidency."[18] Then, despite promises to replace the wayside signage marking the site of the President's House with a larger display that also acknowledged those enslaved by Washington, INHP officials did not post such signage until after a 2004 *Inquirer* article took them to task for its absence.[19]

Interestingly, the park's choice to brush off the calls to acknowledge the President's House site and its power as a symbol of slavery reflected a similar choice made by those who established INHP in 1947. Before Lawler's archival excavation, the story of the President's House had remained buried from the moment of the park's creation. After the project's boosters persuaded the federal government to consider developing a historical park in the heart of Philadelphia, Congress created an entity called the Philadelphia National Shrines Park Commission and charged it with investigating the possibility of developing the park. Considering the loaded phrase *national shrines* in its title, the commission's recommendation, issued in 1947, was hardly surprising; it urged Congress "to acquire by purchase or condemnation" all the structures and property that fell within the borders of the proposed park, which the commission called the Philadelphia National Historical Park.[20] The commission's report thoroughly outlined the territory for the park and described in great detail the historical relevance of all the sites within its boundaries.

The site of the Presidential Mansion (as it was titled in the report) made the list. In the fourteen-page description of the site, the report gushed about the activities that occurred within the home during its decade as the residence of the nation's first two presidents.

> For nearly ten years . . . the Presidential Mansion occupied a position of paramount importance in national life. Moreover, these were the critical years when the Constitution itself was on trial. The question was: could the United States government operate successfully under its system of checks and balances? . . .
>
> The threshold of this mansion was crossed by the members of President Washington's cabinet, who, while differing in their political expressions, were united in the will to support and defend Constitutional government. The names in the first cabinet shine with brilliance on history's pages: Thomas Jefferson . . . , Alexander Hamilton . . . , Edmund Randolph . . . , Henry Knox. . . .
>
> The future of America was a prime topic of conversation at [Washington's weekly dinners]. The President's home was a meeting-place for the greatest minds in the nation. . . .

It was in the Presidential Mansion that George Washington prepared the second inaugural address, delivered by him at Congress Hall. It was in the Market Street house that he had drafted his Farewell Message to Congress. And from this same house, he departed to resume his private life as a Virginia gentleman-farmer at Mount Vernon.[21]

Given the home's role in the early years of the republic, the report concluded, "The site of the Presidential Mansion is hardly surpassed in importance by any other historical site in America. The eminent personages who lived here and the decisions affecting the future of the nation that were made here have caused growing interest in the Presidential Mansion and the ground upon which it stood. It is a distinguished historical site."[22]

Then, as in the recent past, those entrusted with the power to tell the story of the nation's beginnings chose to ignore both the President's House site and the fact that Washington relied on enslaved Africans to provide much of the labor in the house. In the early 1950s, as in the early 2000s, the power of the iconic (and existing) Independence Hall and Liberty Bell, and the desire not to deviate from already-established plans, overwhelmed any desires to interpret more fully the emergence of the executive branch within the park. In 1952, as the envisioned mall was being shaped through the demolition of structures seized by eminent domain, the Philadelphia chapter of the American Institute of Architects (AIA) urged the Commonwealth of Pennsylvania to take heed of sites such as the President's House. Ernest Howard Yardley spoke for the local AIA affiliate when he declared, "It is most unfortunate that the demolition is progressing with no regard, on the part of the State Director of the Project, for the several other important buildings within the area which were of decided prominence during our early history."[23] On Washington's birthday of that same year, James R. George worried that "unless some one hurries up and notes the location [of the President's House], the site will become an indistinguishable part of an open space in the Mall." Writing in the *Philadelphia Inquirer,* George noted: "Right now, that site—formerly 526–528–530 Market St.—is marked by the following: One 2-by-4 plank, about 12 feet long; heaps of broken brick and concrete; and a rusted iron door. For the three business buildings that occupied the site are gone and bulldozers have been clearing the ground for the new Independence Mall."[24]

Similarly, Lawler's work revealed that the 1947 Shrines Commission report noted the presence of enslaved Africans in the President's House—a fact that was reframed in the same manner as it was in the early 2000s. The report enumerated the inhabitants of the mansion, including "fifteen other servants, white and negro," and quoted correspondence from Washington to his private secretary, Tobias Lear, in which the president proposed places to house these servants.[25] While the term *servant,* both in 1947 and in Washington's time, would accurately describe the indentured servants working in the home, it could hardly be interpreted as anything more than a euphemism for *slave* when the servant was described as black and the leader of the estate was a Virginian who enslaved hundreds of Africans. Yet the use of the term provided cover for those who wished to filter the history of slavery from the American consciousness.

Unlike the mid-twentieth-century efforts, however, the more recent work paid dividends. What made the difference this time? To a large extent, the answer lies in how advocates for recognizing the house and the enslaved developed a compelling public message. They were also especially determined to share this message frequently and with people who possessed the political juice to shape INHP decisions that were, as noted in the preceding chapter, largely impervious to forces external to the park. After outlining how the rhetoric of President's House advocates tapped into deeply held beliefs about American political and educational cultures, I point to the many ways in which their messages resonated among those who could exert more direct political pressure on INHP officials.

Telling Stories about Our Past

Public memory is contested because many groups seek to control the past. The story of any public memory site, then, is really the tale of how many stories are distilled through a lengthy and contentious process involving conflict, argument, negotiation, compromise, and the exertion of power. Given their typical location on government land, installations at historic sites are often thought of as the product of careful historical research and government oversight. Although these factors undoubtedly play a role in the process of developing places of public memory, the sites we visit are also the result of the jockeying of many groups of interested parties to have their understanding of history told within the site. John Bodnar referred to these nongovernmental efforts as *vernacular discourses.* As he explained, vernacular discourses have significantly contributed to the shaping of public memory despite institutional interests that offered different visions of how the past ought to be remembered.[26]

Vernacular discourses can easily be understood as the opposite of official discourses, suggesting that only two points of view are in conflict. In many cases, however, multiple points of view may well be present in a collection of vernacular discourses—as when advocates for the President's House initially called for a variety of responses to Lawler's findings. The implicit vernacular/official distinction is also misleading in another way: vernacular discourses do not typically present wholly opposing arguments; instead, they frequently embrace parts of the ideas, values, and beliefs embedded in official discourses. Such a strategy carves out a distinct platform for the publics seeking change yet places them at least partially within the less-threatening grounds of official or familiar positions.[27]

In the early stages of the President's House controversy, the different publics seeking recognition of the site employed language that reflected two types of vernacular discourses. First, they embraced the park's identity as the "cradle of liberty" to offer a counter-narrative that argued that "liberty was incompletely enacted" in the house, the sites within the park, and the nation as a whole. In addition, their words revealed a shared commitment, called a representative anecdote, to "excavating buried truth." So even though the traditional story of the nation's founding, which had permeated park storytelling over the years, provided park officials with a basis for justifying the status quo, the stories told by advocates for the President's House project provided government officials with a way to define the messages of the advocates as politically appealing and park officials with a means of preserving face after their early missteps.

Redefining Independence National Historical Park, and the Nation's Foundations, through Narrative Vernacular Discourse

Counter-narrative: "Liberty Has Been Incompletely Enacted"

As I noted in Chapter 2, no memory site can hold every story associated with the site. As a result, those whose stories have been slighted, ignored, or omitted will seek to have them heard by producing counter-narratives that challenge the officially embedded story while affirming their understanding of the past.[28] Such efforts have generated revisions, and even renaming, of established memorials (such as Little Bighorn Battlefield National Monument), the development of new government-funded memorials (such as Manzanar National Historic Site), and the rise of nonprofit foundations seeking to emplace additional memories within sacred ground (such as the Women in Military Service for America Foundation). In each of these cases, advocates urged the inclusion of untold stories because those stories both challenged simplified tellings of history and reflected fundamental principles honored in official narratives (e.g., heroism, justice, honor). As Stephen Legg argued, these *counter-memorials* "mark times and places in which people have refused to forget. They can rebut the memory schema of a dominant class, caste, race, or religion, . . . [but] they must also draw on existing memories and intuitions to be a success."[29]

Such an approach is based on what Kenneth Foote called symbolic accretion, or the act of drawing on symbols from one memory site to use at another place of memory.[30] Symbolic accretion, Owen Dwyer elaborated, can be used to enhance dominant discourses or to "contradict or otherwise adjust the conventional message of the monument."[31] President's House advocates, of course, employed the latter approach by drawing on the symbolic resources of the nearby Liberty Bell, as well as the entire park's nickname of the "cradle of liberty," to suggest that the stories of the enslaved at the President's House represented the untold story of liberty's incomplete enactment.

To begin, advocates focused on Washington's actions in the home. He not only skirted Pennsylvania law to deny liberty to the nine enslaved Africans who worked in the house but also relentlessly pursued Oney Judge, who escaped servitude to Martha Washington in the President's House and eventually settled in New Hampshire. The nation's first president, advocates noted, helped his own cause in his quest to find Judge when he signed the Fugitive Slave Act of 1793, which gave bounty hunters legal permission to cross state boundaries, kidnap individuals who seemed to have escaped enslavement, and return them to slaveholders—"even if captured in a state that had abolished slavery."[32]

But Washington's actions became only a small part of the story as advocacy efforts unfurled. *Philadelphia Tribune* columnist Linn Washington, Jr., for instance, noted that other members of the nation's first government also ignored the Pennsylvania law and denied enslaved Africans their freedom as they worked in the city during Philadelphia's time as the federal capital. Yet, he continued, INHP refused to acknowledge this fact. "U.S. Park Service officials defiantly sidestep these stories," Washington pointed out, "shirking their legal duty to faithfully present the full history of the multiple struggles for liberty at the Bell site."[33] The planned interpretation for the LBC, as Washington's complaint suggests, was singled out for its incomplete story about liberty. "Curiously," he observed, "while Park Service rangers tell Liberty Bell visitors about anti-slavery activists embracing this icon, Park Service officials resist prominently incorporating the facet of slavery at the site into the story they will tell inside the new Bell pavilion."[34]

On the other hand, Washington argued, the U.S. government's actions in 2002 were consistent with those of the nation's first legislators. "The short shrift U.S. Park Service officials currently give to the George Washington slave quarters site," he wrote, "is comparable to attitudes pervading the U.S.

[Continental] Congress in the late 1770s when that body met in Independence Hall—located across Chestnut Street from Washington's slave quarters. Congress, for example, in January 1800 indignantly rejected the first petition sent by African-Americans to that body asking for the abolition of slavery by an 85–1 vote."[35] Instead, the nation's early legislators held firm to the terms of the Constitution, drafted and debated on the grounds of the park, which forbade any legislative discussion about prohibiting slavery until at least 1808.

These references also underscored how the President's House served as a symbol for the entire nation's immoral embrace of slavery; the story of liberty denied at the President's House was a microcosm of the scope of the counter-narrative. "You can't tell the whole story on that mall [in the park]," asserted Harry Harrison, president of the African American Museum in Philadelphia.[36] Nevertheless, the President's House provided an opportunity to begin telling a story that was not often told in any other venue. For example, Karen Warrington, director of communications for U.S. Representative Bob Brady of Philadelphia, used the President's House controversy to wonder "how educators here and around the country have been able to disconnect American history and African American history. The two are inextricably bound, one unto the other."[37] In one particularly telling example of disconnection, Ray Raphael explained that even though many persons enslaved in southern states escaped to fight for the British (and for their freedom) during the Revolutionary War, his survey of thirteen K–12 history textbooks revealed that "only one mentions that more blacks served with the British than served with the patriots. Not one mentions that some who fought for the patriots were sent back into slavery at war's end. Not one mentions that twenty of Washington's slaves and at least twenty-three of Jefferson's slaves are known to have fled to the British."[38]

These holes in history, *Milwaukee Journal Sentinel* columnist Eugene Kane asserted, need to be filled by more fully acknowledging the role of slavery in U.S. history: "It's time to put slavery into its proper perspective in stark, uncompromising truth. In other words, tell the truth: it wasn't just in the Deep South. And, it wasn't just a small number of plantation owners who benefited."[39] Indeed, "many of what later came to be called manors and landed estates [in the North] were full-fledged plantations that held African-American slaves under conditions similar to those in the south."[40] Slavery did not end in the original colonies of New Jersey and Delaware until 1865, and Pennsylvania's Act for the Gradual Abolition of Slavery was, in typical legislative fashion, crafted with so many exceptions that it did not end slavery and free all the enslaved persons in the state until 1847.[41] The truth of slavery, as the discussion around the President's House revealed, is that the entire nation's economic development depended on the practice of denying liberty to generations of enslaved Africans. American capitalism, democracy, and slavery are "organically connected," asserted the Harvard economic historian Sven Beckert.[42]

The counter-narrative of "Liberty has been incompletely enacted" found its home in the President's House, but it resonated throughout the park and across the nation. While the story of liberty has echoed throughout the nation's traditional stories about itself, the President's House controversy revealed that stories of liberty being sought and denied remain to be told. This strategy of leveraging the powerful yet ambiguous story of liberty served President's House advocates well, just as it had in other situations where African Americans sought to make a place in the American scene. The Lincoln Memorial, for instance, served as a prominent place for the civil rights movement to ground its claims because it contained "cherished American values" whose ambiguities could be mined "to circumvent opposition, unify coalitions, and legitimate black voices in national politics."[43]

In embracing the irony of liberty denied on the doorstep of the nation's foremost symbol of its espousal of liberty, President's House advocates reflected—whether consciously or not—the same sort of approach employed by nineteenth-century African Americans who sought the abolition of slavery before the Civil War and equal treatment for formerly enslaved Africans after its conclusion. In both cases, advocates relied on the African American practice of signifying "that draws on the ambiguity and indeterminacy of language and suggests that the oppressed can gain rhetorical power by appropriating the discourse of the oppressor."[44] The counter-narrative of liberty incompletely enacted not only references the ambiguity of the idea of liberty;[45] it also borrows from "canonical texts of white America . . . in challenging and undermining conventional interpretations" of the term.[46] Moreover, the ironic use of liberty in the counter-narrative offered contemporary advocates the same strategic advantages enjoyed by their nineteenth-century counterparts: (1) "an essential form of protection, to say what they otherwise could not" by using the language of the oppressor,[47] and (2) symbolic distance from the object that they addressed to reduce perceptions of "bias," for irony is a trope that requires a detached perspective.[48]

Representative Anecdote: "Excavating Buried Truth"

At the same time, the counter-narrative of "Liberty has been incompletely enacted" was not some magical elixir that suddenly erased all resistance to acknowledging the President's House and its inhabitants. Disputes about how to recognize the past are embedded within contemporary concerns. As a result, the counter-narrative was not widely accepted among individuals who believe that the nation currently offers abundant opportunities for liberty to its citizens. In Philadelphia, the most outspoken early opponent of the drive to tell the story of slavery in INHP was Robert Morris, a descendant of the colonial Robert Morris who allowed Washington and Adams to use the home as their executive mansion. Morris penned several letters to Philadelphia newspapers complaining that the story of slavery was overwhelming the history of the executive branch and the earlier history of the home. He wrote, "Independence National Historical Park, in coordination with the city, has kicked Morris out the story of his own house in favor of Martha Washington's maid [Oney Judge]."[49]

As a partial remedy to such complaints, representative anecdotes offer familiar, recurring, and overarching stories that provide reassurance for groups struggling to deal with social and cultural stresses; they "resonate with the needs of a people by situating them within a familiar, coherent form."[50] These anecdotes are not necessarily explicitly apparent in discourse but often instead diffused across different public utterances. In the case of the President's House, advocates routinely utilized language that urged the benefit of "excavating buried truth." This anecdote contained the familiar and compelling notions that we should seek truth and that excavation produces new knowledge about the past. Understood within the context of the President's House, the story underscored the need to engage in what Derek Alderman and Rachel Campbell called symbolic excavation, or "the resurrection of difficult and long suppressed (and repressed) historical narratives."[51] Symbolic excavation offered a compatible, if less political, counterpart to the counter-narrative; a symbolic excavation of the past would reveal the untold (within the commemorative landscape) story of the nation's incomplete enactment of liberty.

In addition, advocates sought a literal excavation of the President's House site, both as a sign of symbolic excavation and for the possibility of unearthing buried truths about life in the house. The presence of a public restroom on the location of the house fueled the call for literal excavation; advocates suggested that INHP had covered the site with literal as well as figurative dirt. The figurative dimensions of dirt are more important than its literal manifestation in this case. The anthropologist Mary Douglas suggested that, symbolically, dirt is a concept that represents disorder; things that are dirty are those that do not fit within an established system. Kenneth Burke used similar terms to suggest that violations of social hierarchy pollute the social order and require purification to restore the system.[52] In the United States, the binary of White/Not White has long represented a cultural distinction of Pure/Dirty. Immigrants, lower-class white people (i.e., "white trash"), and African Americans have all been—and often continue to be—classified as out of place or dirty in the United States. The history of slavery and segregation is a lengthy and painful lesson in how white Americans sought to remain culturally pure by both physically separating themselves from black Americans and concomitantly defining blacks as genetically inferior.

Paradoxically, although dirty people are assigned such a status because they *appear* different in some way, they are typically treated like physical dirt in that they are both literally beneath and generally unnoticed, unless they soil something of value to those who consider them dirty. This scenario parallels what Bradford Vivian described as "the politics of seeing and being seen," or the symbolic construction of ways of knowing and seeing social structures and those who supposedly belong in certain places within them.[53] Members of so-called dirty groups see themselves within these constructions and grow wary (and weary) of what McCann called "the threat of erasure" because of desires for purity. Given this threat, dirty groups may see conspiracies where others do not—as McCann illustrated in his analysis of how Nation of Islam members responded to suggestions that the CIA was behind the crack cocaine epidemic.[54]

In the case of the President's House, some public pronouncements simply suggested that the site should not be covered while others went farther and suggested a cover-*up*. That the history of the house was covered by a public toilet—suggesting filth, not just dirt—made the matter worse. Given these circumstances, advocates urged an excavation of the site so that the whole truth could be revealed, or made visible, to a nation that had kept its dirty secrets segregated from its commemorative landscape.

Covering History

As Lawler's findings began to circulate through academic circles and the community of Philadelphia, historians and community activists urged the government to excavate the history buried within the borders of INHP. "Our memory of the past is often managed and manipulated," asserted historian Nash early in the controversy, "[but in INHP] it is downright being buried."[55] Earlier Nash had co-authored an opinion column in the *Philadelphia Inquirer* with the Saint Joseph's University history professor Randall Miller in which they gave voice to the image of buried truth: "The historical memory of the place where George and Martha Washington lived in Philadelphia when he was the nation's first president has been buried for a long time. More troubling, so has the history of the many slaves and servants who resided in and behind the Robert Morris house Washington leased during his stay—now the site where the new Liberty Bell pavilion will soon rise."[56] The two scholars then invoked the image of INHP literally and figuratively covering up the truths buried on the site: "The Park Service decided to 'preserve [the buried site of the slave quarters] in place,' which is to say cover them over and put up the [Liberty Bell Center]."[57]

This theme was echoed in the comments of people who signed IHA's online petition as well. "What a lost opportunity this would be if it is paved over again," lamented Kathleen M. Urban. "We need to remember our history in order to progress and go forward," urged Karen Edery. "We cannot simply ignore it or cover over it!" Other petition signatories used a familiar metaphor to accuse INHP of wanting to avert discussion of slavery within the park: Richard Cullen said, "Let's not sweep history under the rug, or under the Liberty Bell Pavilion," and Geraldine Perkins commented, "We can't afford to sweep our racism under the rug and pretend our past didn't exist."[58] In more pointed language, Michael Z. Muhammad referred to "the plan of the National Park Service and the Independence National Historical Park to yet again sweep Black history under the rug: in this instance, to literally bury it."[59]

Cover-up

Such sentiments lurked beneath the repeated use, with different connotations, of the phrase *cover up*. Some petition signatories used the phrase rather innocently, such as Lisa Franklin's lament: "What a tragedy if we were to cover up this integral piece of our history." Others, however, couched the phrase in more conspiratorial tones:

Don't cover up history. Preserve it. Let our children know the truth. (Tina Dambach)

Covering up the past only does a disservice to us all. (Bobby Keller)

Don't cover the truth, seek it out!! (John Ferguson II)

Covering up and ignoring such information is beyond ridiculous. It's a travesty. (Don Scott, Sr.)

We shouldn't cover up the fact that the "Land of the Free" was a Slavery nation. Show the facts! (Scott)

In fact, concerns about a cover-up eventually gave rise to rumors "that the skeletal remains of slaves lie beneath the earth of Independence Mall"[60] and, in particular, that those enslaved by Washington might be "buried in the third block of Independence Mall, beneath the site of the new National Constitution Center."[61] IHA petition signatory Rosalinde Weiman suggested that they were buried even closer to the President's House site: "I imagine that the black graves they excavated across the street for the new [visitor] center were probably some of his slaves, a fact not mentioned anywhere." In short, "they took the metaphor [of burial] and tried to turn it into a reality," observed INHP supervisory ranger Joe Becton.[62]

None of the individuals enslaved by Washington were buried anywhere near the house, but the rumors were fueled by the combination of distrust of INHP and the memories of how the park had just mishandled an excavation controversy down the mall at the site of the National Constitution Center (NCC). That site was once part of a thriving free African community in Philadelphia. In fact, the home of James Oronoko Dexter, a freed slave and co-founder of St. Thomas African Episcopal Church, once stood on the place where a bus drop-off zone was going to be built. The park resisted calls for excavation at first but relented after intense lobbying from local African Americans, including representatives of two churches founded in the late 1700s by members of Philadelphia's free African community. In an "I told you so" moment, the excavation produced significant artifacts from the colonial period in which Dexter lived.[63]

INHP archaeologist Jed Levin later noted, "[The excavation] brought to the broader public this notion of a hidden African American history below ground."[64] Undoubtedly, an earlier federal government controversy involving excavation, this one in New York City, also lingered beneath the surface of the President's House debates. In 1990–1991, when the General Services Administration sought to construct an office tower in lower Manhattan, the discovery of what is now the African Burial Ground National Monument was poorly handled. Insensitivity, disrespect, and sloppiness permeated the decision making during that process, culminating in an infamous photograph of a backhoe that had inadvertently, but vividly, scooped up remains of enslaved Africans who had been buried at the site.[65]

As these rumors suggest, INHP's reluctance to dig into the past of the President's House site resonated among those who recognized a systematic disregard for African American experiences across U.S. history and throughout the nation's commemorative landscape. That those experiences had been treated, in Douglas's terms, as dirt was underscored in INHP because the President's House site had been covered by a public restroom. As Rich Hall noted when he signed IHA's online petition to commemorate the President's House: "The site is notable as the only place swept not only under the rug, but under the toilet." A good deal of public commentary in the initial stages of the controversy highlighted the impropriety of placing a restroom on the site. "The bathroom should be torn down immediately!" argued D. F. Holly. "What a sacrilege that it was ever built on the spot where Washington and Adams had their White House." Other individuals who signed the IHA on-line petition to commemorate the site agreed:

> I am sure I am not the only one that is bothered by the fact that a toilet has sat on the first location of the executive branch of our government for the past 50 some years. (P. Georgelos)

> This hallowed land now serves as the woman toilets for visitors to the Liberty Bell! (Douglas)

> It seems almost sacrilegeous [sic] to have a toilet on this site. Get rid of it!!!! (Rhonda Field)

> A public bathroom? What a shame! (Renee Holloman)

> What a crime that the first white house is now a Urinal! (Michael diPilla)

> I think it's quite distasteful to maintain a public urinal (restroom) on the site of President Washington's formal home as first President of the United States! (Alexander Mastrando III)

The appropriate solution to this filthy situation was to dig. An excavation of the site, both literally and symbolically, could purify the tainted actions of INHP and the polluted/incomplete story of U.S. history by uncovering the buried past and revealing that which had been kept from view.

While much of the advocacy for excavation called on INHP to make the past visible by acknowledging the President's House site and its inhabitants, this call for a symbolic unearthing of buried history was supplemented by a desire for a literal excavation of the site. Both desires were undoubtedly motivated by an urge to expose that which INHP had been hiding since the park's inception. "We should excavate the site," urged Linda Banks in her petition posting. "We too have a history worth probing, preserving and REMEMBERING." Other petition signatories concurred. Amanda DeLoatch pointed out that "covering the slave quarters and Presidents house will hide our past. . . . The grounds surrounding it should be excavated for potential archaeological finds." And Leslie Greene asserted: "The house of our first president should be both archeologically investigated and then preserved in some meaningful way. It symbolizes both the grand and the shameful beginning of who we are today."

Each of these comments demanded a physical dig, yet they also pointed to the ways in which an excavation would serve as a symbolic action: the beginning of coming to terms with, in Greene's words, the paradox of "the grand and the shameful beginning of who we are today." Digging through the dirt, in other words, would expose any physical remains of and from the house *and* the buried history of slavery. Several petition signatories embraced this visible/invisible metaphor in their postings:

> Obscuring the slave quarters with the Liberty Bell center communicates a profound inability to engage this aspect of our national heritage. (Dr. Ellen Fernandez-Sacco)

> After reading Ed Lawler's article I am convinced that some action must be taken to memorialize the president's house in Philadelphia in a way visible to everyone who visits the site. (Doris F. Zimmermann)

> Preserve the history of the slave contribution to the country during the Revolutionary Period. Make history visible. (Debra Calhouon)

In making history visible, as Calhouon suggested, INHP—and the nation—would be completing the story of liberty, just as the counter-narrative urged. Gene Dyer, for example, pointed out: "If by burying a foundation they are trying to cover slavery it won't work. We need to see all of history, not selected parts." Similarly, Jay Buckwalter declared: "I am absolutely in favor of bringing to the light of day for the current and future generations the full story of the President's House!"

Buckwalter's phrase "the full story" revealed another element of the representative anecdote of excavating buried truth: exposing the invisible elements of the nation's early history would make whole a story filled with holes. "If you tell the story of the President's House, please tell the whole story which should include commemorating the slaves who lived there," begged Joann Cliggett in her IHA petition entry. Undoubtedly, telling the whole story would be painful, observed *Philadelphia Inquirer* columnist Acel Moore: "We are still reluctant to tell the whole story. But telling it is a debt owed not only to Americans of African descent but also to all citizens of America."[66] As

Moore implies, completing the story of liberty would acknowledge holes in the nation's foundation narrative while also recognizing that we continue to encounter the legacies of slavery in the United States today.

The site of the excavation was seemingly perfect for this monumental task: the executive mansion of Washington and Adams, next door to the nation's icon of liberty, *and* the home of enslaved individuals who were residing in a state that exemplified the nation's unease with slavery by virtue of its law granting gradual freedom to the enslaved. Indeed, this tantalizing prospect endowed the advocacy efforts with an urgent, almost spiritual quality as advocates called forth language echoing the biblical injunction that "the truth shall set you free."

In fact, Michael Coard repeatedly urged, "You have to tell the truth, the whole truth and nothing but the truth."[67] "We have to tell the truth, whether it hurts or not," asserted Charles Blockson.[68] Echoed Harry Harrison of Philadelphia's African American Museum, "There is a responsibility to tell the truth, describe the situation, illustrate the drama in a way where we can at least be honest."[69] Similarly, Lawler aired his frustration with park officials by saying, "I just want them to tell the truth about this place."[70]

The truth, of course, is that slavery was deeply embedded in the President's House, as well as in the nation's founding and subsequent history. Observed Amanda DeLoatch on the IHA petition, "It seems as if the Park service is trying to build over this site to cover up the TRUE history of America and its Presidents." Telling the truth of slavery, moreover, would require INHP to touch on contemporary as well as historical concerns, as Virginia S. Cameron pointed out: "We have to face the truth of slavery in order to dismantle the racism of today which is its legacy."

Cameron's concern both reflected the determination of those advocating for recognition of the President's House and its inhabitants and pointed to the difficulties that lay ahead for the project: namely, the enormous and occasionally conflicting ambitions for what the installation could accomplish. Meanwhile, the righteousness of the advocates' cause was recognized seemingly everywhere but inside the administrative offices of INHP. Throughout the early years of the controversy (roughly 2002–2005), INHP came under pressure from governmental bodies at all levels.

Pressuring Public Officials

NPS chief historian Dwight Pitcaithley, like his counterparts in the Ad Hoc Historians group, quickly recognized the symbolic value of Lawler's findings. After the Ad Hoc Historians alerted Pitcaithley to the INHP's refusal to share the interpretive script for the planned LBC interpretation, Pitcaith-ley demanded the script and, on reviewing it, immediately determined that the interpretation would ring hollow given Lawler's findings. In a strongly worded letter to Aikens on April 3, 2002, Pitcaithley described the planned interpretation as overly celebratory and insufficiently complex, and concluded, "There is much work to be done on this exhibit before it is ready for public display." More pointedly, he urged INHP staff to embrace the story of slavery as practiced in the President's House: "We will have missed a real educational opportunity if we do not act on this possibility."[71] Aikens's guest editorial in the *Inquirer*, published four days after the date on Pitcaithley's letter, defended the park's actions and revealed how strongly his suggestion was taken. More pertinent, on April 22, she told a group representing the Ad Hoc Historians that INHP "would not contemplate any major changes inside the pavilion be-cause 'the plans and specifications for the Liberty Bell Center were completed on March 22, 2002,'"[72] even though INHP's historian (Anna Coxe Toogood), chief of cultural resource management (Doris Fanelli), and an African Ameri-can supervisory ranger (Joe Becton) had never seen that script.[73]

As Aikens prepared to move to a new NPS position in Washington in 2002, she handed the political hot potato to her deputy (and soon-to-be interim successor), Dennis Reidenbach, at the end of April. Pitcaithley, meanwhile, began to intervene more forcefully. He repeatedly met with park officials and NPS regional supervisors during April and then attended a May 13 meeting among INHP staff and interested parties designed to produce a breakthrough in the stalemate over the proposed interpretation for the LBC. According to Nash's account of the meeting, little progress had occurred when the group agreed to take a break for coffee. During the break, Nash noted, Pitcaithley visited "with recalcitrant INHP staffers" and apparently directed, persuaded, or motivated them to consider the perspectives of non-park employees at the meeting (which included three people representing U.S. Representative Bob Brady). After the break, Nash explained, INHP officials at the meeting agreed to integrate discussions of slavery into interpre-tation both inside and outside the LBC. In addition, the proposed interpreta-tion would "be sent out for review by noted scholars of the African American experience and the history of liberty in America."[74] Two weeks later, a group of historians and INHP officials met to begin the process of "rewriting the text, modifying captions, and dropping some images while adding others."[75]

This breakthrough, of course, addressed only the content inside the LBC. During the ensuing months, INHP officials continued to resist entreaties to acknowledge more fully the President's House site itself. Over a period of seven months in 2002, the Pennsylvania House of Representatives, the U.S.

House of Representatives Appropriations Committee, and the Philadelphia City Council all voted unanimously to urge the park to mark the President's House site and to acknowledge that enslaved Africans worked in the house. The City Council resolution called for "the appropriate memorializing of the eight human beings of African descent held in bondage at that site"[76] (Lawler's first article identified eight individuals who were enslaved in the house; his later research identified a ninth person); the state house resolution demanded "the placement of a permanent commemorative plaque recognizing the site of the slave quarters";[77] and the U.S. House vote, which carried more weight considering its location in an appropriations bill for the Department of the Interior, instructed the NPS to "appropriately commemorate the concerns raised regarding the recognition of the existence of the Mansion and the slaves who worked in it"—and, in a statement indicating that the park was to take the directive seriously, to provide a progress report within one year's time.[78] Meanwhile, petition drives sponsored by Avenging the Ancestors Coalition (ATAC) and the IHA collected thousands of signatures, and public events sponsored by ATAC generated significant media attention.[79]

At the same time, NPS officials in Washington filled the open superintendent's position by bypassing interim superintendent Reidenbach in favor of a park outsider, Mary Bomar, who came to Philadelphia from a post as the first superintendent of the Oklahoma City National Memorial. Bomar quickly demonstrated an awareness of the stakes in the controversy, listened to the concerns of those advocating for recognition of the President's House site, and worked to facilitate their ideas as the process moved forward. (Bomar was so widely admired for her work at the park that she was promoted to director of the Northeast Region of the NPS only two years after starting at INHP.)

The combination of public, city, and state pressure, along with strong encouragement from Washington and the arrival of a new park superintendent, eventually produced funded mandates to build an installation on the site of the President's House. Initially, Philadelphia mayor John Street engaged in a bit of political payback against INHP when he used the occasion of the grand opening of the LBC in October 2003 to pledge $1.5 million in city funding for a commemorative site. Reading a letter he had written to Coard's ATAC group, Street said:

> This letter is to confirm my support for your position that a commemorative project to honor the 8 enslaved Africans who resided at George Washington's White House be established at the Executive Mansion site. . . . When the country's greatest symbol of liberty is moved to its new home, we must fully include the plight and contribu-

tion of African Americans as a critical part of American history. As the home city of the Liberty Bell and the buildings in which the founding documents of our nation were written, we want to insure that the full history of the spirit of liberty and the struggle for equality is told.[80]

Street also promised to lobby federal government officials for additional funds. Street's advocacy efforts for the project bear a striking resemblance to the work of New York City mayor David Dinkins when the African Burial Ground National Monument controversy in Manhattan was in its early stages. As with Street's decision to get involved in the President's House controversy, Dinkins's participation in the burial ground dispute both asserted local authority on land owned by the federal government and, ultimately, generated a response from federal officials.[81] In Philadelphia, U.S. Representative Chaka Fattah, representing a Philadelphia district, announced on September 6, 2005, that he had secured $3.6 million in federal funding for the construction of a President's House installation.[82]

With funds in hand, the next questions were, what kind of installation would be constructed and who would oversee the project? The answer to the first question, as the preceding pages have suggested, is that the installation would strongly emphasize the nine enslaved Africans, both as individuals and as representatives of the nation's institutionalization of slavery. All parties involved in the controversy quickly recognized this fact, Lawler and IHA webmaster Doug Heller told me over lunch on Memorial Day in 2011. Indeed, INHP's Doris Devine Fanelli reported that of the 248 attendees at a public discussion in the fall of 2004, "no one in the audience called for explication of the executive branch of government or for discussions of Washington's and Adams's presidencies."[83] Adams, she continued, was barely mentioned in any of the park's public meetings, while Washington's story— Coard pointed out—needed amplification only in terms of his role as an enslaver of humans: "It truthfully can be said that Washington was great. But his greatness was as a patriot, a general, and a president. His greatness was not as a man—that is, if greatness is measured by how a man treats his fellow man or woman, even if he or she happens to be black and enslaved."[84]

The second question was more difficult. While INHP administrators would have to be involved in the development of the installation, their resistance to the project had engendered tremendous distrust. In fact, in a January 2003 public meeting, park officials had presented an unfunded conceptual plan for an installation (a response to the March 2002 congressional demand that a plan be developed within one year), which was created by a team led by the urban planning organization responsible for redesigning the

mall. Despite the plan's many laudable elements, and the fact that its interpretive themes were developed with the input of many of the principals who
had advocated for the building of an installation, the lack of goodwill previously exhibited by INHP officials (and perhaps more important, the lack of
acknowledgment of the slave quarters in the preliminary design) ensured
that the proposal was met—to the surprise of INHP officials—with much
skepticism and, in some cases, outright hostility.[85] *Inquirer* reporter Stephan
Salisbury noted that individuals "in the largely black audience accused park
officials of duplicity and racism" and that "park officials appeared, by turns,
glum, chalky-faced and frustrated." Community activist Reggie Bryant asserted, "None of this [design] happened until there was great pressure applied. . . . The promises made here are tantamount to those made in the back
seat at a drive-in movie."[86]

As a result, supervision of the project largely fell to the city, despite its
significantly smaller financial contribution to the project. Although INHP
remained involved, the call for proposals at the end of September 2005 came
from the mayor's office and opened with the words, "The City of Philadelphia (the 'City'), in partnership with the National Park Service ('NPS') and
Independence National Historical Park ('INHP'), invites teams interested in
providing design, exhibit and installation services in a design-build format,
to submit a letter of interest and statement of qualification for consideration
regarding: The President's House: Freedom and Slavery in Making a New
Nation."

The project's ungainly and unspecific name (was it a monument, memo-
rial, or neither? *Inquirer* architecture critic Inga Saffron referred to it as "the
Thing That Is to Be Built"),[87] its lengthy list of core design requirements (six
themes and five cultural values), and the establishment of a fourteen-person
Oversight Committee composed of representatives from advocacy groups,
the park, the city, and Fattah's and Brady's offices (members included Lawler,
Coard, and Blockson) gave more than an inkling of the difficulties to come.
The fights over the President's House were just beginning.

5

Shaping the Place

The Design Competition

"The Thing That Is to Be Built" first had to be designed. And, at this point in the process, that was no easy task. "Independence Mall," opined Inga Saffron, "feels less like an historic site and more like an ideological minefield."[1]

Initially, more than twenty teams stepped foot into the minefield by responding to a Request for Qualifications (RFQ) issued at the end of September 2005. From that group, six were selected as semi-finalists and announced to the public on March 28, 2006. The semi-finalists (which were whittled to five when one team later withdrew from consideration) were invited to create three-dimensional models that were displayed from August 16 to September 19, 2006, at the National Constitution Center, and from September 20 to October 1, 2006, at the African American Museum in Philadelphia. Brief descriptions and selected images of the models were also displayed on the city of Philadelphia's website.

The five semi-finalist design teams faced a significant pair of challenges: how to honor the nation's first two presidents as well as the nine individuals enslaved by Washington in the President's House, and how to remember the nation's first executive mansion as well as the country's ignominious embrace of slavery in its founding. More specifically, the design teams were asked in the RFQ to clearly mark the footprint of the building and slave quarters while integrating six themes (five of which had been developed for the 2003 preliminary design) and five cultural values. The six themes were "the house and the people who lived and worked there; the Executive Branch of the U.S. Government; the system and methods of slavery; African-American Philadelphia (including an emphasis on free African-Americans); the move to freedom; history lost and found (how knowledge of the President's House and the presence of slavery was forgotten and recovered; why we must remember)." The five cultural values were identity, memory, agency, dignity, and truth.[2]

At a larger level, the designers faced "a series of impossible questions" similar to those encountered by Germany after World War II: "How does a state incorporate shame into its national memorial landscape? How does a state recite, much less commemorate, the litany of its misdeeds, making them part of its reason for being? Under what memorial aegis, whose rules, does a nation remember its barbarity? Where is the tradition for memorial mea culpa, when combined remembrance and self-indictment seem so hopelessly at odds?"[3] Given these challenges, the number of responding teams was astounding.

The designs of the five semi-finalists—Amaze Design, Davis Buckley, EwingCole, Howard+Revis, and Kelly/Maiello—met these challenges in a variety of ways, and each, as we'll see, generated a similar variety of reactions from those who evaluated their designs.

Amaze Design

The design from Amaze Design did not attempt to provide a concrete impression of the house (see Figure 5.1). Instead, the designers noted, "we have made use of horizontal and vertical planes to suggest the form of the original footprint. Minor elevation changes in the ground planes along with changes in paving and plant materials suggest various 'rooms.'" The slave quarters and smokehouse areas, for example, were marked with a reflecting pool "to signal the sanctity of this ground, a place upon which we do not tread." The primary structural component of the installation was the Liberty Memorial, a steel tower placed at the site of the kitchen and servants' dining room. To signify the role of the enslaved, nine chairs were placed in the vicinity of the tower while, at the edge of the installation, nine columns "carry the biographies of the enslaved people who lived in the house."[4]

Figure 5.1. Amaze Design's entry: nine chairs, representing the enslaved Africans who worked in the Washington household, sit empty near the Liberty Memorial tower. (Courtesy of Amaze Design, Inc.)

Davis Buckley

The Davis Buckley design "focus[ed] on the enslavement of Africans within the executive mansion during the formative years of this nation" (see Figure 5.2). The entrance of this design featured two bronze figures on either side of a glass wall with a center opening. Embedded in the glass wall were images of 1790 slave censuses in the thirteen states and Mount Vernon. The house floor plan was marked with black granite in the plaza, and the rooms were noted with bronze letters in the plaza. In particular, the slave quarters site was covered with glass, with soil from Africa below the glass covering. The east and west edges of the design were marked by glass "Pillars of Truth," each of which "presents its own theme revealing the contradictory values and ideals that were present during America's first decade."

EwingCole

The EwingCole design emphasized a storytelling approach in which "ten primary stories up to two minutes each will be developed (see Figure 5.3). Each will be marked on the site by a granite icon." Speakers placed in walls throughout the installation would transmit the stories. Interestingly, the

Figure 5.2. Davis Buckley's entry: a glass entryway with black granite marking the floor plan of the home and glass pillars along the east and west edges. (Courtesy of Davis Buckley Architects and Planners.)

Figure 5.3. EwingCole's entry: concentric circles of glass, with images of free and enslaved Africans, underneath trellises. (Courtesy of EwingCole.)

volume level would be different at each story site, with the loudest volume (normal conversational level) in the state dining room and the softest volume (whispers) in the slave quarters area. In addition, the site incorporated a trellis and plantings in order to provide shade and a sense of enclosure for the site.

Howard+Revis

The Howard+Revis design used sculptural figures engaged in the work and history of the house to show how the activities in the house reflected the dichotomous struggle between freedom and slavery (see Figure 5.4). "These sculptural figures are not monumental 'frozen' statues," the designers claimed, "but are engaged in the work of the day, the business of running the Executive Branch of Government contrasted with the business of supporting Washington's household. Their thoughts and activities appear as quotes inscribed into the granite that forms the plaza." In addition, the design contained a bas-relief sculpture with images of each of the nine individuals enslaved by Washington in Philadelphia. On the rear of this sculpture, "a multi-generational struggle beginning with the capture and transport by sea of Africans to the New World and culminating in the contemporary protests of the slave's descendants, the activist groups that brought this commemoration into being," was presented. The house floor plan was marked with bricks in the plaza.

Figure 5.4. Howard+Revis's entry: bricks marking the floor plan of the house and sculptures representing the inhabitants of the house at work. (Copyright © Howard+Revis Design Services, Inc.)

Figure 5.5. Kelly/Maiello's entry: doorway, windows, walls, and fireplaces suggesting the shape of the house when it served as the executive mansion. (Courtesy of Kelly/Maiello, Inc., Architects & Planners.)

Kelly/Maiello

The Kelly/Maiello proposal featured sound recordings, LED screens, graphic panels, and cast impressions in eight places to highlight presidential decisions, slave experiences, the free black community in colonial Philadelphia, and contemporary "contests over freedom" (see Figure 5.5). Its structural components provided representations of fragments of the building, including windows, an entranceway, pillars, and a stairway to the second floor. "As visitors move through the ghost of the building," the designers noted, "its architectural fragments reveal the traces of momentous decisions, heart-rending conversations, and the passing details of everyday life and work in a complex human community."

As these models were displayed in person and online, viewers were invited to offer their evaluations of each of the semi-finalist designs. Each evaluation card contained four items: (1) overall impression of the models; (2) how well does each model commemorate the lives of all the people who inhabited the President's House? (3) what features do you particularly like or dislike about each model? (4) additional comments. The first two items had four response option categories (including a space for comments),[5] while the third item offered the categories of *Like* and *Dislike* and the opportunity to write comments. The city posted on its website 994 completed evaluation cards as eleven batches, each batch in a PDF file (another 138 cards were shared with only members of the Oversight Committee because those who completed the cards requested anonymity).[6] Of the published cards, 780, or 78.47 percent, contained comments as well as marks in the option categories for the items. In the remainder of this chapter, I examine those 780 cards to illustrate how public memory places in general and the President's House site in particular can generate a variety of meanings from those who encounter them.

Because these evaluation cards encouraged people to share their impressions of the designs, I analyzed the cards with the assumption that we have what Sara Ahmed calls affective investments that "stick" when we encounter symbols that move us.[7] More specifically, I embrace the suggestion of Carole Blair, Greg Dickinson, and Brian Ott that "Ahmed's question 'what sticks?' should be supplemented . . . by the questions 'what makes it stick? how? and with what effects?'"[8] And, I would add, "for whom?" because different groups of people will find a single place of public memory more or less compelling. Answering these questions highlights the complex nature of meaning embedded in public memory sites and offers new ways of thinking about the ever-slippery definition of what constitutes a or the *public* and *public sphere.* To that end, let me begin by outlining how I define those terms and then work with them in the remainder of this chapter.

First, I presume that places of memory are sites where a variety of circulating discourses and memories converge and then collide in a symbolic centripetal explosion that reveals the affective investments held by different groups. In this respect, places of public memory are *public spheres,* sites in which competing voices vie to see whose perspective gains currency in the moment. Public memory is, after all, "a site of struggle, a dynamic field of competing and intersecting meanings and discourses, constructed by diverse publics, and articulated through varied media and texts."[9] These competing discourses are pulled to the site in a variety of ways. To begin, the sponsoring agencies spell out parameters (such as requests for proposals) that include and exclude particular voices, perspectives, histories, and so forth. The designers, of course, make their own choices about how to respond to those parameters, in turn offering a range of possibilities for visitors, who bring their own experiences to the site. Through these processes, a place of public memory functions as a permeable container for the past. Not surprisingly, then, the meanings of a memory site resist easy categorization; each place holds *entangled memories* in which "simple narratives cannot take hold."[10]

Second, the centripetal collision of discourses and memories exposes the constellation of multiple *publics* whose members share distinct affective investments in their interpretations of the meaningfulness of the memory place.[11] These publics do not necessarily exist prior to their experience with the memory site; they "emerge in relationship to discourses, events, objects, and practices."[12] Their emergence, as noted in Chapter 2, is also not solely dependent on their members' contemporaneous experience of a memory site; publics materialize when those experiences harmoniously converge with their members' histories, politics, and values.[13] One can thus identify a public by how its members share a contemporary understanding and how that understanding is infused with other discourses they have encountered. In this respect, Kendall Phillips argued, the controversies surrounding public memory sites should "be thought of less as 'oppositions' to some order and more as moments where a multiplicity of orders come into open conflict."[14]

Finally, the open conflict cannot accommodate every public's position; some investments will stick and others will be expelled. Those that are dislodged do not simply disappear, though. Instead, they continue to circulate within the larger public sphere, remaining poised to be pulled into other controversies.[15] For example, as I noted in Chapter 2, the development or revision of some memory sites is often in part motivated by the efforts of those who do not feel invested in an existing memory place (e.g., the building of the Korean War Veterans Memorial and the National World War II Memorial was motivated, in part, by the desire to have more uplifting counterparts to the stark Vietnam Veterans Memorial).

Thus, even though places of public memory are designed to reflect a collective "us" in some form, they often do not succeed. Some of us will feel affectively invested, and some of us will feel no investment in the stories told at the sites. In this respect, memory sites reflect *concord,* or the existence of a democratically produced decision in which certain points of view prevail over others.[16] In the case of the President's House, those ideas that were rejected during the selection of a design continued to circulate among discussions about the site, often reemerging during subsequent steps of the site's development.

Identifying Affective Investments during the Design Competition

As I reviewed the 780 evaluation cards that contained comments, I embraced Gerard Hauser's counsel that scholars enact "an empirical attitude toward the ways in which publics, public spheres, and public opinion are manifested . . . [because] the meanings a critic finds in a text are not necessarily those found by its consumers."[17] Therefore, I treated the comments about the designs as empirical evidence of individuals' affective investments in the designs' meanings. In so doing, I heeded Mark Porrovecchio's point that much scholarship about publics tends to erase the individual by obscuring his or her participation in publics or neglecting to examine how individuals may not participate in a definable public.[18] After all, as I noted in Chapter 2, the collective memory pioneer Maurice Halbwachs emphasized that our group memories are composed of individual memories in interaction.[19]

I found seven primary themes that appeared both uniquely on single comment cards and in combination with other themes on the same card.[20] Each theme is identified below, along with the total number of times it appeared on a comment card and the number of times it was the only theme apparent on a single comment card, respectively.

Feel the Site—the design had aesthetic dimensions that suggested a positive/negative experience in visiting the completed design (291, 154)

Slavery—the design featured the institution of slavery and/or the enslaved residents of the house (115, 41)

Re-create—the design featured evidence of the elements and/or floor plan of the original home (115, 35)

Ethos—the design provided a good fit with INHP and/or historical Philadelphia (96, 28)

Insufficient—the design lacked important elements (66, 12)

Balance—the design balanced the conflicting demands of the project, primarily the executive branch and slavery (51, 11)

Too Much Slavery—the design overly emphasized the institution of slavery and/or the enslaved residents of the house (21, 4)

I reexamined each of these themes to ensure that they represented distinct and unique perspectives on the President's House designs. I noted that almost every comment in the *Insufficient* theme asserted that the designs did not adequately convey the terror of slavery; as a result, I relabeled the theme *Insufficient Attention to Slavery*. I then observed that the remaining *Insufficient* cards shared much in common with the language used on the *Too Much Slavery* cards and on the *Balance* cards. Those cards were combined to develop a new category: *Insufficient Focus on the Presidency*. The final collection of themes was *Feel the Site, Slavery, Re-create, Ethos, Insufficient Attention to Slavery,* and *Insufficient Focus on the Presidency*. Each of these themes appeared as the only theme on a comment card at least twenty-eight times (the two new themes developed after reexamination of the initial themes—*Insufficient Attention to Slavery* and *Insufficient Focus on the Presidency*—showed up on twenty-nine and thirty cards, respectively).[21]

These cards represent collections of individuals who shared perspectives on how the President's House and its inhabitants should be remembered; in short, each theme represents a public with a particular investment in the design of the installation. I also wanted to know if particular publics preferred one or more of the designs as well as why any preferred design might appeal to their interests. So I returned to the cards representing each of these publics to count the favorable votes for each design in terms of *Overall Impression* and *Representing All Inhabitants*. As I describe each of the publics in more detail in the following pages, I also make note of which designs received favorable votes from more than half the members of the public. Interestingly, although not every person completing a comment card listed his or her hometown, the large number of cards that indicated Philadelphia as the commenter's place of residence, and the importance of the site to local residents, suggests that most of the members of these publics were local; they envisioned the designs and the site as part of their *city* as well as an element of INHP.[22] Accordingly, as I discuss the six most prominent publics—three of which featured discourses primarily concerned with aesthetics and three of which featured discourses primarily concerned with politics—I pay careful attention to how local affective investments also may have contributed to each belief about how the past should be presented.[23]

Aesthetics-Driven Publics

Publics interested in aesthetics demonstrated little concern for the messages and/or proposed interpretive material within the five design models. Instead, members of these publics offered comments that focused on the anticipated experience of visiting the President's House site as it was imagined in the models. In this respect, individuals in these publics approached the designs as casual tourists might, although many of their comments also reveal intense local concerns as well. One public (Re-create) displayed a concern with experiencing the *house,* as much as possible, within its original structure. A second public (Feel the Site) focused on the sensory experiences of visiting the *site* as suggested by the models. A third public (Ethos) expressed concern with how the President's House would fit within the larger *area* of INHP and/or structures outside but near the park that represented colonial Philadelphia. I conclude this section with a brief illustration of how the issues that matter to individuals in these publics often overlap.

Re-create the House

Throughout the design process, and even after the construction of the project broke ground in August 2009, some individuals expressed the desire to—as much as possible—develop a design that provided an accurate representation of the house as it existed when Washington and Adams used it as the nation's executive mansion. In fact, especially after the foundations of the mansion were unearthed in the summer of 2007 (the subject of the next chapter), some visitors to the IHA website urged the complete re-creation of the house.[24]

This public likely referenced memory discourses from, and surrounding, other historical sites, whether they are found within the boundaries of INHP (such as Franklin Court, which features a well-regarded Robert Venturi and Denise Scott Brown design that uses a skeletal structure outlining the suggested shape of Ben Franklin's home), at other NPS sites, or in private commercial ventures (e.g., Colonial Williamsburg). The desire for authentic experiences, the ability to touch the past (literally), undoubtedly drives these preservationist discourses. Indeed, as noted in the preceding chapter, at least one commentator bemoaned the destruction of the remaining one or two walls of the house (they were attached to other buildings at that time) when hundreds of buildings were destroyed to create Independence Mall in the 1950s and 1960s.[25]

These concerns reflect discourses of preservation, which typically seek to retain that which is authentic so that history or memory is not lost. Our search for authentic reminders of the past, in fact, is what drives much of the historical tourism industry.[26] When the authentic past is not available, individuals often are content with re-created structures that offer an *aura* of authenticity if not the real thing itself, such as the popular Colonial Williamsburg, where a number of visitors believe they are in the midst of original structures.[27] The NPS, in fact, has historically struggled to honor visitors' desires for a feeling of authenticity with historians' commitment to representing the past accurately—as INHP's decisions to reconstruct the Graff House (where Thomas Jefferson worked on the Declaration of Independence) but not Ben Franklin's house illustrate. (This desire for authenticity is, no doubt, why the blended public of Re-create/Feel the Site, which is briefly discussed at the end of the "Aesthetics-Driven Publics" section, also exists.)

As required by the RFQ, all the semi-finalist design models marked the footprint of the house, but only the Kelly/Maiello design provided faux architectural remnants—such as window frames and a staircase—designed to give a sense of the long-destroyed building. Not surprisingly, then, 86.7 percent of the individuals within this public had a favorable impression of the Kelly/Maiello design, and 68 percent thought it represented all the inhabitants well. "The Kelly/Maiello is the only design that gives any architectural sense to the house," wrote Deborah Sullivan (all names are used unless a respondent requested anonymity, in which case no name is attached).[28] Other comments about the Kelly/Maiello design within this public revealed similar sentiments: "It looks like a house" (Dorothy E. King); "Kept the house shape" (Adam Bowers); "Structure of house remains!"; "Fullest representation of house"; "Sense of house is apparent."

Referencing the Franklin Court design, Alisha McCann praised the Kelly/Maiello design: "A la Franklin Court, helps visitor to imagine the house and how occupants lived in and used it." Similarly, another respondent disliked the EwingCole design because the "sense of building is completely lost"; the Kelly/Maiello design, on the other hand, "uses the house as a platform for interpretation" and "is hands down the best design." The only other design to reach the 50 percent threshold within this public was Howard+Revis, which found 50 percent approval in both the *Impression* and *Inhabitants* categories (all percentages are reported in this order).

For members of this public, then, merely marking the outline of the house was insufficient. Their desire for a fuller sense of the structure reflects the broader notion of sense of place. While park visitors can stand in Independence Hall or visit Washington's version of Camp David in Germantown to experience an authentic place from the past, they must engage in some exceptionally difficult imaginative work to get a sense of place from the outline of a long-gone home. A yearning for *authentic* experience among members of this public differentiates it slightly from the members of the next public, who seek felt experiences not specific to a particular place in history.

Feel the Site

When William Penn planned Philadelphia, he sought to combine a country-and-town feel by interspersing green spaces throughout the city. That idea is perhaps most visible today in Independence Mall itself, but its historical roots are evident in Independence Square, located behind Independence, Congress, and Old City Halls in INHP, and in the adjacent Washington Square (as well as the more distant Rittenhouse Square). Penn's vision of pastoral patches within a city has influenced nearly all the planning for how INHP will be landscaped over the years. In 1960, for example, Philadelphia's *Bulletin* reported that plans for the third block of the mall, which was largely composed of green space, "were symbolic of William Penn's gridiron and park system plan for old Philadelphia, drawn up nearly 200 years ago."[29]

Penn's work, and its legacy in INHP, highlights how many individuals prefer experiences that engage the senses, especially within urban and/or historical landscapes. Not surprisingly, then, individuals within the Feel the Site public offered comments that attended to the subjective, aesthetic dimensions of the design models as a whole rather than commenting primarily about the site of the house. While these types of comments reflected an age-old concern that a memory site should provide a moving experience, recent commemorations have more fully embraced the notion that emotion is a vital part of any memory site experience.[30] Beginning with the Vietnam Veterans Memorial and the AIDS Quilt, a number of other public memory sites (e.g., the U.S. Holocaust Memorial Museum, the Oklahoma City National Memorial and Museum) have been designed to generate intense, emotional experiences. The virtual tour of the Oklahoma City National Memorial and Museum, for example, describes parts of the site as possessing "peaceful serenity" and offering "a powerful experience."[31]

Similarly, individuals in this public imagined how future visitors to the project would emotionally experience the installation. The idea of *feeling* the site, then, refers not as much to the tactile desire to touch a re-creation of the house (as in the Re-create public) as to a craving to be *touched by* the site as a whole. For example, historian David Glassberg, in discussing what he calls a sense of history, pointed out, "Although a sense of history is not based in physiology like a sense of smell or sight, reminders of a past event not experienced can evoke sensations deeply felt, such as feelings of loss, or reverie, or intense pride."[32]

Given the breadth of responses that could be evoked within this category, it was easily the largest public among the six discussed here, with no single overwhelming favorite among the designs. The Howard+Revis design received the most support (67.6 percent [*Impression*] and 72.7 percent [*Inhabitants*]), followed by Davis Buckley (65.7 percent and 54.9 percent); Kelly/Maiello was favored by 57.6 percent and 58.6 percent in the two categories, while EwingCole received 50 percent and 49 percent. Framing the wide-ranging comments about how the models "felt" is challenging, but my examination of the positive and negative evaluations of the models pointed to two prominent pairs of themes: (1) inviting vs. cluttered and (2) powerful vs. cold.

Some individuals expressed preference for designs that felt open, inviting, and engaging. Art Stiefel, for example, praised the Kelly/Maiello design for its "nice use of open space combined with interactivity," while Richard deCampo agreed that "Kelly/Maiello's design is the best combination of things to see and hear. I would feel drawn to enter to the footprint to see what it's about." Another person praised the EwingCole model because it was "futuristic, open, modern," while another voter gushed that it was "clean, clear, open, visitor friendly." Dave Wisniewsky liked Amaze Design's model because it was "activity friendly; use of open air space, garden," while another voter said of the Howard+Revis model, "I like its simplicity—we do not need more structures and buildings cluttering the area."

Other individuals, however, disliked designs that they perceived as too cluttered. One voter complained that Amaze Design had "too much structure" and Howard+Revis had "too much paving," while another person said the Amaze Design model had "too much stuff," especially compared with Davis Buckley's design, which "tells the story simply and uncluttered." G. Murphy also disliked the Amaze Design model because it had "too much going on," just as the EwingCole model was "too busy." In an especially critical comment, one individual complained that the Amaze Design model was "too cluttered—closed in—resembles an outhouse!"

Another group of individuals in this public indicated that a compelling design should generate a powerful emotional response. Those designs that failed to do so were described as "too cold, too stark" or "cold, barren, nothing special," as these anonymous comments about Amaze Design's model illustrate. EwingCole's design was panned by Anjela Rush-Jackson for its "coldness," while Davis Buckley's model was described as "too stark, no heart." Other individuals used similar language in their comments of the semi-finalist designs: "too sterile" (Eleanor Brennan's description of Kelly/Maiello), "too bland" (Sara Mathews's indictment of Davis Buckley), or just "plain" (Teal K. Ellington's comment on Amaze Design, EwingCole, and Kelly/Maiello).

When individuals perceived that a design "lack[ed] mood and feelings," as a voter complained about the Amaze Design, Davis Buckley, and EwingCole models, they implicitly indicated that the designs should evoke a powerful emotional response. As Edward L. Williams explained, "While I kind of like all of the designs, none jump out at me. To come close to the pain of slavery and being from the South, I thought that after looking at them I would feel some—I did not." When individuals were not emotionally affected by a design—"There's no life to it," asserted Sara Matthews about both the Amaze Design and Davis Buckley models—they complained that a design (in this case, Kelly/Maiello) was "not moving, compelling" or, perhaps more tellingly in this comment about the EwingCole model, remarked on the design's "resemblance to an office building or food court."

Instead, individuals in this public preferred designs that were "powerful" (Howard+Revis), contained "powerful images" (Howard+Revis), or offered the "power of simple figures at crossing of threshold" (Davis Buckley). A powerful design could promise "visual/auditory impact [that] excites visitors" (EwingCole), but it was more likely to be described as "very moving" (Howard+Revis) or "simple, yet moving" (Davis Buckley). A design that offered a powerful feel, in other words, suggested a profound experience for visitors. For example, one person described the Kelly/Maiello design as "heartwarming, yet solemn," while another said the Howard+Revis design "reminds me of the impact of the FDR memorial in D.C."

Members of this public thus focused all their attention on the characteristics of the installation itself, not just on the house, as those in the Re-create public did. They also displayed no overt interest in the political ramifications of how the design would interpret history, nor did they raise concerns about the site's fit within the surrounding landscape. Individuals in the Ethos public, however, very pointedly evaluated the designs on the basis of the issue of fit.

Ethos of the Area

Individuals in the Ethos public expressed a desire to have the design of the President's House site fit well within the surrounding landscapes. "Fit well" is, of course, a judgment that relies on one's understanding of the meanings of the surrounding environment,[33] and in Philadelphia the range of landscapes is most definitely rooted in the historical. "There is some sense," wrote Philadelphia native Steven Conn, "in which the Philadelphia region steeps more in its own past than any other place in the nation."[34] Given this context, we can consider the landscapes surrounding the President's House to entail the structures of INHP, including those adjacent to or near the site; the historical structures of Philadelphia that symbolically reference colonial times; and the greater Philadelphia area's historical sites.

This public pulled in a slew of memory discourses, ranging from the park's interpretive themes—under the General Management Plan of 1997, for example, INHP emphasized that "eighteenth century Philadelphia was the political, economic, and cultural center of colonial America"[35]—to the park's location near the Old City neighborhood, an area locally embraced because "its history dates from the city's beginnings."[36] Independence Visitor Center's mission to promote both the park and the surrounding historical sites speaks to this expanded sense of landscape. The Visitor Center's website, for example, designates nonpark destinations such as the Betsy Ross House and Elfreth's Alley ("known as the oldest continually inhabited street in the country") as "must see" historical sites within the city, while elsewhere it encourages trips to historic sites outside the city.[37] The votes of individuals within this public indicated general approval with two designs: Kelly/Maiello with 68.2 percent and 58.8 percent, and Howard+Revis with 54.5 percent and 70.6 percent.[38]

Within this public, some individuals indicated a preference for the design to mesh with existing INHP structures. They pointed out that the project should not distract future visitors from the impressive collection of buildings within the park. Dirk Allen, for instance, wrote: "It [the winning design] should serve to educate and complement what is there already, not detract or isolate from the overall park experience." Similarly, Amanda Rodriquez preferred the Howard+Revis design because it "will clash least with the entire Independence area," while another person liked this model because "it fits into exhibits in [the] area." One person praised the EwingCole model because it "works well with [the] Visitor Center." Two other voters liked Kelly/Maiello's design because "the Colonial style [is] in keeping with the Park" and it "blends in with [the] mall."

Other individuals expressed concern with how some of the designs would harmonize with the colonial ethos of historical Philadelphia. As Tyrone Brown observed, "Some of these models do not fit in with the colonial era." Within this public, the primary complaint about the designs was that they were "too modern" to fit well within the larger area. Stephanie Kirkpatrick summarized this concern: "All of the displays appear to be much too modern. I don't want to see modern architecture when viewing a house 200+ years old." Ewing-Cole's model, which featured trellises and a garden-room concept, was called "too hi-tech to represent a house from 1790" by Erika Peres, while another individual claimed that the Amaze Design model's abstract rendering of the site, featuring a prominent steel tower, was "too modern a design for the setting/topic." Another voter offered an apt summary of the collective opinions of this public by noting that the Amaze Design model was "too modern," the EwingCole design was "too busy, too modern," but the Kelly/Maiello design possessed a "clear message, in keeping with neighborhood and historical period."

Throughout the park area's history, governmental entities have striven to offer a consistent and historical look in the area.[39] The members of this public must surely agree with the intent of those efforts, for their comments display a clear concern with developing a site that is visibly harmonious with its surrounding landscapes. As one person, who preferred both the Howard+Revis and Kelly/Maiello designs, explained, the design should be "a good historical addition to Philadelphia landmarks." In this respect, this public's interests bear some resemblance to both the Re-create public (a concern with the visual) and the Feel the Site public (a desire for sensory experiences). Given these similar concerns, I was not surprised to discover that two subsidiary publics expressed interest in aesthetic concerns and that their concerns merged the interests of two of the three primary aesthetics-driven publics.

Blended Interests

In a number of instances, the comments on the evaluation cards reflected individuals' interests in two of the three topics addressed by the aesthetics-driven publics; thirty-six people uniquely expressed a desire for a design that addressed the concerns of both the Re-create/Feel the Site publics, while another twenty-seven people offered comments that suggested their investment in both the Feel the Site and Ethos publics. Given the popularity of these two combinations, I want to note briefly how these individuals' comments reflected the interests of both publics (I consider these blended groups to be distinct publics with interests that overlap with the other two publics). In so doing, I hope to underscore the overlapping investments in meaning that inevitably occur across distinct publics and to illustrate how aesthetic issues in particular are not easily separated.

Re-create/Feel the Site

Individuals in the Re-create/Feel the Site public were primarily advocates for re-creation of elements of the house—which is likely why the Kelly/Maiello (85.7 percent and 68.6 percent) design was easily the most popular model for them; Howard+Revis (65.6 percent and 53.1 percent) was the only other design to reach the 50 percent threshold—*because* such a design would provide the best feel for life in the house, especially compared with the other choices. As Allen Hoover argued, the Kelly/Maiello model was "closest to what the building actually looked like, but with a modern feel," while Davis Buckley's design was "too plain," EwingCole's was "too confusing," Amaze Design offered "no re-creation of original building layout," and Howard+Revis provided "not enough re-creation." Similarly, another voter claimed that the Kelly/Maiello design "provides the feeling you are in a house" whereas other designs were "too vague," (Amaze Design), "too sterile" (Davis Buckley), or "too futuristic" (EwingCole).

Feel the Site/Ethos

Those individuals whose comments revealed a concern with both the feel of the designs and their fit with the area either evaluated a single design for its ability to move potential visitors and mesh with its surroundings *or* remarked on one design's ability to move visitors and another design's fit within the environment. Interestingly, the Davis Buckley (85.7 percent and 86.4 percent) design was a clear favorite among this public, even though it was not the top choice of either the Feel the Site or the Ethos publics. Kelly/Maiello (67.9 percent and 58.3 percent) and Howard+Revis (60.7 percent and 78.3 percent) also received significant positive evaluations among the members of this public. Joe Shearn was among those individuals who revealed concerns about both the feel and fit of the projects in their evaluations of single designs. He disliked the Amaze Design model because it was "ugly—[and] doesn't fit in with area or transition well to Liberty Bell," and he panned the EwingCole design because it was "too much—takes away from Liberty Bell Center." This type of evaluation was also evident in an individual's praise for the most popular choice among this public, the Davis Buckley design: "Simplicity, dignity. Moving, relates well to Liberty Bell Center."

In summarizing this discussion of the three aesthetically oriented publics, I want to emphasize that these publics' concerns with aesthetics are not exclusive of political concerns, for issues of authenticity—which reverberate throughout the Re-create and Ethos publics, in particular—most certainly possess political undertones. Similarly, as we shall see, design issues are also relevant to political concerns. The aesthetic dimensions of a memory site design, especially as they are configured in relation to its location to other places, "value and legitimate some views and voices, while ignoring or diminishing others."[40] For example, discourses of Re-creation and Ethos certainly imply a concern with respecting, rather than challenging, the traditional stories of INHP, as two of the politics-driven publics desired.

Politics-Driven Publics

Publics driven by politics expressed little direct interest in the aesthetics of the designs but instead shared their perceptions about which messages were featured (or not featured) within the designs and the proposed interpretive material. If the comments of the aesthetics-driven publics represented the perspective of casual tourists as well as local residents, the language of individuals in these politics-driven publics reflected both the politics of power in Philadelphia and the interests of historically minded tourists. One public (Slavery) was pleased to see designs that devoted attention to the enslaved who lived and worked in the President's House as well as to the institution of slavery in general. A second public (Insufficient Attention to Slavery) found all the designs lacking because they did not offer unvarnished accounts of the horrific practice of slavery in the United States. A third public (Insufficient Focus on the Presidency) was dissatisfied that many of the designs did not give Washington and, especially, Adams their due as the first chief executives of the nation.

Slavery

Individuals who praised designs for their attention to slavery—especially those of Howard+Revis (81.3 percent and 79.3 percent) and Davis Buckley (75.8 percent and 67.7 percent); no other design reached the 50 percent threshold—expressed satisfaction with the projects' acknowledgment of the enslaved in the design or, in a slightly different vein, with the models' depiction of the experience of slavery. Their focus on this element of the project suggests that these respondents were less interested in the official role played by the executive mansion and more interested in how the design would offer rhetorical reparations for the nation's original sin of slavery.

In this respect, these individuals reflect what Carole Blair and Neil Michel identify as the trend toward increasingly democratic representations in public memory sites.[41] In other words, such sites designate the contributions of a variety of individuals, not just elites, as worthy of commemoration. In addition, this public likely pulls in memory discourses from other public memory controversies, historical and contemporary, in which vernacular interests were ultimately integrated within final designs and decisions.[42] Finally, some individuals in this public undoubtedly represent local Philadelphians' interest in telling the stories of the city's first black residents; both ATAC and Generations Unlimited strongly advocated for such recognition.

Those who were pleased to see slavery acknowledged in a federal memory site seemed to reflect the general sentiment shared by this individual: "I like how they are placing slavery into more importance." Such language reflects what Blair and Michel called the increasingly popularity of "commemorative works . . . undertaken to honor the 'dispossessed.'"[43] These works, often fueled by grassroots efforts, point to the urgency and intensity behind efforts to reclaim the stories and actions of those who have heretofore been neglected in mainstream memories.

Not surprisingly, then, individuals within this public tended to praise the statuary in the Davis Buckley and Howard+Revis design models—features largely absent in the other three designs—for both humanizing the enslaved staff in Washington's house and drawing attention to their individual stories. Those who commented on the Davis Buckley design, for example, noted "the statues of Hercules and Oney Judge [two of the nine enslaved individuals in the house]" (Gaylord B. Gray), "the glass with the number of slaves in 1790 in front," and the "listing of slaves, bronze statues." Similarly, the Howard+Revis design was praised for "the statue of the struggle with the 9 slaves who lived in the President's House" (Lorraine M. Sheaff), "the monument to the enslaved people" (Ronald C. Padgett), and "the commemorative sculpture; all the slaves standing together" (Queen Marshall).

The Howard+Revis and Davis Buckley models were also singled out by individuals who believed that those designs captured the experience of slavery. Specifically, individuals within this public indicated that the struggles and sufferings of the enslaved were best represented within these two designs. As one individual claimed, "The design by the team Howard+Revis best depicts the true history and brings to life the enslaved people." Similarly, Donald L. Johnson, Sr., wrote that "the Howard+Revis model in my opinion captures the essence of the struggle enslaved Africans endured just to get to America from West Africa," while Sharon Stewart asserted that "only the Howard+Revis model fully depicts the suffering of the nine enslaved Africans who were part of George Washington's household. (This is clearly an example of a picture (relief) being worth a thousand words.)." The Davis Buckley design, argued Naomi E. Ware, depicts "a true picture of slavery," and Jennifer Herring noted, "I love the design by Davis Buckley the most because it shows how the slaves were accounted for. Davis Buckley model displays the truth that America wants to ignore."

Most efforts to make places for untold stories within the commemorative landscape—especially those that are federally funded—are what Kenneth Foote calls "oblique" and promote "the heroism, fortitude, and sacrifice" of those honored rather than directly challenge the deeply ingrained or ignored memories that have held sway over the years.[44] The comments quoted in the preceding paragraph suggest that the quoted individuals see the Howard+Revis and Davis Buckley designs as challenges to the deeply ingrained public memories celebrated within INHP. Indeed, the very existence of the installation is a challenge to those memories. At the same time, however, their use of the words *truth, struggle,* and *suffering* also indicates that these design responses, while more than oblique, are not forceful and direct either. For some individuals, a bold and graphic story of slavery was required at the site.

Insufficient Attention to Slavery

For most of these individuals, the idea of speaking truth to power seems to motivate their interests, and suggests that they view the President's House design process as a forum for addressing the denial of human rights then and now. Members of this public might well have been among those advocates for the President's House in the preceding chapter who urged INHP to "tell the truth" about what happened at the site, but the individuals in this public typically used more passionate and powerful language indicating that acknowledgment of the role of slavery within the house and across the nation was simply not enough.[45]

Members of this public were not excited about *any* of the designs. The highest percentage of positive impressions of the design belonged to Howard+Revis at 38.5 percent, while the same percentage favored Davis Buckley's treatment of all the inhabitants. "All of the models," wrote Rod Mitchell, "are at best, remotely suggestive of the indignities suffered by enslaved Africans and their opposition of their condition to the professions of the 'Founding Fathers.'"

In particular, most of the individuals in this public took exception to the designers' choices to valorize the enslaved who worked in the President's House without a more direct treatment of the lived experiences of the enslaved in general. This public sought a treatment of slavery at odds with the traditional tendency in public memory work to praise the work of those, especially African Americans, whose lives and achievements had been heretofore neglected, perhaps because they embraced a more recent trend in the design of public memory sites: the desire for "therapy and healing" through commemoration.[46] The goal of a therapeutic monument, explained Kirk Savage, "is not to celebrate heroic service or sacrifice, as the traditional didactic monument does, but rather to heal a collective psychological injury."[47]

In this case, the general discourses of therapy and healing are likely also interwoven within political discourses of confession, truth, recognition, and reconciliation. Much of the rhetoric found within this public reflects discourses also found in the controversies surrounding South Africa's Truth and Reconciliation Commission. Deborah Posel, for example, unpacked the myriad ways in which testimony to the commission featured discourses of confession that were aligned with discourses of truth—much as many members of this public sought to equate confessions of the sins of slavery with the idea of a cleansing truth.[48] Similarly, some members of this public suggested that the horrors of slavery were not sufficiently *recognized* by the designs, a discourse also evident in Erik Doxtader's thoughtful analysis of how testimony offered to the Truth and Reconciliation Commission underscores the need to have recognition precede reconciliation.[49]

Members of this public seem more than wary of the ability of the President's House site to serve as a place of potential reconciliation, likely because they saw all the designs as insufficiently confessing the sins of slavery and/ or recognizing the horrors of slavery (and their historical legacies).[50] Sacaree Rhodes, for example, liked "nothing" about all of the models and urged the selection committee to "show the inhumanity against Black Enslaved Persons." Another individual argued that the collection of models "does not show the horrible things that happened to Black people held as slaves by George Washington," while another person complained, "I feel this is not showing the terrorism and rape against Black people."

Individuals within this public argued that the evils of slavery had been withheld from the designs. Many of the comments offered by members of this public echoed the tensions in discourses identified by Nathan Austin in his analysis of visitors to Ghana's Cape Coast Castle, a fort used for slave trading during colonial times. According to Austin, some African American visitors felt that whites "should not be allowed to enter the site" while some white visitors attempted "to de-racialize the history and events associated with the site."[51] Members of this public undoubtedly were concerned with designs and interpretation at the President's House site that diluted the horrors of slavery. In the words of Janet Powell Dailey, the designs provided "a sanitized depiction." Or, as Deanne Cardwell argued: "The models do not depict the true story. It makes it seem as if slavery was a wonderful institution. The designs are great structures, but the wording is unacceptable. They do not depict the struggle of my ancestors who were treated like animals." Accordingly, C. Keller reminded the selection committee that "slavery was not a picnic. Even free Africans suffered intense discrimination. Please do not 'white-wash' it!" Added an anonymous respondent, clearly referring to the enslaved, "The structures have no meaning in the absence of the truth about their lives, suffering, treatment, and roles."

A slightly different, but still dissatisfied, response emerged from individuals in this public who felt that a more complete historical account of African American contributions should have been included in the models. While the former group embraced a more tragic account of slavery's role in the United States, this group used language that suggested a progressive story in which the enslaved contributed to the development of the United States. For example, Rashima Jonson argued, "The President's House design competition does not teach me anything on how African Americans played a vital role in history. We were more than 'slaves,' we built this nation and we still are building it." More generally, Henry Goodley asserted that the designs "don't show anything about our culture. They don't show African slave hardship, suffering, and contribution to this country." In some respects, then, these individuals fall between those in the Slavery public and the more passionate voices in this public; they simply want more stories of the enslaved than what they saw in the designs. As Arthur E. Edens summarized, "Not enough historical facts about G. Washington's and wife's slaves."

As noted in Chapter 3, while African Americans generally consider the institution of slavery to form a significant foundation for the group's collective memory, individuals within the group possess many perspectives on where, how, and if slavery should be acknowledged.[52] Non–African American voters, too, likely held a variety of perspectives on slavery's place in the commemorative landscape generally and in INHP and the President's House site in particular. Certainly, some individuals who completed comment cards expressed disappointment that many of the designs, in their opinion, overly emphasized slavery at the expense of the executive branch.

Insufficient Focus on the Presidency

Individuals who offered comments indicating that one or more of the design models devoted insufficient attention to the presidency expressed concern with how the designs—from their perspective—minimized the development of the office of the presidency by Washington and Adams. These individuals, who favored only the Kelly/Maiello design (73.3 percent and 80.8 percent), likely harbored more traditional sentiments toward commemorative practices in that they seemed to embrace the idea of what Foote labeled sanctification, which includes the praising of heroes and/or ideas at the memory site.[53] In some respects, this discourse of memory harbors traces of the once-prevalent "great man" theory of history popularized by Thomas Carlyle in the latter half of the nineteenth century—that is, the great moments of history are the products of heroic individual efforts, such as Washington's leading the military efforts for independence and then serving as chief executive of the new nation (while refusing to serve beyond two terms).[54]

In addition, the memory discourses reverberating throughout this public seem to embrace the traditional discourses of interpretation used in INHP. "In the early 1970s, the story visitors heard at Independence National Historical Park was one of freedom, liberty and opportunity as reflected in the pale faces of Washington, Jefferson, Franklin."[55] Even as the park was developing its revised General Management Plan in 1997, three of the five primary interpretive themes focused on Independence Hall as the "birthplace of modern democratic government worldwide," the park as the site where "the founding documents of the United States" embraced limited government and popular sovereignty, and the Liberty Bell as "a symbol of liberty . . . [that] has weathered threats and has endured."[56] Although the entirety of the 1997 Liberty Bell theme's wording leaves open the possibility of acknowledging that the bell earned its name from abolitionists in the 1830s, the supporting explanation in the GMP makes no mention of this fact. Indeed, as I noted in the preceding chapter, INHP included more discussion of slavery and the abolition movement in its interpretation for the 2003 opening of the LBC only after much public pressure to do so. Historically, INHP has served as a site in which only the positive features of the nation's founding have been celebrated.

Accordingly, individuals in this public pointed to one of three concerns in the other four designs: (1) slavery was emphasized more than the presidency; (2) issues involved in the establishment of the office of the president were not given their due; (3) John and Abigail Adams were not sufficiently acknowledged.

The first issue produced a significant share of the comments offered by members of this public. G. A. Pataki argued that the problem, from his perspective, was rooted in the design requirements for the installation: "The words 'enslaved, slavery, bondage' are used more than a dozen times in the core Design Requirements; 'Washington' twice; and John Adams, Abigail Adams, and Martha Washington not at all." Another person also argued that slavery was emphasized at the expense of the presidency: "Slaves, unfortunately, were commonly found around the country. There is only one 1st president[;] therefore, I am opposed to any exhibit of the President's House that makes the slave story seem to be the most important."

As this person notes, most individuals in this public were not opposed to the incorporation of slavery within the design models; instead, they believe that one or more of the designs devoted too much attention to slavery. For instance, Bill Clossey claimed, "These [design models] are terrible! The emphasis should be on the President's House, including the slave quarters, not just slavery," and Doris Z. Taylor asked: "Why must slavery be the primary thing commemorated at this site? George Washington and John Adams seem to be lost in the shuffle."

In a related complaint, other individuals bemoaned the seeming lack of attention devoted to the development of the presidency in relation to the emphasis on slavery. Alison Gay, noted, for example: "Without a doubt [slavery] is a very important issue to address. But slavery should not overshadow all the other issues surrounding this house. Washington really defined the Presidency. I'd like to examine the ways in which he did this. Adams passed the Alien and Sedition Act. He also dealt with the XYZ affair and the Quasi war with France." Similarly, M. Hughes argued that the perceived imbalance between the presentation of slavery and the presidency actually detracts from the former: "Without sufficient commemoration of the presidential aspect of the site, the slavery aspect is reduced from tragedy to irony, from truth to complaint. These projects diminish slavery by failing to dignify the Presidency's founding." As another evaluator complained, the perceived imbalance oversimplifies the complex history of the house: "[I] would like to see more emphasis on other aspects of President's administration. Too much focus on just slavery. I'm sure the house has more of a storied history than just the fact that slaves lived here."

Some individuals who expressed displeasure with the attention accorded the presidency in the design models were especially bothered by the lack of interpretation regarding the anti-slavery president John Adams and his wife Abigail. Asserted one voter, "I dislike the lack of anything on J. Adams." Added another, "None of these exhibits highlight John & Abigail Adams!!

Abigail was an abolitionist who lived in this house and they *never* owned slaves!!" Similarly, Stuart Howard urged, "Whatever design you ultimately choose, I beg you to give John Adams the respect and prominence he deeply deserves. . . . Also, by emphasizing his lifelong opposition to slavery and the fact that there were *no* slaves in the President's House during Adams' tenure, you will build a monument that unites rather than divides our people." Perhaps the general absence of the Adamses contributed to the overwhelming support of the Kelly/Maiello design model within this public. For example, one individual noted the lack of recognition of Adams as a weakness in all the models except for Kelly/Maiello's design. Interestingly, and perhaps not coincidentally, David McCullough's popular biography of John Adams— which featured correspondence between John and Abigail Adams—had reached the top spot on the *New York Times* bestseller nonfiction list shortly before Lawler's research became public, and McCullough's 2005 account of the pivotal year of 1776—which devoted much attention to George Washington—had achieved the same status during the time in which voting on the semi-finalist designs occurred.[57]

As the comments from individuals in this set of politics-driven publics reveal, the most significant point of controversy in the design process mirrored the original dilemma faced by INHP administrators: how do we create an installation in which the most strongly held affective investments—the traditional idea of the United States as the land of liberty brought into being by great men and the more complex fact that this land of liberty denied freedom to much of its population—are at odds with one another? As *Philadelphia Inquirer* architecture critic Inga Saffron noted during the voting, "the need to satisfy many interest groups" meant that finding a satisfactory design "might well be impossible."[58] Nonetheless, one of the five semi-finalist designs was destined to become the foundation for a permanent installation in INHP.

Picking a Winner: Concord and Centrifugal Discourses

How would the winning design be selected? Would the public voting determine the winner? Would the public voting even contribute to the decision? Much of the deliberation that occurred between September 2006 and February 27, 2007 (when the winning design was announced), occurred behind closed doors, which makes "understanding how one or more positions gain relative dominance" difficult.[59] We can tell, however, that the public voting demonstrated clear preferences for some designs over others. My analysis of the favorable and not-favorable votes for the five designs revealed that three of the models (Howard+Revis, Kelly/Maiello, and Davis Buckley) were more

TABLE 5.1. TOTAL FREQUENCIES AMONG ALL COMMENT CARDS FOR "OVERALL IMPRESSION"

Design Firm	Love	Like with Reservations	Neutral	Don't Like	Not Evaluated
Amaze	98	159	163	319	138
Davis Buckley	204	253	123	169	129
EwingCole	169	165	145	265	134
Howard+Revis	291	224	123	145	95
Kelly/Maiello	211	233	154	145	135

TABLE 5.2. TOTAL FREQUENCIES AMONG ALL COMMENT CARDS FOR "REFLECTS ALL INHABITANTS"

Design Firm	Exceptionally Well	Well	Adequately	Not Well at All	Not Evaluated
Amaze	60	145	183	257	233
Davis Buckley	168	192	176	130	212
EwingCole	147	151	181	180	220
Howard+Revis	281	202	129	94	172
Kelly/Maiello	178	211	149	132	208

TABLE 5.3. MEANS AMONG ALL COMMENT CARDS FOR "OVERALL IMPRESSION" AND "REFLECTS ALL INHABITANTS"

Design Firm	Impression	Inhabitants
Amaze	2.95	2.99
Davis Buckley	2.34	2.40
EwingCole	2.68	2.45
Howard+Revis	2.16	2.05
Kelly/Maiello	2.31	2.35

positively evaluated than the other two (Amaze Design and EwingCole).[60] The Howard+Revis design was clearly the most popular in both the *Overall Impression* (item one) and *Reflects All Inhabitants* (item two) categories. In the *Overall Impression* category (see Table 5.1), Howard+Revis received the most votes in the *I Love It* column (represented by a score of 1). When the total votes received in the two columns indicating positive reactions were counted, Howard+Revis was also the most popular design. In the *Reflects All Inhabitants* category (see Table 5.2), Howard+Revis was even more clearly the collective top choice of those completing evaluation cards. The means for each of the three designs, in which 1 is the most positive score and 4 the least positive score, reaffirmed these totals (see Table 5.3).

On the basis of the total number of votes cast, Howard+Revis appears to be a fairly clear "people's choice" as the best design for the President's House project. Given that the Howard+Revis design was favored by a majority of the members in the Feel the Site, Ethos, and Slavery publics, we might tentatively conclude that—among the population of voters—the following impressions "stuck" or gained relative dominance: the best model did not need to re-create the house, but it did need to offer a powerful aesthetic experience that was at once consistent with the surrounding architecture and emphasized the institution of slavery as well as the particular individuals enslaved in the house.

A second, and more concrete, means of assessing relative dominance is to examine (as much as possible) the less visible processes of deliberation and decision making that occurred after the public voting. In early November, Howard+Revis, Kelly/Maiello, and Davis Buckley were all given the opportunity to respond to concerns raised by the Oversight Committee, the city, and INHP officials. In identical language, Davis Buckley and Kelly/Maiello were asked for "more emotional impact" because "the full impact of what it meant to be enslaved in the President's House is not yet adequately conveyed at an emotional, visceral level." In addition, Davis Buckley was directed to broaden its treatment of the executive branch, mark the footprint of the house more fully, correct errors in its text, and explain how the text in its proposed glass pillars could be "read in bright daylight." Kelly/Maiello was also asked to explain how its extensive use of audio and video would work in a noisy, outdoor installation. Howard+Revis was told to integrate its proposed elements more fully so that visitors would have "a unified emotional or visual experience."[61]

On the basis of these directions, one would be tempted to think that the Howard+Revis design had an edge among those officially charged with making recommendations and, ultimately, a decision about who would design the installation. At the least, the team had fewer issues to address than the other two teams. Each of the three teams had only a short amount of time, and space, in which to respond to these directives. Following a conference call shortly after receipt of the letters outlining the concerns, the teams had two weeks to share new sketches (but not models) and/or an explanation of no more than three pages. After sharing their responses, the teams waited patiently as members of the Oversight Committee evaluated their work and then shared their assessments with the city and INHP.

More than two months elapsed between the Oversight Committee's final review and the announcement of the winning design. Notably, no one in the city or INHP produced any data regarding the results of the "people's choice" voting, nor were the deliberations of the Oversight Committee shared with the public either at the time or after the fact (my Freedom of Information

Act request for the minutes and votes of members of the Oversight Committee's deliberations was denied),[62] nor did Mayor Street refer to any comments made by members of the Oversight Committee when he announced on February 27, 2007: "I am proud that—at the end of a tough national competition—the consensus winner is headed by a local, African American–owned firm—Kelly/Maiello!"[63]

Given that public reaction to the design models was so assiduously courted, the question arises, why was the Kelly/Maiello design chosen when it was clearly a second—nearly third—choice of the voting population? One answer may be that the selection of Kelly/Maiello's design *did* take public commentary into account, either directly or indirectly, because (1) it acknowledged the concerns of a wider variety of publics (both the Kelly/Maiello and Howard+Revis designs were favored by a majority of four of the six prominent publics, while Davis Buckley's design found majority favor within only two of the six publics) and (2) it was the *only* design favored by the Re-create and Insufficient Focus on the Presidency publics. Indeed, Emanuel Kelly told me that he thought his team's design prevailed because it "lay the full floor plan in the site," its use of faux fireplaces with video screens gave the site "presence," the videos allowed for the possibility of changing the interpretation without changing the site's design in future years, and—perhaps most important—it achieved all the values and themes identified in the RFQ.

Perhaps part of the answer also lies in more contemporary political concerns. Dana Cloud's critique of the democratic idea of concordance is valuable here, for she notes that some seemingly democratic processes (such as offering opportunities for individuals to evaluate the semi-finalist designs) "offer the façade of democratic compromise" as decisions are made in ways that benefit those with more political, social, or economic power.[64] In a city whose politics have long been both racial and parochial, where African Americans constitute "perhaps the most powerful voting bloc,"[65] and where Street infamously ad-libbed at an NAACP meeting in 2002 that "the brothers and sisters are running the city,"[66] the mayor's language in announcing Kelly/Maiello as the winner revealed the political dimensions of the decision: the firm was the only semi-finalist both headquartered in Philadelphia and owned by an African American. As early as 2004, INHP notes from an October public meeting asserted that "there is a marked interest in having African American designers and contractors create the site."[67] One year later, Coard's ATAC issued a statement in 2005 demanding "that Black architects, Black designers, Black construction firms, Black historians, and other Black workers be selected to play a 'substantial, significant, and prominent' role in the slavery commemoration project."[68]

Part of the reason for such a demand was historical; the need to right past wrongs in the present. Coard argued, for example, that "because our enslaved ancestors were forced into unpaid labor in the past, their descendants must be selected for paid labor in the present."[69] Part of the reason reflected contemporary political concerns. The project required skilled laborers, and—at the time of Street's announcement—Philadelphia was just over a year away from the eruption of long-simmering tensions between African American laborers who resided in the city and the largely white unions whose members lived in the surrounding area but enjoyed the fruits of the unions' vast political influence within the city.[70]

The same kinds of tensions permeated Philadelphia's architectural community at the time of Street's announcement. Gus Baxter, former head of Philadelphia's Architect's Workshop, argued in 2003 that black architects in Philadelphia faced "a wall of exclusion" when they tried to earn bids for public and private projects within the city. He pointed in particular to the dismissive response he received when he asked why black architects were not involved in the ill-fated first plan to develop a site for the President's House in early 2003. The lead architect, Baxter recalled, "gave me some nonsense about not knowing any minorities . . . the same stock answer that they always give."[71] Street, noted Linn Washington, Jr., in his *Philadelphia Tribune* op-ed on the subject, was being criticized at that time for not being "aggressive enough to break down . . . the 'wall of exclusion.'"[72] The selection of a design for the President's House site, then, was a process bursting with politics, from both the past and the present.

All these factors were on display during the question-and-answer session of a June 5, 2006, public meeting, held more than two months before the public display of the design models. Rather than ask questions of the two guest speakers, who had been brought to town to talk about lessons from past commemorative projects involving African American history, many of the crowd members who spoke passionately expressed their desire to see black Philadelphians working on the installation. In fact, when representatives from the five semi-finalist teams in attendance were asked to stand to be recognized (most of the representatives at the meeting were white), they were greeted with a chorus of angry shouts and a smattering of boos from the largely African American audience.[73]

Jeff Howard of Howard+Revis and Davis Buckley told me that they were shocked by the reaction but later understood the frustration in light of the larger context surrounding the project. Howard said he "felt a level of anger and distrust" throughout the crowd that evening. "As the evening wore on," he added, "it became clear to me that the spokespeople for the Black community were mad for a handful of reasons well beyond the simple fact that the design teams appeared to be predominantly white. There was talk of the need to ensure that black contractors, for one, be hired to implement the project with mention of a painful legacy of white-led unions boxing them out of such jobs."[74] The sixth semi-finalist design team, however, decided to withdraw from the competition because of the reception it encountered that evening. In their letter of withdrawal, three principal members of the team wrote, "It was made quite clear at the June 5th public meeting that the most vocal, organized and disruptive stakeholder group—[who], ironically, should be commended for bringing the project into fruition—will insist on the telling of one story, built by one demographic."[75]

In this context, the selection of Kelly/Maiello offered the possibility of a win-win: local black voters would finally see the possibility of breaking whites union members' near-monopoly of skilled labor jobs on a public project, and members of publics who favored aesthetic elements and had concerns about giving the executive branch its due would see a design they generally favored (the Kelly/Maiello design had over 50 percent approval from the three aesthetics-oriented publics and the Insufficient Focus on the Presidency public). At the same time, however, the choice of Kelly/Maiello's design also hinted at future trouble. While the project was clearly going to feature the stories of the enslaved, only 12.5 percent of the members of the Insufficient Focus on Slavery public and 31 percent of the Slavery public gave the Kelly/Maiello design positive marks.

Thus, although the selection of Kelly/Maiello's design generated a seeming moment of concord, "concord is neither harmonious nor inevitably fair or equitable. . . . Concordances are therefore always open to dispute and in play."[76] Indeed, as the Kelly/Maiello design was altered and implemented, and interpretation was embedded within it, disputes about the project continued. As we see in Chapter 7, many of the same concerns expressed by members of the six publics outlined here reappeared as the installation moved toward and then reached completion. But, between the selection of Kelly/Maiello and the beginning of construction, all the controversy surrounding the project briefly, and literally, disappeared into a hole.

6

Revealing the Foundations

The Excavation of the Site

When Mayor John F. Street broke ground on March 21, 2007, for the archaeological excavation at what would become the President's House site, few people expected that the dig would reveal much of interest. Despite the mass of artifacts unearthed at the James Oronoko Dexter house excavation near the NCC and the discovery of remains of the President's House ice house during the excavation preceding the construction of the LBC, park officials were, according to the park's archaeologist, Jed Levin, "cautious and pessimistic" about the President's House excavation.[1] They observed that the LBC dig on the site of the President's House outbuildings had revealed little evidence of the buildings' existence. Moreover, they noted that eighteenth-century structures had been replaced by buildings with deeper basements in subsequent centuries.[2] So, Levin concluded before the excavation, "we cannot confidently predict that research excavations will yield information that will substantially increase our knowledge of the site and the people who lived and worked there during the President's House period."[3]

Yet, in early May, "against virtually all expectations, the archaeological excavation of the President's House . . . uncovered powerful physical evidence evoking presidents and slaves": foundation remains of the original house—a discovery that Levin conceded was a "long shot" when he was planning the excavation.[4] Visitors began streaming to the viewing platform that park officials had constructed in advance, but officials surely were not expecting the surge of interest that followed each revelation: first, at the start of May, the wall of the kitchen where the enslaved chef Hercules labored; then, one week later, the bow window that Washington had installed in the dining room to create a more inspiring space for meeting the public (and which likely served as a precursor to the Oval Office in the White House); finally, an underground passageway used by the servants and enslaved to move between the main house and its attachments. (The passageway became known, inaccurately, as the "slave passage/way" in public discourse, largely because of an Associated Press story that ran early in the excavation process.)[5] Responding to the intense interest, INHP opened the viewing platform on the weekends. The excavated hole, which was scheduled to be filled at the end of May, was instead left open for another two months as the viewing platform became one of the park's hottest attractions.

By the time the remains were reburied to prevent their exposure and decay, more than a quarter of a million people had visited the viewing platform, and countless others had watched the excavation via a live webcam on the IHA website. "Nothing [in the President's House saga]," wrote the *Inquirer*'s Saffron, "has gripped the public imagination more than the current excavations."[6] Project director Rosalyn McPherson, whose consulting firm was hired by the city of Philadelphia in 2005 to oversee the construction of the installation, noted that while the project was initially funded to satisfy local African American residents, the excavation prompted interest in the site among white residents as well: "I watched people realize that the whole issue of slavery was real. The project took on a new life."[7]

From an aesthetic perspective, the site was not much to see (see Figure 6.1).[8] The wall foundations arose no more than a foot or so from the base of the pit; the bow window remains were even less striking. The temporary viewing platform looked a bit like a rectangular version of a backyard gazebo, with a few interpretive panels mounted on plywood along the rail (see Figure 6.2). So what drew an average of over 2,500 people per day to the site from May through July? The answer, I believe, lies at the convergence of three powerful symbolic currents.

To begin, the removal of the earth in front of the LBC underscored the fact that the President's House project was physically and symbolically changing the identity of INHP. The act of digging disrupted the park's self-definition as the "cradle of liberty" by literally tearing up a vital part of the ground on which that political myth had been planted. The hole in the ground, in other words, was far from empty; instead, its openness served as a material portal into a revised understanding of the past. Excavation, observed

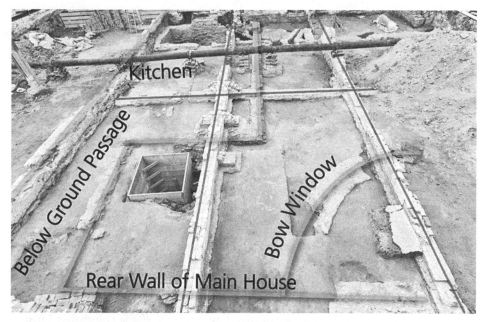

Figure 6.1. Excavated remains of the foundation of the President's House. (Courtesy of Independence National Historical Park.)

Figure 6.2. A crowd of visitors on the viewing platform at the excavation site on July 4, 2007. (Copyright © by, and used with permission of, the Independence Hall Association; on the web at www.ushistory.org.)

archaeologist Gavin Lucas, is an intervention into the physical world as well as a displacement of what we thought we knew to be true. Once an excavation occurs, he argued, the site is forever changed, as is our understanding of the history that is revealed by the removal of the earth.[9]

Next, because every excavation is unique, Lucas asserted, we need to comprehend its displacement in relation to the histories and cultures of those who are invested in the site. In the case of the President's House, the physical act of excavation meshed well with the symbolism of the dig. While Levin's initial predictions framed the excavation largely in terms of its research potential, his discussions with the Oversight Committee convinced him that "the act of looking [beneath the surface of the site] would itself be a significant act of respect."[10] These discussions, no doubt, were grounded in the notion of unearthing buried history, as outlined in Chapter 4. In short, the act of digging beneath the physical surface of the INHP terrain represented a commitment to revealing stories that had not been told before in the park or across the national commemorative landscape. *Tribune* columnist Linn Washington, Jr., affirmed this assessment, telling a colleague as the excavation commenced, "This dig is more symbolic than anything else, but we should not let the lack of finding anything diminish the significance of the monument being built."[11]

Finally, precisely because *something* was found in the President's House excavation—discretely potent symbols of slavery and executive power—the symbolic force of the excavation was amplified. Suddenly, the five years of public talk about the intertwining of the abstract concepts of freedom and slavery was visibly manifest. "Pointing out the foundations that survive and telling the story of what they represent has meant telling long-buried truth about the presidency, slavery and the formation of the nation," noted Cheryl LaRoche, an archaeologist who served as public-outreach cultural heritage specialist for the dig.[12] Visitors to the platform apparently agreed. Three of them, in fact, used language similar to the vernacular discourses described in Chapter 4. A twenty-five-year-old graduate student from North Carolina said the excavation provided "the whole picture of history," a retired federal government employee noted that "this part of history has not been told," and a fifty-eight-year-old physician affirmed that "truth buried will at some point rise."[13]

The material elements of the site—namely, the hole and the remains—provided only a fraction of its visual experience, for the convergence of the currents of excavation as displacement, symbolic commitment to unearthing the nation's buried past, and revelation of the remains of the foundation generated a distinctly immaterial experience: seeing that which was *not* present.

Viewers of the site used the excavated remains as a prompt to imagine the people, places, and activities in the house during its time as the nation's executive mansion; "seeing the foundations helps spark imagination," claimed visitor Ed Hart.[14] Here—without glass, panels, or tour guides mediating the experience—viewers could envision Washington and Adams greeting honored guests in the formal dining room and, only a few feet away, imagine the presidential chef Hercules preparing meals for the man who enslaved him.[15] In short, visitors were seeing things. But how?

Seeing Things at Public Memory Sites

Ruins, James E. Young explained, "are haunted by the phantoms of past events, no longer visible, but only remembered."[16] Speaking even more broadly, Michael Mayerfeld Bell suggested that *all* places are imbued with what he calls ghosts, or "the sense of the presence of those who are not physically there."[17] Neither Young nor Bell, of course, is referring to apparitions that are, in Bell's terms, typically envisioned as "scary spirits of the unsettled dead."[18] Instead, they point to the undeniable experiences of the immaterial that we encounter as persons-with/in-places, whether those experiences be memories of our past experiences in places (such as our childhood homes and schools), projections of how others inhabited the places (such as tours of homes for sale, offices used by others, and historical sites), or even more general feelings of the past's presence in a place. In each of these cases, we visualize the immaterial to make it more real, perhaps quasi-material, through remembrance and/or imagination.

Places of public memory, of course, are overflowing with possibilities for such visualization. Every memory site evinces a "surplus of memory,"[19] in which "the absence of these past 'other' meanings haunts the presence of the material now."[20] These *absent presences*[21] provide a basis for engaging the selective picture of the past presented at a memory site—"even at these sites," noted Tim Edensor, "the excessive material, sensual, semiotic and epistemological effects of words, places and things escapes attempts to stabilize memory"[22]—and, as the President's House excavation demonstrated, a possibility for acknowledging that which has been buried beneath those stabilizing stories.

The idea of absent presences is grounded in Jacques Derrida's notion of the *hauntological,* or the homophonic idea of ontological indeterminacy: we cannot fully ascertain what is tangibly real.[23] The hauntological refers to the simultaneity of absence and presence, in which neither is completely evident. As Warren Montag, whose interpretation received Derrida's stamp of approval, summarized: "Ontology speaks only of what is present or what is absent; it cannot conceive of what is neither."[24] In this respect, places of public memory, where traces of the past linger unspoken and unrecognized among the inevitably limited and selective accounts of the place's past, are haunted by the "unseen but nonetheless felt."[25] Considered in these terms, the traditional public memory binaries of visible/invisible and remembered/forgotten seem insufficient; they are grounded in a material mentality that has no room to account for the immaterial. This material mentality is at once understandable yet also oddly inappropriate for the study of something as immaterial as memory.

In this respect, the unearthed remains offered material phenomena that provided a gateway to immaterial experiences. The remains also accomplished one of the primary purposes of classical persuasion: "giving presence to the *unseeable*—something not yet or capable of being seen—or to the *unseen*—something visible but ignored,"[26] but in this case the work of seeing fell to those who viewed the remains. They envisioned much more than remnants of the President's House foundation; by remembering/imagining, they made the past visible in the mind's eye. They also engaged in the process of re-collection by drawing on the stories surrounding the President's House controversy and the historical landscapes of freedom and slavery embedded within that conflict, for their words reflected some of the same desires that emerged during the design competition: re-creation, powerful emotional experiences, and acknowledgment of the work done by those who inhabited the house during its time as the nation's executive mansion.

To illustrate how these processes unfolded on the viewing platform, I rely on the classical notion of *phantasia,* which has been translated as "'imagination' (and *phantasma,* 'image'), and sometimes 'impressions,' 'outward show,' or 'appearance.'"[27] Perhaps the most concise definition, by Martha Nussbaum, is simply "'what appears,' and context must determine its usage."[28] Phantasia appeared in the writings of several classical scholars, including Quintilian and Longinus,[29] but Aristotle offered the most thorough theoretical account of the concept, describing it as both a psychological process (in *De Anima*) and a persuasive effect (in *Rhetoric*). Even though Aristotle wrote about phantasia in both *De Anima* and *Rhetoric,* Nussbaum argued in 1978 that "there seems to be no canonical theory of *phantasia* in Aristotle, but rather a number of assorted observations, sometimes apparently inconsistent, of varying length and technicality."[30]

In the years since this observation, other scholars have offered additional interpretations of Aristotle's writings on phantasia.[31] I refer to some of their ideas in the following pages, not to offer a canonical interpretation but to illustrate how the concept of phantasia can explain the powerful effects that occur when absent public memories haunting our collective consciousness are made present. Although most scholarship, understandably, has implicitly treated phantasia as something created by a speaker, the idea of re-collection suggests that we should work with phantasia as something that viewers create in the mind's eye, as both a persuasive and a psychological phenomenon. Specifically, I demonstrate how the President's House remains provided a powerful *presence* that brought authentic evidence from the past into the present. Next I use the notion of *ideal presence* to illustrate how visitors to the excavation imagined the past in the present. Finally, I point out how the presence of the remains encouraged a type of *sublime* experience that promoted acknowledgment of the pernicious and still-lingering effects of enslavement on African Americans.

Phantasia and Appearances of the Absent

Presence

The idea of presence, originally introduced by Chaim Perelman and Lucie Olbrechts-Tyteca to describe a feature of compelling argumentation, has been traditionally employed to explain why some elements of persuasive efforts stand out compared with others.[32] This "standing out-ness," as Robert Tucker called it, works as the equivalent of the figure in a figure-ground relationship.[33] In most cases, presence is invoked as a means of highlighting how choices made by speakers, designers, and curators serve to foreground and/or background particular ideas.[34] In the case of the President's House remains, however, presence works with phantasia to allow visitors to make present the absent figures of the executive mansion, particularly the nation's first two presidents and the individuals enslaved by George Washington. As John Brinkerhoff Jackson observed about ruins generally, they are "venerated not as a work of art or as an antique, but as an echo from the remote past suddenly become present and actual."[35]

The phantasma of the remains provided a tangible presence, not merely symbolic suggestions, of the birth of the executive branch (the bow window), the institution of slavery, and the lives of those enslaved by Washington (the kitchen and passageway). Inga Saffron, the *Philadelphia Inquirer* architecture critic, observed early in the excavation process: "The house's form has emerged over recent days like the details of a photograph in a developing bath: Here's the floor of the kitchen in which Washington's enslaved African chef, Hercules, toiled. Over there is the outline of the curving neoclassical window that inspired the White House's Blue Room and Oval Office."[36] As Saffron's words suggest, the remains helped to make imaginatively visible other portions of the house and the actions of those who worked within its absent walls. Presence works in much the same way. Those who experience presence rely on imagination to conclude that they have encountered "the real."[37]

"The real," understood within the context of places of public memory, underscores the desire for authenticity as the past is re-presented.[38] Museums, for example, strive to preserve and present real/authentic elements of the past,[39] and—as the preceding chapter pointed out—visitors to memory sites reported that they "valued authenticity highly."[40] Strikingly, the words of visitors to the President's House excavation reflect how the remains triggered their imaginations, which in turn prompted conclusions that they were witnesses to authentic traces of past places, people, and practices. Their comments, retrieved from newspaper articles and a message board hosted by the IHA, demonstrate how the remains evoked emotional responses that made absences present to them. D. F. Holly, for instance, urged, "The slave passage is the ONLY physical evidence that survives of the enslavement of these 9 human beings in Washington's presidential household. It is precious, and should become the centerpiece of the slavery section of the President's House memorial."[41] Holly's use of all capital letters suggests the urgency to preserve these authentic elements in the design of the site. Similarly, David G. Orr, a former NPS supervisory archaeologist who described himself as a frequent visitor to the excavation, used capital letters to underscore his profound reaction to witnessing the remains: "Here we have an unrivaled entryway into the rich and complex history of our early republic. A wondrous sampler of diverse stories powerfully told USING the REAL material culture of the period; not a restoration."[42]

The vivid presence of the remains was thus described as a more real experience than anything suggested by the design for the site. "It was clear to many," wrote the *Inquirer*'s Saffron, "that the rough, time-scoured foundations speak far more articulately and movingly than the planned . . . structure."[43] Not surprisingly, then, visitor Mary Trahan advised officials to "keep it real" when evaluating whether/how to integrate the uncovered remains into the design of the site: "The site should allow visitors to clearly see the slave passage recently uncovered—and not just through a glass floor that distances the viewer from the experience and gives an unrealistic visual perspective."[44] As Trahan's words suggest, the lack of a barrier between the visitor and the remains as displayed during the excavation generated emotional reactions rooted in a feeling that visitors were sharing space with/in the past. An individual named Dana, for instance, described the excavation as "a tangible link to our past. . . . To know that you are standing where George Washington stood, where the slaves that ran his household walked, where our very history took place is an overwhelming feeling."[45]

Indeed, presence "is a felt quality in the auditor's consciousness."[46] That viewers felt the presence of these absences speaks to the hauntological experience of seeing the remains. As visitors gazed at the protrusions at the bottom of the hole, they were not witnessing re-constructions or structured interpretive displays, yet they could envision the extant house and its occupants. Even those presences contained absences, however, for the historical figures were not physically present, nor were other elements of the building. In what seemed to be an effort to rectify these additional dimensions of absence, some individuals shared even stronger sensations of haunting within the hole; they not only imagined the presence of the structure and its inhabitants but also imaginatively saw and heard the absent historical figures.

Ideal Presence

In this respect, the remains as phantasia were even more evocative than the notion of presence would suggest. Such powerful imaginative work points to the relevance of what the eighteenth-century scholar Lord Kames called *ideal presence*.[47] Ideal presence engages phantasia through the *incompleteness* of the phantasma. The incompleteness is sufficiently evocative that those who experience it are encouraged to fill in the details of the suggested scene through imaginative work. Although Kames wrote about ideal presence largely within the context of art and fictional representations, he emphasized that "it makes no difference whether the subject be a fable or a true history: when ideal presence is complete, we perceive every object as within our sight."[48] Although the visual sense may dominate the experience of ideal presence, we may also become so immersed in the experience that other senses operate as well.[49]

Using poetry as an example of the experience of ideal presence, Eric Rothstein asserted, "The reader's imagination supplies what the poet can not," much as Nussbam explained that phantasia is at once a perceptual and interpretive experience.[50] These experiences of completion are present in historical sites as well as in the arts. Visitors to sites of memory possess a "desire for an affective connection with an earlier time" and use their imaginations to facilitate such connections.[51] John Gatewood and Catherine Cameron called this desire "numen-seeking" because such visitors sought a numinous experience at historic sites: "They enjoyed the experience of transcending the present and leaping back into the past, imagining the lives, feelings, and hardships of people in earlier times."[52]

The presence of authentic elements from the past assists in this process. In their large national survey of Americans' uses of the past, Roy Rosenzweig and David Thelen discovered that heritage tourists "feel connected to the past in museums because authentic artifacts seem to transport them straight back to the times when history was being made."[53] Rosenzweig and Thelen offered some examples of how survey respondents expressed their desire for unmediated experiences at historic sites. They quoted two Sioux respondents, for instance, who shared their experiences about visiting the site of the Wounded Knee Massacre. "You can almost hear the voices. You can almost see the events taking place," said one. Another said, sensing "the feel of the ground and the wind and how cold it was, . . . [I] could put myself back there and not feel how they felt but get an idea of how they felt."[54]

In this respect, the experiences of visitors at the President's House excavation were not unique but were perhaps an ideal manifestation of ideal presence. The foundation remains could certainly not make material the historical sights, sounds, and activities of the house, but they undoubtedly *invited* individuals to imagine and interpret these things.[55] Specifically, those who encountered the remains engaged in a bit of experiential time travel in which they (1) imagined themselves *in the house in the past,* when it served as the executive mansion, and (2) imagined the remains of house, and its inhabitants, *speaking to them in the present.*

To begin, some individuals saw the remains and imagined themselves moving to the past. As visitor Shamyra Gunn told a reporter: "I really think this is amazing to know we're *standing in history,* where slaves were, where our president was."[56] Megan Townsend suggested that the site be designed to take advantage of this imagined experience. She wrote: "Let the viewers actually feel like they are standing in George Washington's home. When you are doing tours you could say something like 'we are now standing in the parlor.' And people could look down and see the actual foundation of what was the parlor."[57] Similarly, Gerald D. Klein proposed a redesign of the installation in which "the President's House and many of its wings and structures could be simply framed to rise above their original foundations."[58] The effect of this structural skeleton, he continued, "would enable a visitor to feel what it was like to stand on this very property in the late 1790s, and to imagine what was

occurring in its different buildings and rooms."[59] Indeed, part of the evocative power of memory sites emanates from such point-of-view experiences.[60]

As we imaginatively take the place of those who came before us, we are
both here and there, then and now. For example, Irene Coard, mother of
Michael Coard, said the excavation allowed her to imagine the past in the
present—as evidenced in her mixed verb choices: "This *is* where George
Washington *was* with his slaves."[61] As viewers gazed at the kitchen foundation remains, some of them envisioned Hercules at work. "'Hercules would
have cooked here,' [archaeologist Jed] Levin, of the National Park Service,
said of Washington's renowned—and enslaved—chef, as he pointed to the
remains of an L-shaped stone foundation wall, which outlined the kitchen's
boundaries."[62] Similarly, Jeffrey E. Finnegan, Sr., urged INHP to "let people
see the passage way. It's probably the one that Hercules slipped out for the
last time!"[63]

As the foundation remains evoked imagined scenes from the house in the
1790s, the voices from the house echoed throughout the excavated site. Some
visitors described how history could be heard through the remains because
those remnants, like spectral presences, would "speak" to visitors about the
past. Rather than fill the site with suggestive design elements, wrote Adri-
ane S., "let the bricks speak for themselves."[64] This suggestion was echoed
by other individuals. Chris Day proclaimed that "the actual house conveys
much more sense of history and meaning than any mere architectural rendering could provide. Please do not fill in the dig upon completion."[65] Alan
Markley declared: "If these remains could talk—what a story they could tell!
These (bricks, mortar, etc.) [were] made, set in place and used by real people
(famous or not) of a long ago, significant time in our nation's past. Please
preserve the site and leave the excavations open for all (now and in the future)
to see and imagine! That would really be experiencing history."[66] Part of the
experienced and imagined history, as noted earlier, involved envisioning the
activities of those who worked in the house. Karen Warrington, a member of
the Oversight Committee for the installation, viewed the remains and heard
the voices of those individuals, the enslaved in particular, as well. "Looking
at the site, she said, evoked 'those people reaching up out of the soil, telling
their story. It's a monument of what happened.'"[67]

Warrington's phrase "those people reaching up out of the soil" underscores the hauntological nature of the excavation. The imagined presence
of the absent people defines the site as haunted by memories. Even more,
however, the imagined time travel experiences shared by those touched by the
site point to the hole as a place that is not entirely of the present or the past;

viewers are physically moored in the present but imaginatively float through the past at the same time. The intensity of this imagined movement helps individuals learn from their experience. "For Kames," Robert Miles argued, "ideal presence is ultimately a scene of moral instruction."[68] In the case of the President's House hole, the instruction occurs by virtue of the relationship between phantasia and the traumatic sublime.

Phantasia and the Traumatic Sublime

The idea of the sublime can be traced at least as far back as the writings of the Roman scholar Longinus, who suggested that skillful speakers could evoke "a transforming moment of self-reflection" through "'rhetorical visualization,' or 'phantasia.'"[69] While Longinus's classical approach to the sublime assumes "an elevation of the self," Kimberly Wedeven Segall outlined a more contemporary variation that she called the traumatic sublime, in which "images of victimized persons create startling symbols of remembrance, and these reminders of someone (or some event) suggest an unresolved issue or past injustice, which is now being re-visited."[70]

Segall's description of the traumatic sublime eloquently captures the experience of viewing the remains, particularly of the kitchen and passageway, at the President's House. Those "startling symbols of remembrance" vividly reminded viewers of the past injustice of slavery, which remains largely unresolved in the nation's collective conscience. The very physicality of those ruins did not permit evasion or denial of the past; "the reality of the physical place gives authority to the story."[71] That the remains did so without words speaks to the power of the visual to show what is difficult to tell.[72] "'Here,' said one man on the platform, pointing to the window, 'the powerful.' Sweeping his finger over to point at the kitchen, 'Here, the powerless.'"[73] Moreover, the very act of looking *down* on the remains mirrored the type of gaze required at the traumatic events of funerals and burials. Ronnie Polaneczky reported "an unexpected lump in my throat,"[74] and Roger Reddick said he "felt as though I had been at a viewing."[75]

Segall's description of the traumatic sublime underscores the hauntological nature of the remains as well: "Because these disturbing memories are not easily ignored nor assimilated into a narrative of identity, these mnemonic images resist a complete erasure of the past."[76] When ruins emerge as a physical reminder of those uncontained memories, Dylan Trigg observed, the place "'punctures' the broader region surrounding that event, effectively acting as a spatiotemporal gathering source."[77] Accordingly, the remains encouraged visitors to *hear* not just the voices from the past but contemporary perspectives that challenge the traditional narrative of national identity told within INHP.

Segall's argument offers a powerful means of understanding why the remains of the kitchen and passageway generated many of the contemplative moments experienced at the excavation site. In fact, the unassimilated spectral images associated with the traumatic sublime mean that "the troubling voices and haunting bodies of the oppressed are the central figures of the traumatic sublime."[78] While the bow window's association with Washington and the contemporary Oval Office makes it compelling viewing, the other remains served "as a tactic of interruption and ghostly presence"[79] because they confronted viewers with the absent presence of slavery in the nation's foundational myth as told at INHP.

Even though the passageway was used by free servants as well as the enslaved, it was widely, if erroneously, recognized as yet another means by which Washington sought to hide his use of enslaved Africans in the executive mansion. In this respect, the revelation of the passageway served as a powerful reminder of the nation's symbolic burying of the individual identities of the enslaved as well as the institution of slavery. Accordingly, Diane Komadina urged, "The hidden passageway used by slaves should be incorporated into the new exhibit at the site."[80] Andrew Kafel's call to "the custodians of the President's House to preserve the 'slave passage' in any restoration of the site" illustrated how the "interruption and ghostly presence" of the enslaved contributed to the traumatic sublime.[81] "As a 'white' American," Kafel continued, "I consider it to be a particular responsibility to promote the recognition of the grievous injuries inflicted on 'blacks' in the name of racial superiority. The President's House has an opportunity to help set the historical record straight."[82]

The debate over setting the historical record straight at the President's House site had begun long before the foundation remains were revealed, but their visible presence served as a cathartic reminder of the long-standing absence of honest dialogues about slavery and its haunting legacies. As the *Philadelphia Inquirer*'s Saffron pointed out: "Those old stones testify to the site's multiple and conflicting meanings. In one glance, you can see the outline of both the oval room where George Washington learned to practice democratic accountability and the kitchen where his illegal slaves were kept hidden. Where else is America's noble experiment so bluntly juxtaposed with the evil institution of slavery?"[83] As Saffron's phrase "at one glance" suggests, the elements of the remains were at once spatially distant and interconnected. While the closeness of the remains to the visitor bolsters the power of the experience,[84] this visual panorama also offered an epiphanic example of the difference between abstract ideals and lived experience that images of the civil rights movement—especially the published photos of Emmitt Till's broken and battered body—similarly provided.[85] With such powerful visual evidence present, no one could deny the absence of the nation's celebrated ideals.

As such, the remains contributed to a contemporary acknowledgment of the nation's incomplete confrontation of slavery and its enduring legacy. Indeed, "ghosts . . . are a reminder of unfinished business."[86] In her call to preserve the passageway remains in particular, Diane Komadina remarked that they "will serve as a reminder of the distance we have yet to travel."[87] Archaeologist LaRoche, who spent a great deal of time on the viewing platform while serving as an expert resource for visitors, told a reporter that the platform provided a space in which the echoes of slavery could be more directly addressed:

> LaRoche said discussions of race between blacks and whites were often impeded by a "guilt component" in whites and a "shame component" in blacks. But the viewing platform at the President's House has provided a way around such emotional blockage. This dig "is creating a space—I don't want to say of comfort, that's not the right word—it's creating a space of possibility for discussion," LaRoche said. "It's an opportunity to touch a chord in the past, and it's an opportunity to touch a past that's been so maligned and hidden, buried and walled away."[88]

The excavation site, then, served as a place in which uncomfortable absences in the nation's history were *acknowledged*. Acknowledgment, noted Michael Hyde, is more than recognition. The distinction, he argued, is critical—and often misunderstood. While acknowledgment cannot occur without recognition, the latter is "the mental process of identifying what has been known before" and thus "is only a preliminary step" on the way to the acknowledgment.[89] For example, individuals in the Slavery public identified in the preceding chapter were satisfied with recognition of slavery's existence within the President's House, while individuals in the Slavery Insufficient public likely sought acknowledgment of slavery's pervasive and historical influence in American life both during and after its legal practice. Acknowledgment occurs, Hyde continued, when "people can take the time to know together some topic of interest and, in the process, perhaps gain a more authentic understanding of, and feel more at home with, those who are willing to contribute to its development."[90] Acknowledgment requires that we *hear others*.

From all accounts, a lot of listening occurred on the excavation's viewing platform. Newspaper stories, reports from archaeologists who answered questions on the platform, and web postings all noted the remarkable fact that strangers on the platform frequently engaged in unprompted, heartfelt discussions—not arguments—about race, slavery, and freedom. Retired INHP chief of interpretation and education Steve Sitarski said he had never seen anything like it during his years working for the NPS. "Without anybody prompting them," he said, "people were debating and discussing the stories on the stage that was constructed to watch the dig."[91] Doug Heller, of the IHA, was so moved by the experience of what he called "sharing awe" on the platform that he frequently visited the dig to hear "conversations about the most difficult topics in American history—slavery and race. Blacks and whites, kids and grown-ups all together sharing their thoughts and asking hard questions as they . . . witnessed history being uncovered and exposed."[92] "People who normally probably wouldn't speak to each other on the street," recalled retired INHP supervisory ranger Joe Becton, "were on the platform together discussing their histories and their various perspectives."[93] LaRoche, who spent a great deal of time on the platform, noted, "Archaeologists and interpreters on the viewing platform witnessed, and supported, countless individual struggles with centuries-old historical tropes glorifying Washington, excusing slavery, and tolerating slavery at the founding of the nation."[94]

While the *recognition* of others' contributions to the collective has been increasingly a part of public memory practices, or what Barry Schwartz and Todd Bayma called "the politics of recognition," those efforts tell us what we have known before (i.e., slavery was pervasive in the early United States); they do not always generate *acknowledgment* of others' perspectives.[95] Instead, at such places of public memory, contemplative efforts are typically directed toward the self rather than others "because social inclusion and self-esteem are political needs."[96] Although some places of public memory may encourage self-reflection through contemplation of others' tragedies,[97] acknowledgment is not often encouraged by, or found in, completed public memory installations and practices, especially on issues surrounding race and/or widespread oppression of others on the basis of culture and ethnicity. In these cases, dominant interpretations of the past are typically superimposed on and/or elide the experiences of those who were collectively traumatized.[98]

The traumatic sublime, however, is likely to promote acknowledgment more than recognition because it at once forces confrontation with the past injustice of slavery and makes contemplation of slavery and its legacies more palatable. Within the traumatic sublime "the focus shifts from oneself to another";[99] its presence encourages one to consider the experiences and perspectives of others. At the President's House excavation, visitors were almost forced to consider others' perspectives because the platform was the only physical place to gather to see the ruins. Visitors not only stopped moving as they settled in on the platform; they also viewed the painstakingly slow process of archaeological excavation below them. Both activities provided a counter-experience to what Robert Hariman and John Louis Lucaites called "the kinetic quality" of contemporary political spectacle. "Amidst this [typical] torrent of sights and sounds," they wrote in their discussion of the experience of viewing iconic photographs, the visual image "can induce a consciousness that is almost a form of slow motion." Accordingly, they argued, the slower experience "might nurture a reflective, more deliberative mentality"[100]—one that, in the case of the President's House remains, prompted visitors to consider carefully the nation's legacy of slavery.

Moreover, the nature of the excavated site also contributed to the likelihood that acknowledgment would occur among those gathered on the viewing platform. Slavery is neither present in the remains nor absent from them; the remains instead contain only haunting traces of the "unresolved issue," which makes contemplation of its horrors slightly less painful, and thus more likely to occur, in viewers' unavoidable confrontation with the past, with its presence in the present and even each other. Indeed, the echoing presence of slavery in contemporary society was acknowledged by a platform visitor interviewed by *The New York Times*: "'It's up to us now to look at our own lives,' said Tom Hill, 55, an accounting manager from Petersburg, Ky. 'Someone may look back at us and say, "How could those people have done that?"'"[101]

As Hill's comments suggest, acknowledgment requires an admission that past practices continue to echo into the present and that they are not easily resolved. Roger I. Simon observed, for example, that museum displays of lynching photographs "acknowledge past injustice and the continuing affective heritage" of the images.[102] After viewing the President's House remains, Craig Ostlund made this point explicitly in his impassioned plea to include the passageway foundation remains visible at the site:

As is often said, we stand on the shoulders of those great or small, who have come before us. With humble and seldom spoken gratitude, it is well past time to acknowledge the global contributions of peoples who are commonly known as "slaves," and their lives of suffering, injustice, torture, and restraint from liberties. . . . Let us not forget the man we revere, George Washington, would not have been that able man were it not for his slaves. That we as a nation would not be that "able" nation, but for the individual forced economic contributions of Africans whose investment and wealth have enriched our country, indeed the world, with their dividends. Include all history in your endeavors; save the tunnel![103]

The possibilities of acknowledgment were represented by the exchange between two men who visited the viewing platform at the same time. As reported in *The New York Times:*

> Two other Philadelphians, Bill Hempsey, 78, a retiree who is white, and Wayne Gibbons, 58, a doctor who is black, stood at the edge of the excavation, listening intently.
>
> "It's part of history, and it's been underground," Mr. Hempsey remarked.
>
> Dr. Gibbons said, "Truth buried will at some point rise," and added, "Independence Day is something to celebrate, but in the context of understanding the price paid for freedom."
>
> The men, who had met for the first time only minutes earlier, ended their conversation shaking hands.[104]

This exchange, punctuated with a handshake, strikingly reveals how the traumatic sublime encouraged, perhaps demanded, collective contemplation and acknowledgment on the viewing platform. As one anonymous reader of the *Inquirer* commented online, the viewing platform was "a spot where visitors of all colors have stood shoulder to shoulder to actually view the contradictions in our history. There is great value in this—in a small way, it helps mend the national fabric."[105]

Significantly, none of the contemplative work in evidence here suggests that the remains *healed* these festering wounds; such traumas are "unassimilable breach[es] in the collective narrative."[106] To what extent every one of the approximately 250,000-plus platform visitors, and the uncounted webcam viewers, were moved to acknowledgment by the presence of the remains is, of course, unknowable. Nonetheless, those who publicly shared their impressions of the remains provide compelling evidence that the excavation evoked powerful responses and interactions among many individuals.

Keeping the Remains (and Slavery) Visible

"Slavery," asserted Steven Conn in his discussion of the President's House controversy, "may well be the ghost that haunts this nation more than any other."[107] The excavation of the President's House site proved a promising step in exorcising this ghost of collective memory. After years of intransigence on the part of INHP, distrust among historians and local Philadelphians (especially African Americans), and acrimony among all who thought the site should be remembered in a particular way, the platform experiences at the excavation injected a remarkable dose of common ground into the discord. As public fascination with the excavated foundation grew over the late spring and early summer months of 2007, nearly everyone involved in the project realized that the unexpected discoveries must somehow be incorporated into the Kelly/Maiello design.

In a letter to Mayor Street and Park Superintendent Dennis Reidenbach urging the two "to allow the design team to respond fully and professionally to the newly uncovered richness of the site," the Ad Hoc Historians group reminded the decision makers that park officials' reluctance to embrace Lawler's research and their prioritizing of the Liberty Bell Center over the President's House site "combined to obscure and nearly re-bury the story of liberty and slavery on this site."[108] The necessary reburial of the remains at the end of July served as a physical reminder of the symbolic burying of slavery, and was motivation for decision makers to respond. No one wanted to see the planned Kelly/Maiello design built on top of what had been unearthed.

The IHA listed a number of redesign concepts on its website and encouraged people to post responses to the possibilities. As with the excitement at the viewing platform, the online reaction was overwhelmingly positive and powerfully worded. For example, one online visitor asserted, "The archaeology is too important to be covered up. The National Park Service has (figuratively) buried the history of these slaves for decades, and now it may (literally) bury the only physical evidence of their existence—the slave passage."[109] Two *Inquirer* readers used similar language in their pleas to integrate the remains into the design: "To cover it would be indicative of the way America has come to face all of its problems or embarrassments. Out of sight out of mind"; "To cover this sacred site over, as if it never existed, would be to pretend that slavery never happened."[110]

The concern, this time, was unwarranted. On June 5—one month after the first foundation remains were exposed and almost two months before their reburial—representatives from the city, INHP, Kelly/Maiello, and the Oversight Committee had met to discuss whether and how the foundation remains could be used as part of the installation's design. As indicated in the notes from the meeting taken by a Kelly/Maiello architect, everyone who spoke indicated a desire to explore the possibility of including the remains in some way. Only two issues emerged as these discussions unfolded. First, as McPherson noted afterward, some disagreement centered on the degree to which the remains would be featured in the completed installation. While some sentiment favored including as much of the archaeology as possible, McPherson said, "Most people on the Oversight Committee, especially the African American members of the committee, did not want the archaeology to become the dominant piece of this."[111] Second, the question of who would design the revised installation emerged. In one exchange during the June 5 meeting, the politics of choosing a designer outlined in the preceding chapter briefly reappeared when an attorney working for the city asked if the group was considering the idea of seeking new design proposals from other teams. Despite Kelly/Maiello's initial reluctance to redesign the site,[112] the query was met with these two statements: "It will be Kelly/Maiello" (Tanya Hall, executive director, Philadelphia Multicultural Affairs Congress) and "We have the design team" (Ramona Riscoe Benson, president and CEO, African American Museum in Philadelphia).[113] So, on July 18, while the excavation was still open to the public, project manager McPherson convened a design charrette to begin brainstorming ways to integrate the foundation remains into the design—even though no funding was immediately available to support construction of an installation in which the foundations would remain visible.

Kelly/Maiello spent the early fall months researching, pricing, and envisioning five alternative designs. A clear favorite among the five quickly emerged, largely because it kept many of the features of the original design while offering the lowest additional cost and fewest engineering complications.[114] On December 13, the addition to the installation was revealed: a glass vitrine would encase a small excavated area that would include the three significant features revealed during the excavation. An *Inquirer* editorial spoke for many when it expressed relief that history would not remain buried: "A unique reworking of the design for the President's House memorial at Independence Mall means there will be no coverup—quite literally—of the little-known story of George Washington as a slave owner."[115]

After the announcement, one nagging question yet remained: who would provide the money for the redesign? After some moderate success in garnering corporate and private donations at a September 2008 fundraising event,[116] advocates for the President's House project found an unlikely financial savior early in 2009: the Delaware River Port Authority, the board that manages the funds generated by bridge tolls over the river separating Pennsylvania and New Jersey. The toll business had proven so successful that the board had millions of extra dollars in its coffers, and a mandate to spend some of that money on economic development projects as well as maintenance of the bridges. On February 18, 2009, with Pennsylvania governor Ed Rendell's blessing, the board voted to provide $3.5 million to the President's House project.[117] With the additional funding in place, the long-awaited commemorative site could finally be completed. The targeted date for a grand opening was July 4, 2010.

It didn't happen.

7

Telling the Stories

The Opening of the Installation

onstruction projects rarely unfold as anticipated, and the President's House installation was no exception. In the late summer of 2009, Lawler and other members of the IHA sought to review final plans for the installation. They discovered that, nine weeks earlier, Kelly/Maiello had distributed plans to contractors interested in bidding on the project, yet the plans had not been shared with the Oversight Committee, nor were they apparently accessible through INHP. After tracking down a copy of the final design, Lawler and the IHA were stunned at what they saw.

Complaining of "serious flaws and historical inaccuracies" in the final design plan, the IHA Board of Directors fired off a letter on August 11, under the signature of board chair James S. Cassano, to the superintendent of INHP, Cynthia MacLeod. Specifically, the board pointed to three concerns: (1) two feet had been shaved off the front of where the house's historical footprint lies on Market Street; (2) the size and shape of the bow window had been altered to "an easier-to-build 'bay' window"; and (3) the site of the slave quarters had been moved. Acknowledging the various sources of pressure the park and city were under to complete the installation, the board nonetheless warned MacLeod that "it could end up being an embarrassment for the Park Service to proceed uncorrected due to expediency." The letter concluded with a call for a meeting of involved stakeholders so that changes could be made to the design "in keeping with historical accuracy."[1]

The IHA's demand for a meeting produced the desired result: a meeting was scheduled for August 25. At the same time, however, the IHA's concern about historical accuracy was not widely shared by some of its allies in the push to mark the President's House site. Two members of the Ad Hoc Historians group, for instance, suggested that the IHA's issues were nothing to get overly concerned about. "I wish people would pause, take a deep breath, and look how far we've come," said Gary Nash. Added Randall Miller, "Let's get real. . . . You're not going to tear up Market Street" to build the installation.[2] Michael Coard acknowledged that the IHA "criticism is sincere and well-intended," yet he noted that "hyper-technical replication must sometimes give way to practical-minded accessibility." The most important issue, he emphasized, was telling the story of the home's inhabitants: "Although the house matters, the people who were inside it matter more."[3]

As these comments suggested, the IHA did not have a very receptive audience for its concerns. Although INHP superintendent MacLeod indicated in e-mails that she was concerned about issues of scale, and even liked some of the suggestions offered by Lawler and the IHA to address the discrepancies between the installation design and the historical evidence of the house's structure, project manager McPherson believed Lawler was pushing to delay the project for some unstated reason.[4] One month after the stakeholders meeting requested by the IHA Board, the city and INHP put out a press release in which they outlined how the physical design issues were going to be addressed. In short, the project would go forward as planned. A majority of those attending the meeting, the release noted, "reaffirmed the importance of dimensions that were as accurate as possible, even if not exact. . . . [Yet] the main purpose of the site is to tell the stories of the people who lived and toiled at the site, especially the enslaved Africans who lived the hypocrisy of slavery in a new nation built on the ideals of freedom for all men."[5]

The convergence of the language in the release and the public comments of Nash, Miller, and Coard suggested a meeting of the minds regarding the installation's narrative focus on the home's inhabitants, yet in fact it merely presaged another controversy that was beginning to brew behind closed doors: members of the Oversight Committee, as well as other city and INHP officials, were not happy with the interpretation being developed by the consultant hired to complete that portion of the project. In a series of meetings throughout the fall of 2009, the local stakeholders argued both with each other and with the New York City consultant, American History Workshop, over whose stories would be told and how. According to Coard, the conflicts split along racial lines: "A lot of blacks thought the project might be too white, and a lot of white folks thought the project might be too black."[6]

More specifically, in a debate echoing the design selection process, conflicts emerged about how much interpretation should be devoted to the executive branch compared with the enslaved as well as in how much detail the story of slavery should be told. "It's shaping up to be a true battle," opined Karen Warrington, chief of staff to U.S. Representative Bob Brady and a member of the Oversight Committee. For Warrington, the President's House represented an opportunity to tell "the true story of the enslavement of Black people. . . . This is one of the few times that Black people have really had an opportunity to impact slavery." On the other hand, Lawler agreed that the story of slavery needed to be told but worried that "coming on too strong is just going to alienate people rather than intrigue them." Moreover, he added, the site should not downplay its role as the place where the executive branch was developed in practice. Despite all the attention devoted to Washington in the commemorative landscape generally, Lawler noted, "Washington's presidency is interpreted nowhere else within the National Park Service."[7]

American History Workshop's efforts to balance these conflicting desires largely failed—in no small part because its leader, Richard Rabinowitz, was perceived by others involved as more interested in telling than listening. Despite his successful curation and writing of the popular *Slavery in New York* exhibit at the New-York Historical Society Museum and Library in 2005–2006, those inside the President's House discussions were not impressed by his work on the INHP project. They expressed anger because he at once seemed to be telling prominent African American leaders how slavery should be interpreted and, in Nash's words, "blew off his advisory team" while developing a "deeply flawed interpretive script."[8] Eventually, despite the fact that Rabinowitz had been working with Kelly/Maiello from the beginning of the design process, American History Workshop was fired from the project.

At the same time, INHP officials struggled to be heard during the deliberations about interpretation, largely because many people in the room—as project manager McPherson noted in a 2008 Oversight Committee meeting—still did not trust them after the park's stonewalling years earlier.[9] Steve Sitarski, the park's chief of interpretation and education at the time, noted that park staffers had the last word, but not primary control, during the development of the site. While he urged that the site display concise interpretive material, he said that some members of the Oversight Committee took "concise" to mean the elimination of important elements of the stories—and each member of the committee represented a constituency that was invested in a particular story and its telling. In addition, Sitarski pushed for interpretation that would both connect the President's House site to other elements of the park, including the Deshler-Morris House (Germantown White House) and provide a variety of perspectives about life in the house, but he noted that Oversight Committee members "weren't real receptive" to this approach.[10]

Push finally came to shove in two December meetings of the Oversight Committee in which the heat in the room compensated for the chilly weather outside. The minutes from those meetings show members frustrated with having the same debates each meeting and concerns that politics were coming before history and vice versa. INHP continued to urge that the interpretation be connected to the park as a whole. Emanuel Kelly, whose focus throughout the project, according to McPherson, was more on the architecture than the interpretation,[11] wanted more focused direction from the committee instead of a list of uncoordinated suggestions. He later told me that he had hoped to offer a balanced interpretation but that he had to include the Oversight Committee's desires; working with the large and diverse membership of the Oversight Committee, he said, was the most challenging task he had encountered in his forty years in architecture.[12] Meanwhile, another consultant (representing the Kansas City firm Eisterhold Associates) attended the second meeting, leading one member of the committee to wonder who was in charge of interpretation at that point.[13] The lack of progress finally prompted the city and INHP to announce that the projected opening date was being pushed back from July 4, 2010, to the fall of that year.

Such disagreements were not entirely unexpected, and they were certainly not unprecedented. Derek Alderman reported similar debates about the images and text that were to be used in a Savannah, Georgia, monument that connected slavery to contemporary African Americans. That controversy, Alderman noted, revealed that "representing the traumatic slave experience is not only a historical project but also a political one."[14] Meanwhile, in Philadelphia, the hiring of Eisterhold Associates, a firm with extensive experience in developing public installations about African American history, was confirmed and the difficult task of telling incompatible tales continued.[15] As winter turned to spring in 2010, those involved in the planning process finally felt sufficiently comfortable with a draft interpretation plan and announced that it would be on display in the Independence Visitor Center from April 23 to May 3. As with the semi-finalist design competition, the draft interpretation was also posted online at the IHA and city websites, and individuals were provided comment cards to complete as they visited the display.

Unlike the case of the design competition, however, completed comment cards were not made available to the public, although I was able to review fifty-one cards provided to me following a Freedom of Information Act request. The comments on those cards largely reflected the concerns of the three politically oriented publics that emerged during the design process.

Some individuals praised the draft interpretation for its acknowledgment of the sin of slavery ("African American slavery being put in forefront to the public, as never has been before"; "To know that so many people will finally know the true history—I was bursting with pleasure/happiness"), while others suggested that the story of slavery was insufficiently detailed ("The 9 who suffered here. When will this country tell the truth about these atrocities?" "Why [do] white historians resist telling the truth?") or overwhelmed the also important story of the presidency ("the lack of balance and one side of the story"; "To focus exclusively on [Washington's enslavement of others] as if it were the whole story is inappropriate, sensationalistic, and unserious").

The reactions that emerged after the display of the draft interpretation concluded were more polarized. At a public meeting following the end of the display period, both Emanuel Kelly and Mayor Michael Nutter's chief of staff, Clay Armbrister, were shouted down by a crowd whose members were furious with the proposed interpretation. Even after audience members lined up to ask questions, their statements reflected anger, including about the name of the installation. "Several critics spoke contemptuously of any characterization of the house as 'the President's House'; they called it 'the house of bondage' or 'the house of horrors.'"[16] Charles Blockson, who had resigned from the Oversight Committee in protest during the fall, asked a journalist before the meeting: "Why are we honoring that house of bondage? Do Jews rebuild concentration camps?"[17] On the other end of the ideological spectrum, Rob Morris—a descendant of the home's owner when it was leased to the federal government—was equally incensed by the proposed interpretation. "The memorial is ugly, misleading, and highly political," he wrote, "in other words, a perfect metaphor for the forces at work in its creation. So come one come all, come on down to Slavery Mall."[18] Blogger Ken Finkel, meanwhile, noted that despite INHP officials' unheeded pleas for concise storytelling,[19] "the commemoration seems unable to accomplish its task succinctly. In all, 10 panels in an open-air plan are weighed down with 5,600 words. That's 1,150 more than the U.S. Constitution; it's 20 times longer than the Gettysburg Address."[20] In short, the proposed interpretation was paradoxically assessed as both overwhelming and insufficient, with the target of those adjectives varying depending on one's perspective. No wonder that INHP superintendent MacLeod had, the summer before, presciently noted, "In reality, this exhibition will not be perfectly balanced for every consumer."[21]

City and park officials eventually recognized that more civic engagement (which had been required by the NPS) would only perpetuate disagreements about the interpretation, and they faced end-of-the-year contractual deadlines[22]—Kelly noted, "We had to come to a decision" at some point because there was "not an endless amount of money"[23]—so they moved forward without further public input. Among the changes made during this time were the refinement of the images and captions for the displays, revision of wording on the displays, and the development of seventeen colored glass panels with illustrations and brief narratives (approximately 50–75 words) about important events surrounding the inhabitants of the house (see Figure 7.1). These glass panels were developed by Eisterhold Associates, project manager McPherson said, "to make the walls less sterile . . . to let them talk."[24] The work of developing the final interpretation was a collaborative effort among INHP staff, Eisterhold Associates, and selected members of the Oversight Committee.[25] Among their primary challenges were finding images that did not depict eighteenth-century African Americans as submissive or as caricatures[26] and connecting "executive branch critical decisions with African American history in Philadelphia and the nation."[27] In late July, the city and park announced that final plans had been submitted and approved, with an opening slated for sometime in the fall.

On December 15, 2010, after what park officials charitably called "eight years of vigorous public participation," the installation was officially opened.[28] Despite cold temperatures and snow flurries, a large crowd turned out for the occasion. Mayor Nutter delivered "an eloquent speech" that "moistened many a cheek,"[29] in which he observed: "We gather today at this historic place in Philadelphia not for presidents but rather on behalf of millions of silenced voices—the enslaved Africans upon whose backs great wealth was accumulated, both here in the North and in the South."[30] Coard, who also spoke at the dedication, pointed out that all the residents of the home before Washington and Adams had been involved with slavery, as either slave owners or slave traders. "Because slavery permeated the President's House," he asserted, "it must permeate this project." In addition, he continued, public memory sites "dedicated to George Washington can be found everywhere in America. But where are the monuments, the memorials, and the museums on federal property that acknowledge the all-consuming horror of and the courageous resistance to and the long-overdue abolition of slavery? They are nowhere—at least not until right now, right here."[31]

Located, as promised, directly between the Visitor Center and the Liberty Bell Center, the installation hewed closely to the original Kelly/Maiello design (see the cover photo). Lines on the pavement and approximately two-foot-high brick walls suggest the walls of the structure as they once existed. Taller elements of the installation, also made of brick, suggest exterior chimneys and interior fireplaces. Video screens, which have not always functioned properly, are located above the faux fireplaces on the interior side of the taller elements.[32]

"Freedom might be too great a temptation"

Hercules, Washington's enslaved chef, asked that his son Richmond be brought to Philadelphia. If Hercules wanted Richmond to witness free people of African descent in Philadelphia, his wish ended after a short period of time. Washington sent Richmond home after writing of his fear, quoted in the letter below, that his enslaved people here would seek freedom. Despite his precautions, Washington's concerns later became reality when Hercules successfully escaped.

"The idea of freedom might be too great a temptation for them to resist. At any rate, it might, if they conceived they had a right to it, make them insolent in a State of Slavery."

Figure 7.1. One of the seventeen colored-glass interpretive panels at the President's House. (Photo by the author.)

Each of the screens displays short scenes of contemporary actors representing the home's inhabitants (primarily the enslaved) or, in one case, of prominent free African Americans in Philadelphia discussing slavery (a large free African American community resided roughly four blocks from the house). Much of the remaining interpretive material presents information about the individuals enslaved by Washington in the house (a separate, granite memorial wall in the installation lists their names) and about the institution of slavery in general. Thus, despite concerns about insufficient interpretation of the presidency which were raised in 2008 by some Oversight Committee members, as well as by the park and Kelly at various points, "slavery," according to one critic, "permeates every aspect of the President's House."[33]

The final design contained some noticeable physical changes as well as alterations in the draft interpretation presented earlier in 2010. The most prominent addition, aside from the vitrine housing the foundation remains, was the presence of the illustrated glass panels.[34] Meanwhile, the stairwell suggesting the home's second floor and the table and chairs in the Family Dining Room had been earlier erased from the design due to safety and security concerns (respectively, children falling or jumping and burns from the hot metal in the summer), the height of the walls had been reduced for security purposes (the site is open to the public at all hours so unobstructed views of the installation's interior were necessary), and the memorial wall with the names of the enslaved and indentured servants had been revised, at the Oversight Committee's direction, according to Kelly, to include only the names of the enslaved servants. And, of course, the shape of the bow window, the dimensions of the house, and the location of the slave memorial remained a bit off from their original location as calculated by Lawler.

As you enter the installation's front door along Market Street, you can move to either the right or the left. To the left is the area of the Entry Hall, which contains one panel interpreting the executive branch and six glass panels that share anecdotes about Ben Franklin's funeral (and his anti-slavery work); a Philadelphia protest about a treaty with England negotiated by former chief justice John Jay; Abigail Adams's fear that conflict over her husband's policies with France might tear the United States apart; Washington's signing of the Fugitive Slave Act in 1793; Adams's signing of the Sedition Act; and Samuel Fraunces, the house steward, nicknamed "Black Sam" (historical evidence does not clearly indicate whether Fraunces was white or black, despite his name and his birthplace of Jamaica). To the right of the entrance is the area of the Family Dining Room, where a video monitor on display above a faux fireplace loops the first-person narrative of the enslaved African, Oney Judge, who served Martha Washington directly and escaped

Figure 7.2. The vitrine at the President's House, with a view of the Visitor Center through the openings in the bow window beyond. An interpretive panel is attached to the rail surrounding the vitrine. (Photo by the author.)

from the President's House, eventually settling in New Hampshire.[35] The Family Dining Room contains no other interpretive material.

Moving toward the LBC, you enter the State Dining Room with its bow/bay window straight ahead and another video monitor to the right; the video tells the story of both the rebellion of the enslaved in Saint Domingue (many of the enslaved escaped to Philadelphia from what is now Haiti) and the 1793 yellow fever outbreak in Philadelphia.[36] Two glass panels interspersed between the three window openings interpret Washington giving a peace medal to the Seneca leader Otetiani when he visited the house with other Native American leaders, and Adams meeting with an emissary of San Domingue (no explanation is provided for the San/Saint distinction) to open trade relations between the two countries. The window openings provide a view down into the vitrine so that you can see the remains of the bow window.

As you move to the left from the State Dining Room, the remainder of the vitrine is visible as you enter the Steward's Room area. Panels on each of the three accessible sides of the vitrine interpret the archaeological work involved in excavating the foundations, the findings of the excavation, and the challenges encountered in creating the installation (see Figure 7.2). Another video display tells the story of how leaders in Philadelphia's free African community responded to Washington's death. A large interpretive panel provides information about the house and those who worked in it, and a glass panel outlines Oney Judge's story.

As you move past the vitrine toward the LBC, you enter the Kitchen area. To the left, on the interior side of the memorial wall, a large interpretive panel provides a summary of the slave trade and the efforts of free black Philadelphians. In addition, three glass panels tell the stories of the enslaved chef Hercules and his later escape from Mount Vernon, Washington's duplicity (this panel also lists the names of the enslaved Africans who worked in the home), and how free Africans in Philadelphia feared being kidnapped after Washington signed the Fugitive Slave Act. Straight ahead lies a fourth video, this one featuring Hercules. On the other side of that faux fireplace is a large interpretive panel titled "Life Under Slavery," which outlines both the conditions of slavery and the efforts of the enslaved to seek freedom. After reading it, you turn back toward the LBC and see the slave memorial slightly to the left and, to the right, a wayside marker that tells the history of the house, yet faces the LBC, and notes that "a permanent exhibit is being created here."[37]

Additional interpretive material lines the exterior of the installation along the walkway leading past the LBC and toward Independence Hall. Five glass panels on the exterior of the Entry Hall tell the stories of how free Africans in Philadelphia provided care during the 1793 yellow fever epidemic; how Washington and other Philadelphia elites left the city for Germantown during the epidemic; how white and black residents worked together to host a dinner celebrating the establishment of Philadelphia's first African church; how Philadelphia's population of people of African descent increased following the revolt in (a third version of the name) St. Domingue; and how Oney Judge left the President's House to find freedom in New Hampshire. The exterior of the memorial wall hosts the engraved names of the nine enslaved Africans who worked in the house and a fifth video, in which the stories of each of the nine enslaved Africans is briefly shared.

As this synopsis suggests, the President's House installation does not contain an intuitive path to follow—despite concerns about visitor flow as early as August 2007.[38] The number of possible entrances into the site, largely the product of its open design and the requirement that it be accessible at all hours, prevents visitors from noticing any clear route through the installation. Moreover, the site lacks an exterior sign to mark it (Kelly said the installation's many possible entrances made the idea of posting signage complicated; instead, visitors would discover, he maintained, that "as you walk through, it unfolds"),[39] brochures on site that might orient visitors, or any sort of park ranger presence to help answer visitors' questions.[40] "The President's House is, in the end, an incredibly confusing place," remarked the Temple University historian Seth Bruggeman.[41] One observer posted on the IHA website that the lack of guidance seems to perplex visitors: "The layout is confusing and lacking in direction. . . . The visitors seemed to wander through the site. . . . They followed no consistent route. . . . On the day the site opened, NPS rangers were on-site handing out a booklet about the site and exhibits. That helped. Two weeks ago, no ranger was there but the booklets were available in the Visitor Center. Last visit, no ranger, no booklets in the Visitor Center."[42] An additional layer of disorientation is promoted by the floor plan displayed on one of the interpretive panels by the vitrine. As visitors look down on the remains and then compare them with the floor plan, they discover (or perhaps not) that the map of the home is rotated 90 degrees clockwise compared with the layout beneath them. After looking at the map, I heard one park visitor tell a companion, "The main house was out in the middle of the street right there" as he pointed to Market Street and the Visitor Center.

In addition to orientation issues, the site overwhelms visitors with words; after Finkel decried the garrulousness of the draft interpretation, the five videos and seventeen glass panels were added to the installation. "As histori-cal sites go," noted critic Michael J. Lewis, "the President's House is uncom-monly verbose."[43] Perhaps as a result, the visitor quoted in the preceding paragraph also noticed visitors "focusing on maybe one or two panels, usu-ally looking down into the exposed foundations. None spent more than a few minutes, and none looked at any large portion of the structural elements (or panels). None went into the [slave] 'memorial' cube." The videos, too, seemed to be too wordy for visitors. A local Philadelphia resident using the screen name BenStone noted, "I watched all of them from start to finish on a crowded Saturday afternoon, but there wasn't another person who stayed all the way through a single one of them."[44]

My observations at the site largely mirrored these accounts. During my visit to the President's House over Memorial Day weekend in 2011, I took seventeen minutes to read all the panels without contemplation and another twenty minutes to watch the three videos that were working that day. Even then, the final interpretation represented a reduction in what had been con-sidered earlier in the process. Nash, who was closely involved with the writ-ing and editing of the final interpretation, noted that two problems made reducing the amount of text difficult. First, the wordsmiths working on the interpretation believed that visitors needed to know more about the crises of the 1790s to appreciate the entwined histories of slavery and the executive branch. Second, they struggled to "satisfy the complaints" of critics who were worried that their concerns "were inadequately treated" in the storytelling.[45]

After the editing was completed, project manager McPherson told me, Eisterhold Associates developed a Plan B of sorts to display additional information in a touch-screen kiosk should funding become available in the future.[46]

During one fifteen-minute period in which I formally charted the attention visitors devoted to the video on the memorial wall, ninety-two people passed by without pausing while only eighteen visitors stopped to watch and listen; of those eighteen, only three spent more than thirty seconds attending to the video narrative. In the following fifteen-minute interval, more people attended to the two videos playing in the interior of the installation; a total of forty-five people paused at one of those two monitors (the Oney Judge video in the Family Dining Room was much less popular, likely because most of the interpretive material is to the left of the site's entrance; the Judge video is the only interpretive material present immediately to the right of the entrance), but only six watched for more than two minutes and not one of the forty-five visitors watched either video in its entirety.

On a busy day at the park, such as when I visited, thousands of park visitors daily bypass or overlook the President's House site. As park guests cross Market Street from the Visitor Center (and Sitarski told me that the vast majority of park guests begin at the Visitor Center), they typically use the crosswalk rather than risk a dash across the busy thoroughfare. At that point, they either continue along Sixth Street and then cut across the President's House installation or turn left to follow the sidewalk along Market Street. Those who turn left can enter through the front door of the installation or continue walking another ten to fifteen yards, where they can catch the mall sidewalk that moves past the LBC and toward Independence Hall. During my visit, park guests followed each of these three paths. In one thirty-minute period, in which I spent ten minutes counting visitors on each route, fifty-six people crossed through the site from Sixth Street, sixty entered through the front door from Market Street, and thirty followed the mall sidewalk that passed the exterior of the President's House. A few visitors occasionally found their way into the site from the rear as they strolled along the sidewalk moving from Independence Hall to the Visitor Center.

Those who bypass the President's House site may be in a rush to join the LBC queue or to make their appointment to tour Independence Hall. They may simply not know that the installation is one of the park's more prominent sites. During my visit, the maps dispersed by the Visitor Center staff listed the main attractions of the park but contained no reference to the President's House. As of March 2014, the park had two online versions of the map, but only one marks the President's House, and in 2013 the park's audio tour (via cell phone) explained that "a commemoration is being designed" for the site.[47] The lack of exterior signage and the finished site's absence in other park orientation material means that casual park visitors—or at least those who do not know of the site before their arrival in INHP—may be unaware of its existence. The site's size and verbiage may make some visitors reluctant to enter, whether they know what it is or not. Visitors who made their way through part of the site on their way to or from the LBC, Visitor Center, or Independence Hall were frequently not aware that they had encountered the President's House site. When my interview requests were declined, and these requests were made after individuals had been through roughly half the installation, I heard comments such as "We haven't been through it yet"; "This right here?"; "Honestly, I didn't know what I was looking at." Even those visitors who spent enough time within the site to recognize that it was a distinct installation expressed surprise at what they had stumbled into. "I didn't even really know it was here," said one. "I actually didn't know that this existed here," echoed another. Additional visitors from this second group told me, "I didn't know they actually still had [something] here" and "I was not aware until now that the President's house was right here." Some visitors initially assumed that the site was part of the Liberty Bell Center because the roof of that structure hangs over the back portion of the President's House site. "Trying to figure out what it is," admitted one visitor. "Kind of neat. Trying to see—first I thought that maybe the Liberty Bell was in here." Similarly, another park guest told me, "I actually didn't even catch on to the fact initially that it was the old house site. I was walking toward the Liberty Bell."

Given that few individuals spent a great deal of time within the site, and the variety of paths that individuals followed when they did engage it, I spent nearly three hours attempting to develop a successful strategy for identifying and approaching visitors to ask for their assessments of the site. Eventually, I settled in by the wayside marker under the overhanging roof of the LBC entrance so that I could determine who had spent a good deal of time within the site and offer visitors a respite from the open-air installation's exposure to the sun (see Figure 7.3). This approach proved successful; at the end of my visit to the site I had interviewed eighty-two people.[48] Yet, in a sign of how often the President's House is bypassed by INHP visitors, park attendance figures for the weekend of my visit show that twenty-two thousand people entered the neighboring LBC.[49]

These descriptions of park visitors' encounters with the President's House suggest that the site fails to engage the majority of visitors to the park. Yet "the most powerful kinds of memorials," argued Marita Sturken, "demand forms of reenactment in the sense that they force viewers to participate rather

Figure 7.3. A visitor enjoys the shade near the President's House wayside marker in front of the entrance to the Liberty Bell Center, with the slave memorial to the immediate left. (Photo by the author.)

than to find a comfortable distance."[50] For example, the eponymous memorial to three African American men who were lynched in Duluth, Minnesota, was designed so that the statues representing the three men were looking across the street at the site of the lynching. The designer of the Clayton Jackson McGhie Memorial, Carla Stetson, asserted: "His look forces *you* to look."[51] INHP visitors, however, are offered opportunities to avoid the President's House or, if they enter its confines, to escape easily if they dislike its stories, verbosity, and/or noise.

No wonder that "the President's House has earned near universal contempt in national media," as Seth Bruggeman commented.[52] The *Philadelphia Inquirer's* Saffron found some redeeming elements in the installation but still criticized it as "a pile of bricks . . . far too big for the space . . . [with] crude [glass] story panels [that] look as if they were torn from a bicentennial-era children's book."[53] Edward Rothstein, who disliked the site so much that he twice critiqued it in *The New York Times,* argued that the site lacked "both intellectual coherence and emotional power," displayed illustrations that were "melodramatically contentious," and generally was "subservient to the claims of contemporary identity politics."[54] The architecture historian Michael J. Lewis complained that the site was filled with "didactic material" and was "not so much a memorial as an exposé"; in short, he claimed, the site "has failed badly."[55] Julia M. Klein of *The Wall Street Journal* was troubled by the use of extensive interpretation in an open-air installation, the site's obvious borrowing from another INHP site's design (Franklin Court), and "dramatically inert" videos.[56] The Philadelphia journalist and writer Thom Nickels offered perhaps the harshest published review. He called the site "a disaster on all fronts" and "an intellectual embarrassment" with "grade-school-like 'teaching' storyboards [the glass panels]" and a design that could "also double as a SEPTA [Southeastern Pennsylvania Transportation Authority] subway stop." Nickels emphasized that "it's not that the important story of slavery in Philadelphia shouldn't be told. . . . But the evangelical zeal with which this message is delivered is like getting hit on the head with a hammer."[57]

"Taken in isolation," noted Chris Satullo of Philadelphia's WHYY, "the President's House is a very imbalanced presentation." Yet, he continued, "America's textbooks and shrines have long and culpably undertold the role of blacks, both slave and free, in the nation's founding. In light of that, the President's House is the merest first step to redress. . . . It feels right. It feels like justice, like welcome revelation."[58] In this context, the President's House was especially welcomed by local African American activists and writers; its presence on Independence Mall, on the front porch of the LBC, and a block away from Independence Hall provided a reason to visit the park and to engage the stories of the nation's founding on their own terms. They heaped praise on the site—not necessarily for any of its architectural features but for its very existence, including its telling of the stories of slavery, of the nine individuals enslaved by Washington who toiled in the house, and of the free African American community in Philadelphia. In a *Tribune* column published less than a month after the site's opening, A. Bruce Crawley had words to share with the critics of the site, *The New York Times*'s Rothstein, in particular: "Hey, if just the story of George Washington's nine slaves has surprised and embarrassed Rothstein and people like him, perhaps they should sit back, get comfortable, and open themselves to learning a few new and perhaps very positive things about the entirety of American history, including the Black part."[59] An editorial in the *Tribune* concisely summarized this perspective: "The President's House exhibit tells a powerful, painful but necessary story."[60]

Public memory places that confront difficult histories, such as slavery, force their visitors to engage the horrors of the past, sometimes in visceral ways. These confrontations, Erika Doss emphasized, are emotional because they remind everyone of past injustices (for example, the lynching of African Americans, the internment of U.S. citizens of Japanese ancestry, the massacre of unarmed Native Americans) and challenge those who would prefer to forget or dismiss these injustices.[61] Experiencing such sites forces us to look into the national mirror and to cringe at the seemingly distorted reflection of our national character. The President's House embodies this description. "It really causes us to look at ourselves, who we are, and how we became who we are," claimed INHP retired supervisory ranger Joe Becton.[62] In this respect, sites such as the President's House function as what Michel Foucault called heterotopia.

Heterotopia and Difficult Public Memories

Foucault defined heterotopia as "something like counter-sites," in which other cultural sites are at once "represented, contested, and inverted."[63] In this respect, heterotopia serve as cultural mirrors of a sort; their reflection "exerts a sort of counteraction on the position that I occupy. From the standpoint of the mirror I discover my absence from the place where I am since I see myself over there."[64] As an alternative space that is both real and unreal, the mirror/heterotopia contains all that it reflects while simultaneously reordering/inverting that which it contains. Accordingly, Kevin Hetherington, in his discussion of Foucault's ideas, emphasized that "the important point to remember when considering heterotopia is not the spaces themselves but what they perform in relation to other sites."[65] This point, while slightly overstated, is worth underscoring because of the direction in which it directs heterotopic analysis: the site's meaning and power derive primarily (but not exclusively, as Hetherington's language suggests) from its relation to other places—and, I would add, the narratives contained within those places. I also suggest a minor alteration of the mirror analogy: the mirror can be envisioned as a *funhouse* mirror. As Hetherington stressed, heterotopia—"as spaces of alternate ordering"—are "unsettling," "have a shock effect," and "challenge order" by "revealing what is hidden."[66]

Foucault's principles of heterotopia point to the ways in which confrontational places of public memory may function as such unsettling countersites.[67] His third principle, for example, that "the heterotopia is capable of juxtaposing in a single real place several spaces, several sites that are in themselves incompatible,"[68] reveals that confrontational memory sites offer complicated narratives that are not easily reconciled. These juxtaposed spaces and stories prove shocking because they "function at full capacity when [people] arrive at a sort of absolute break with their traditional time."[69] In this respect, many traditional memory sites may *not* function as heterotopia, given that their primary function is to preserve a seemingly permanent link to the past through narrative continuity. When memory places interrupt those narratives by disconnecting the site from the story and surrounding milieu, much as the Vietnam Veterans Memorial did for the Washington Mall, then the site may work as a heterotopia.[70] When those foundational narratives are challenged, the temporal continuity of a society is also questioned; the social order that these narratives support suddenly seems less permanent. Accordingly, Hetherington asserted, heterotopia are spaces that "reveal the process of social ordering to be just that, a process rather than a thing."[71]

Considering the idea of heterotopia within the context of places of public memory draws our attention to sites in which how "we"—or those who have identified with dominant narratives—have seen ourselves is at once reflected and distorted. Rather than celebrate the past, heterotopic places of public memory force us to confront how selective recollections of the past are more complex, challenging, and disturbing than we wish to remember. The experience of encountering such sites is unsettling because they tell "us" who we are while doing so in a way that disrupts how we see ourselves. "Heterotopic relationships unsettle because they have the effect of making things appear out of place. The juxtaposition of the unusual creates a challenge to all settled representations; it challenges order and its sense of fixity and certainty."[72]

In this respect, heterotopia offer what Kenneth Burke called *perspective by incongruity,* a method of analysis that "refers to the methodic merger of particles that had been considered mutually exclusive."[73] These particles, as

Burke noted in his book *Permanence and Change,* refer to the socially con-structed assumptions and associations we take for granted: "the sense of what goes with what."[74] Rather than try to argue against those assumptions and associations, which are held so strongly that Burke termed them "pieties," perspective by incongruity places them in dialogue with something seem-ingly incompatible. "Perspective by incongruity is powerful," Naomi Rockler said in her synopsis of the idea, "because, if successful, it jars people into new perceptions about the way reality can be constructed and may encourage people to question their pieties."[75]

Three pairs of incongruous juxtapositions, in particular, combine to struc-ture the President's House site as a heterotopia in which pieties may be chal-lenged. First, the shorthand name of the installation, the President's House, promises an interpretive experience that focuses on George Washington and John Adams during their service as the nation's chief executives ("As the years go on, everybody's still going to refer to it as the President's House," Becton predicted).[76] Yet the site's interpretive story—reflected in the second half of the installation's full name—focuses on people of African descent who were enslaved within the house and lived in the nearby neighborhoods as free per-sons. Second, the installation is set within the park's metaphysical scene of the early United States. Yet the scenes of the interpreted stories are located within both the streets of Philadelphia and the African diaspora. Third, the design of the site, specifically its openness and loudness, draws attention to the instal-lation. Yet other elements of the site's design make it indistinguishable from its surroundings. Together these three juxtapositions provide an unsettling experience for those who encounter the President's House; the site's design and interpretation, considered within the context of INHP, do not mesh well nor do they offer a traditional means of narrating history within public space.[77]

Juxtaposition 1: A Promise of Presidents and a Story of Slavery

The most obvious contradiction is between the shorthand name of the site and the interpretive story promised in its full name (which may be one of the reasons that Coard prefers to refer to the site as the Slave Memorial). In all likelihood, most visitors to INHP are drawn to the park to visit its most popular structures. If they run across any reference to the President's House, their first impression will settle on the home as the residence of Presidents Washington and Adams. I overheard the following comments, for example, as I observed visitors within the site: "That's the foundation of the house where Washington lived when he was president," "The presidents lived right there," "You guys are standing in George Washington's house right now." The narrative of the site, however, emphasizes that the house is less the first home of the executive branch or the residence of Washington and Adams, and more the representative anecdote for the nation's historical unwillingness to confront the history of slavery; this move shifts ownership of the park's story, at least in this site, away from its traditional white moorings and toward a more African American perspective.[78]

To begin, the interpretive material within the site depicts both George Washington and John Adams either as passive presidents or, paradoxically, as presidents whose actions were historically questionable and created division within the early United States. The one-term president Adams receives less attention than Washington in the installation. He does not appear in any of the five videos, is mentioned in only seven of the twenty-five interpretive panels located around the site, and is visually represented in five of those panels. In these panels, Adams is portrayed as an alternately passive and divisive president. Despite his reputation as an anti-slavery advocate, Adams's political work in this area is referred to only at the end of one panel, in which he is described as being "strongly opposed to slavery, though [he] made no public move against slavery while president" ("The House & the People Who Worked & Lived In It").[79] When Adams's actions are noted, only those that created division and/or suggested his failure to embrace some of the nation's founding principles are referenced.[80] One color panel, headlined "We shall come to a civil war," quotes Abigail Adams in a letter to her sister as she worried that, according to the panel, her husband's "policies towards France" imperiled the young nation. Oddly, the policies to which Abigail Adams referred are not named or explained, nor is the panel's headline explained in the panel, although it presumably comes from the letter written by Abigail Adams. In another color panel, titled "Suppressing the Opposition," Adams is shown greeting guests at a dinner while, the panel intones, Benjamin Franklin's grandson was being arrested "two blocks away" for libeling Adams and the government. Elsewhere, "The Executive Branch" panel refers to Adams's signing of the Alien and Sedition Acts during his tenure as president, quoting him as saying, "I knew there was need enough for both the Alien and Sedition Acts, and therefore I consented to them."

Similarly, many of Washington's actions as president are framed as divisive. Panels refer to his efforts to suppress domestic political speech and to negotiate a treaty with France. While an older park pamphlet noted that the Congress ratified the treaty and "averted war" with England in 1793, the panel omits that information and instead quotes Thomas Jefferson, who said the treaty was "an act 'against the legislature and people of the United States'" ("The Executive Branch"). In general, the site's interpretation depicts

Washington as a fearful man rather than a courageous political leader. A color panel remembers the yellow fever epidemic of 1793 and points out that "Washington, his staff and cabinet, along with many other Philadelphia upper and middle class residents," left the city for nearby Germantown ("Refuge in the country").

Most prominently, Washington's fear of those he had enslaved, and their possible freedom, is featured throughout the interpretive narrative. One color panel, for example, refers to Washington's return of Hercules's son Richmond to Mount Vernon, quoting Washington as writing: "The idea of freedom might be too great a temptation for them to resist. At any rate, it might, be they conceived they had a right to it, make them insolent in a State of Slavery" ("'Freedom might be too great a temptation'"). One of the larger panels, titled "The House & the People Who Worked & Lived In It," has a small section labeled "Washington's Deceit," in which Washington's desire to keep those he had enslaved unaware of Pennsylvania's Gradual Abolition Act—which would have granted their freedom after six months of uninterrupted residence in the state—is outlined: "President Washington, when reminded of the Abolition Act, chose to rotate some of his enslaved servants to Virginia to prevent them from claiming their freedom." Washington's signing of the Fugitive Slave Act is also featured in three different panels. In fact, Washington himself relied on the powers of the act in his dogged, but unsuccessful, efforts to recapture Oney Judge, who escaped from the house in 1796; the final interpretation of the "Life Under Slavery" panel added an image of a newspaper advertisement seeking Judge's return, which Washington (fearfully?) placed through an intermediary.

On its own, the selection of these moments within the site's interpretation may seem puzzling, but perhaps not shocking or unsettling, to unsuspecting park visitors who are otherwise interacting with sites and stories that promote the nation's celebratory foundation myth. When this material is considered in the context of the dominant narrative of the installation, however, the effect on unwary visitors may well be disquieting. For visitors eager to engage the interpretation, on the other hand, the juxtaposition may be gratifying.

The site's dominant narrative is one in which representatives of a great people—those of African descent—acted with courage and solidarity during terrifying times. This story is not unique to the President's House, of course. In their analysis of what they called "Black-centric" sites of slavery in the South, Jennifer Eichstedt and Stephen Small observed that the interpretation tells stories "of individual struggle and suffering, collective resistance and identity, and human dignity in the face of oppression. At these sites, African Americans are humanized and individualized—we hear of their struggles as human agents in a nation that promised equality but delivered so little."[81] Similarly, the President's House site works diligently to remove any suggestion that the enslaved were victims; instead, they were part of a collective of *people of African descent,* a phrase repeatedly used throughout the site. Changes in the draft interpretation demonstrate the commitment to erasing any trace of a victim narrative while emphasizing a story of courageous leaders. The heading "Daring to Escape" was changed to "Resistance and Escape," a phrase noting that the enslaved "often succumbed" to poor treatment from slaveholders was removed, and the slave memorial's dedication was changed from honoring the nine individuals enslaved at the house to the "millions of men, women, and children of African descent . . . [who] endured brutality and mistreatment for over 200 years even as their labor built and enriched the nation." The courage and solidarity of people of African descent is marked in many other ways within the site, most particularly through the heroic tales of Oney Judge and Hercules, and through the depiction of the free African community in Philadelphia.

Oney Judge comes to life through an appearance in three of the five videos (in one of the five she shares her story in a first-person narrative) and on five different panels. On one color panel, Judge is depicted sitting on a pallet (her bed) at the foot of Martha Washington's bed while "the First Lady read the Bible, [sang] hymns, and pray[ed] with her two granddaughters in the next room" ("'I will fear no Evil'"). Judge, the panel reports, later said that she "had 'never received the least mental or moral instruction of any sort.'" The story of her subsequent escape to New Hampshire, which was facilitated "with the aid of free people of African descent" ("Life Under Slavery"), is mentioned in the video and in three other panels.

The escape of Hercules, who appears in the President's House in two videos and four panels, is a difficult to tale to tell because he apparently slipped away from Mount Vernon sometime after he was returned there from the President's House (Washington suspected that Hercules had intentions of escaping while in Philadelphia). Interestingly, references to his escape within the President's House site omit this fact and allow visitors to assume that the chef vanished while in Philadelphia. One color panel, after implying that "Hercules wanted [his son] Richmond to witness free people of African descent in Philadelphia," and then noting Washington's fears about the enslaved escaping, concludes that "Washington's concerns later became reality when Hercules successfully escaped" ("'Freedom might be too great a temptation'").

Escape, the interpretation emphasizes, was made possible by free Africans located in Philadelphia. Judge, for example, was harbored by free Africans in the city and then hustled aboard a ship sailing north to New Hampshire. As the "Life Under Slavery" panel observes, "The city was a hub of several escape routes for many seeking freedom"; it continues, "Free African sailors, numerous in Philadelphia, helped some escape by boat from the West Indies and U.S. coastal ports to freedom in the North." These free Africans, moreover, are depicted as diligently working to gain the freedom of their enslaved counterparts. A distinct section in the "Life Under Slavery" panel, for instance, discusses the life and work of Richard Allen and Absalom Jones, both of whom were "born into slavery" and then purchased their freedom (as well that of family members). Each then started a church in Philadelphia and, the panel notes, led the fight for freedom that eventually become a global phenomenon: "Jones, Allen, and other free Africans continued to debate, petition, and publish newspapers and pamphlets, arguing for their citizenship and the freedom of all enslaved persons. Ultimately, their work helped to fuel a growing international movement against slavery and inequality."

By repeatedly emphasizing the leadership efforts of Allen and Jones (Allen is also the subject of one of the five videos, in which he argues for freedom for the enslaved), reiterating the escape stories of Oney Judge and Hercules, and using language that speaks to the courage of all free and enslaved people of African descent, the President's House interpretation tells a story that casts the nation's early African Americans as heroes rather than victims—a not uncommon strategy in sites that address topics that challenge a collective's heritage. The tenor of this narrative had long been planned for the President's House. The summary of a 2003 roundtable gathering of INHP and historians—no one from the city was yet involved with the project—concluded that the finished interpretation should "humanize the big stories" and "acknowledge agency and self-determination" among the enslaved.[82] One year later, after five themes for the site had been identified, those attending a public meeting showed no interest in interpreting the executive branch and the most interest in telling stories of free African American Philadelphians.[83] "No one in the audience called for explication of the executive branch of government or for discussions of Washington's and Adams's presidencies," wrote Doris Fanelli, INHP's chief of the Division of Cultural Resources Management, in her summary of the meeting. Instead, those attending the meeting wanted to "shift the focus from master to slave."[84]

The historical culmination of this story is reflected in the addition of the photo of President Barack Obama and his family to the panel titled "The Executive Branch." Positioned below reproductions of historical documents that illustrate the white founders' (Washington's, specifically) fear of "passionate political criticisms," the photo's caption underscores President Obama's legacy as a person of African descent, both by using the phrase and by pointedly including his middle name: "When Barack Hussein Obama II was sworn in as the 44th President of the United States on January 20, 2009, he became the first person of African descent to hold this office."

In telling this story, the President's House interpretation changes the race and perspective of the implied narrator of the traditionally white celebratory story of the nation's founding.[85] The historical actions of African Americans are depicted not from a white point of view, in which they are either invisible or the recipients of white actions (i.e., black Americans were/are victims of slavery and its legacies), but from a perspective in which people of African descent performed heroically, courageously, and in solidarity. Conversely, the white founding fathers are largely portrayed as fearful and morally equivocal. This juxtaposition suggests an alternative social order in which a people who have been historically terrorized, neglected, and dismissed are *better* representatives of the nation's founding ideals; indeed, the inscription on the slave memorial asserts that "their labor built and enriched the nation." Paradoxically, it interrupts the temporal narrative of a nation's inexorable march toward greatness by deconstructing the very foundation of that narrative, simultaneously embracing a narrative of progress—only with different protagonists resisting the tyranny of the powerful.[86] Moreover, unlike many contemporary memorials in which the heroic acts of disenfranchised individuals are celebrated, the President's House does not tread lightly around the topic of slavery. Generally, Doss noted, "like slavery memorials, American slavery museums tend to skirt slavery's trauma in their exhibitions and even their names."[87] The shortened name of the site, *President's House* (which is typically used in place of the site's unwieldy formal title), certainly skirts the issue, but the interpretation—while not brutally explicit—focuses extensively on the slave trade and the lives of the enslaved.

Juxtaposition 2: Birthplace of the United States and Philadelphia/African Diaspora

In addition to replacing the traditionally white founders' narrative with a story of courageous people of African descent, the installation primarily positions that story within different scenes: Philadelphia and the African diaspora rather than the United States. While the site's repeated references to people of African descent certainly suggest its diasporic orientation, other elements of the installation underscore this perspective. The slave memorial, for instance, is covered with the names of African nations and tribes, while the "Life Under Slavery" panel notes that "enslavement interrupted their connections to the rich oral histories of Africa and to the numerous powerful and sophisticated civilizations that thrived there." A graphic called "The 'Dirty' Business of Slavery" panel illustrates how, between 1514 and 1866, "Enslaved Africans" were shipped to North America, Central America, the West Indies, Brazil, and Europe. Color panels, all of which were added after the release of the draft interpretation, point out that "Jamaican-born Samuel 'Black Sam' Fraunces" served as Washington's steward in the President's House ("The Keeper of the House"), that San Domingue possessed a "government led by men of African descent" ("Strengthening Ties with the United States"), and that some plantation owners of that island fled to Philadelphia, with their enslaved in tow, after the revolt there: "As a result, the population of Philadelphians of African descent increased by about one-third" ("The opener of the Way").

Other panels, which discuss the practice of slavery, focus almost exclusively on Philadelphia; only one brief section, titled "Slavery on Plantations," locates slavery within its traditionally understood mooring in the South ("Life Under Slavery"). Meanwhile, the "Life Under Slavery" panel has a section—four to five times larger than the plantations paragraph—headlined "Enslaved in Philadelphia," while a different portion of the panel titled "How Did Enslaved People Become Free?" devotes two paragraphs to the Emancipation Proclamation, two paragraphs to Pennsylvania law, and the rest to emancipation efforts in Philadelphia. Elsewhere the "The 'Dirty' Business of Slavery" panel illustrates both the population of "Enslaved Africans" in the United States and the number in Philadelphia (before and after the state passed its Gradual Abolition Act)—and contains a partial map of downtown Philadelphia in which the locations of prominent African American landmarks are noted; its caption underscores that Philadelphia "provided opportunities for free people of African descent and those escaping enslavement." The slavery timeline on that panel contains eight references to events in Pennsylvania and Philadelphia (seven of them positive) and eight largely negative references to actions taken by the federal government (followed by notations about the Emancipation Proclamation and the passage of the Thirteenth Amendment).[88]

To some extent, this focus on the local is understandable; the site was a jointly funded production of the federal and city governments, and, more important, the project was initiated by, and largely overseen through, the Philadelphia mayor's office. The emphasis on the African diaspora is also not surprising for visitors familiar with the controversies surrounding both the development of the President's House and the salience of African American issues in Philadelphia city politics. The prominent history of African Americans in Philadelphia, highlighted in the displays about the free African community in the city, also explain this focus.[89] In addition, the contemporary identity of *African* American is rooted in the experience of the enslaved ancestors who were born in Africa: "It was slavery, whether or not one had experienced it, that defined one's identity as an African American, it was why you, an African, were here, in America," explained Ron Eyerman.[90]

The juxtaposition between the President's House installation and the rest of the park is striking. In addition to the LBC and Independence Hall, other sites within INHP are firmly situated within the metaphysical scene of the early United States. The Second Bank of the United States, for example, both emphasizes the role of the federal government in the nation's early financial development and contains a "People of Independence" portrait gallery featuring "185 paintings of Colonial and Federal leaders, military officers, explorers and scientists."[91] Congress Hall, which borders Independence Hall on Chestnut Street, and served as the meeting place for the first Congresses in U.S. history, is described as the site of "historic events" such as "the presidential inaugurations of George Washington (his second) and John Adams."[92] The former Deshler-Morris House, which the park recently renamed the Germantown White House, is described as "the oldest official presidential residence [in existence]," the site where Washington "held four cabinet meetings" in 1793, and "a welcome retreat for him and his family near Philadelphia, the Federal Capital" in 1794.[93] (Interestingly, this last line positions Philadelphia within the larger scene of the nation.)

Ironically, while the literature for the surrounding sites in the park highlights their role in the early history of the nation, and thus functions to sever the President's House from the remainder of the park, the Park Service itself has also disconnected the installation from the remainder of the park. Although during my visit the Visitor Center had a wall display about the site—and referred to it within a larger exhibition about race, slavery, the Underground Railroad, and civil rights, and the park's website contains a link to information about the site on its home page—the President's House is nearly invisible to those who are on the grounds of the park. As I noted earlier, when visitors cross Market Street from the Visitor Center, they see no signage indicating that the installation in front of them is the President's House site; the only wayside marker or sign is hidden in the shadows near the entrance to the LBC. In addition, the President's House may or may not be listed on the maps used by the visitors. And, as I pointed out in Chapter 3, the park ranger who led my group's guided tour of Independence Hall omitted the President's House from his spiel about sites to see—which included Valley Forge, more than twenty miles away—even though the house was just one block down the mall (moreover, in his discussions of compromises made during the writing of the Constitution, he referred to the number of terms the president could serve and the development of two legislative houses but said nothing about slavery). These omissions suggest that some park officials may see the site as a "place apart" from the remainder of INHP (Sitarski's concern from the outset), even as it remains firmly situated between the park's most popular destinations: the NCC and Visitor Center to the north, and the LBC and Independence Hall to the south.

Juxtaposition 3: Uniquely Present and Indistinguishable

The final juxtaposition is largely, but not entirely, design-oriented. On the one hand, the President's House is an open, visible, and vocal presence within the park. On the other hand, it is structurally indistinguishable as a unique presence within INHP and relatively closed to other interpretations. To begin, the President's House is structurally distinct from its neighbors along the mall. It is not a preserved historical landmark like Independence Hall, nor is it a contemporary structure like the Visitor Center, NCC, or LBC. Instead, its open design encourages visitors to engage its story at any time. Unlike its mall neighbors, the President's House is an outdoor attraction that never closes; it requires no reservations (like Independence Hall), no waiting (like the LBC), and no admission charge (like the twelve-dollar fee for adults to enter the park's affiliated NCC). In addition, the site possesses a number of possible entrance points beyond its faux front door, and those points can be found on all four sides of the installation. In comparison, the LBC and the Visitor Center—which, like the President's House, border Sixth Street on their west side—have no entrances on Market Street; in fact, the LBC hides behind landscaping on the Sixth Street side. Independence Hall has post-9/11 security barriers in front of the building, and those seeking to enter must meet a park ranger at the rear of the structure before entering there in a group. These structural distinctions, especially when considered in light of the site's narrative distinctions, mark the President's House as a place that wants its story to be heard among the other sites of INHP.

As if to amplify this message, the President's House is loud, especially compared with the fairly reverential, museum-like atmospheres inside the other attractions along the mall.[94] As an open site at the corner of the busy downtown intersection of Sixth and Market Streets, it is saturated with traffic noises. Within the installation, the five video presentations are designed to air in nonstop loops. "The sound of the video," noted *Inquirer* reporter Stephan Salisbury, "is piercingly audible on both sides of the wall, adding to the cacophony now ricocheting through the installation."[95] Both the slave memorial within the site and the forty-eight speakers embedded at shin level in the bench-like walls marking the rooms of the house air snippets of audio from the videos, but those sounds are barely audible over the clamor of traffic and video noise—as was feared during the design competition.[96]

The installation is also visually loud. The seventeen glass panels added after the draft interpretation was revealed are both vibrant and ubiquitous; every brick wall and fireplace contains either a video screen or color panels, or both. Moreover, the large video screens (when working) are never turned off, which provides the site with constant moving images. In the rear of the installation, the exterior glass in the slave memorial is blanketed with the names of African tribes written in orange and the names of African countries inscribed in a bluish/silver color. And, as noted earlier, the installation is packed with printed words. Although not spoken, the volumes of text on the walls fill the site with stories.

Collectively, these design choices seem to make the President's House shout, "Look at me!"—especially in relation to the other, quieter, park structures along the mall. In this respect, the President's House is a challenge to the structural order of INHP. Even though the NCC trumpets "We, the people . . ." as its slogan, an idea celebrated as well in Independence Hall and the LBC, only the President's House offers constant, affordable, and easy access to all people visiting the park. Its narrative message, that all people contributed to the building of the nation, is mirrored through these design choices.

Yet despite—and, in some cases, because of—these design choices, the President's House is also indistinguishable from its surroundings. Initially, as critics of its architecture noted, the President's House looks as if it collided with the LBC, giving the site the appearance of being part of the center rather than a distinct installation. Similarly, the wayside marker for the President's House, which was first posted at the time of excavation, is bizarrely placed at the back of the site near the entrance to the LBC. Not surprisingly, then, I overheard one woman say to a friend, while pointing to the entrance of the LBC, "This is the President's House." In addition, given the open-air nature of the President's House installation, one could easily assume that—like the Visitor Center across the street—it is simply a home to another exhibition about history within the park, one that provides visitors with something to browse on their way to see the Liberty Bell. The absence of signage along the Market Street entrance could certainly contribute to this notion, as could the fact that all the other main attractions along the mall are enclosed facilities.

As a result, visitors who want to move directly to the LBC, and this constitutes a large number of those leaving the Visitor Center, may (and do) easily bypass the President's House and the maze-like barrier that its suggested rooms and walls present by following the walkway that runs the length of the mall. This path requires only a slight detour to the left after one crosses Market Street and, in fact, offers a more direct route to the line to see the bell. Those who come to the LBC from Independence Hall, on the other hand, queue up along the walkway before they reach the President's House site, and then exit the LBC at the end closer to Independence Hall along Sixth Street. There is no signage here to direct visitors north to the President's House site. Thus, visitors to INHP who are seeking to visit its most popular attractions may easily overlook the President's House, even though it is positioned alongside the walkway that connects all these attractions. For example, at 9:45 on the Saturday morning of my visit, the line to enter the LBC was approximately twenty yards long while only four people lingered within the President's House site.

Those who enter the site, moreover, will not likely find the space to be open to contemplation and reflection.[97] Although the President's House is meant to be historically and structurally suggestive—its faux windows, fireplaces, and walls are designed to evoke the sense of the house and its activities—the audio and visual stimuli at once firmly situate the house within a contemporary, technological milieu and fill the site with noise that reduces opportunities for reflection. "Whatever happened to quiet contemplation?" asked one visitor to the site.[98] Only the vitrine and slave memorial offer spaces for imagination and contemplation, but the installation's narrative, which permeates the site, literally surrounds the vitrine while the slave memorial is filled with fragments of audio culled from the video presentations. On one side, a panel section labeled "Discoveries" refers to "African cultural attributes" and "African traditions" being discovered through history and genealogy, without indicating that the excavation revealed nothing of the sort (this panel section was situated in a different context in the draft interpretation). On another side, a photo is captioned: "On July 11, 2007, a West African Yoruba and Pan-African libation ceremony concluded the closing of the archeological investigation" (the photo appeared in the draft interpretation; the caption was added afterward). On the third side, a panel section called "Digging for History," which was added after the draft interpretation, talks about "the challenges of telling the story of Africans and their descendants in Philadelphia and elsewhere" without mentioning the excavated ruins except in an indirect reference in the final line: "the lives of the enslaved people who occupied this house." During my time at the site, most visitors did not linger long at the vitrine, and I noticed only minimal conversation within intact groups—certainly not the spontaneous conversations between strangers, often across races, that was a regular occurrence when the viewing platform was open during the excavation of the site.

As a public place of memory, the President's House is at once exceptionally public (it is open, visible, and voluble), nondescript (it blends into the scenery), and opaque (other interpretations cannot permeate the site). This juxtaposition of seemingly incompatible characteristics challenges the established structural order of INHP and offers a design experience commensurate with the site's contesting narrative, yet simultaneously suggests that the site is nothing special and is uninterested in engaging all its visitors. The nature of the unsettling experience of the President's House, then, is certainly far from settled itself. Indeed, as the next section illustrates, visitor reactions to the site reflect a wide variety of experiences.

Heterotopicity and the President's House

In their discussion of museum exhibits that tackle difficult subject matter, Jennifer Bonnell and Roger I. Simon identify three ways in which such exhibits may earn the moniker *difficult*. First, visitors might "undergo significant challenges to their interpretive abilities" when exhibits offer explanations or perspectives that deviate from traditional depictions. "Such exhibitions may indeed require visitors to engage in the process of confronting and dismantling their expectations and complicating their desire for a particular 'way of telling' the story." Second, visitors might experience "negative emotions" if the exhibit "raise(s) the possibility of complicity of one's country, culture, or family in systemic violence such as the seizure of aboriginal land, the slave trade, or the perpetuation of genocide." Third, "difficult exhibitions may evoke a heightened anxiety that accompanies feelings of identification with the victims of violence as well as a potential re-traumatization of those who have experienced past violence themselves."[99] For different publics, the President's House most certainly meets each of these criteria, not just one.

Its narrative replaces the (white male) founders' story with a tale of courageous people of African descent overcoming adversity. This narrative, moreover, is literally re-placed. Rather than situated within the early activities of the United States, the home is positioned within both the more precise location of Philadelphia and the broader territory of the African diaspora. As such, the installation encourages visitors to reconsider the place of the United States—through its history and character—as a shining city on the hill forged in places like Philadelphia. At the same time, the site can also be experienced as a utopian "no place" that is both narratively and structurally disconnected from the rest of the park. While the narrative replacement offers an alternative order, it also lifts the home from its mooring in the nation's foundation myth. In addition, the various structural elements of the site work to displace it from the rest of the park's installations. As a result, the President's House also has no sense of place.

This overarching juxtaposition is not meant to suggest that visitors encountering the site gravitate toward one or the other extreme. Instead, the merger of these disparate places in one site opens the opportunity for a variety of interpretations about the site's meaning and appropriateness. In short, the social and cultural places from which visitors engage the President's House contribute to their judgments about the site. "Heterotopia always have multiple and shifting meanings for agents depending on where they are located within its power effects," observed Hetherington.[100] Two concepts, in particular, help illuminate this merger of places: *identification* and *kairos*.

First, our experiences position us in socio-cultural places where we will feel more or less connected to the physical place we engage.[101] Indeed, we make decisions about whether we should even experience places on the basis of our expectations of the site's relevance to the places from which we come. After we arrive, "the more [visitors] regard the site as part of their personal heritage, the more interested they are in having the interpretation focus on their heritage."[102] Victoria Gallagher, for example, discovered that visitors to the Martin Luther King, Jr., Memorial in Atlanta interpreted the site differently depending on the degree to which the site reflected their experiences.[103] Similarly, Brent Allen Saindon observed that the Jewish Museum Berlin functioned as what he called a double heterotopia in which different elements of the memory place invited different means of identification for visitors.[104]

Second, we also make judgments on the basis of our assessment of the site's *kairos*, or appropriateness. Kairos is, unfortunately, typically discussed in temporal terms; that is, appropriateness is often defined as a matter of timing.[105] Elizabethada Wright, however, thoughtfully argued that place is also an important dimension of kairos; *where,* in other words, is as much a consideration of appropriateness as *when*.[106] In the commemorative landscape, she continued, judgments about who and what belongs carry significant consequences: "If, however, there is no public place into whose boundaries a rhetorical memory space is deemed appropriate, then the memory . . . can disappear."[107] The idea of kairos as place-based also helps us understand responses to the President's House, in particular, because the connection of place and appropriateness carries the historical weight of segregation. African Americans have heard for centuries that they should "know their place" and stay "in their place." To do otherwise would bring judgments of inappropriateness at best and physical violence at worst. "Place," summarized Kirt Wilson, "determined the spaces that a person could occupy and how one could interact, privately or publicly, with others" during Reconstruction (and beyond).[108]

Just as the President's House possesses both heterotopian and utopian dimensions, visitors to the site bring expectations related to both identification and kairos to the site; judgments of appropriateness are embedded in feelings of connectedness and vice versa. To discern how visitors responded to the President's House site, I interviewed eighty-two park guests in addition to perusing comments posted on the IHA website, the Philadelphia-area discussion blog philadelphiaspeaks.com, the website tripadvisor.com (where individuals can review the places they have visited), and newspaper articles in which visitors shared their opinions of the site. Using the same process outlined in Chapter 5, I identified four distinct publics.

Three publics emphasized the value of telling the story of slavery within INHP; the first two publics were composed primarily of individuals who spoke with me at the President's House site, while the third public's comments are found mostly in online posts. Thus, the nature of their comments may be connected, to some degree at least, to the places in which they shared their views. The first public consists of those who stressed the educational value of the site but who were seemingly reluctant to utter the words *slave* or *slavery;* instead, they frequently used pronouns when referring to the subject of the installation. The second public consists of those who pointedly acknowledged that a discussion of slavery in INHP was welcomed and appropriate. The third public passionately embraced the President's House as a symbol of the nation's long-overdue telling of the story of slavery in the United States. After explaining how each of these publics found meaning in the President's House site, I point out how a fourth public found the installation inadequate.

An Educational Experience

Individuals in the Educational public expressed appreciation for the alternative knowledge gained from the site, but their appreciation is carefully and cautiously articulated. The site contained "so much information about the history of our country" and "we get the complete history of what happened in America." The site "definitely breaks it down and tells you how they, how they lived, and then—I like the way they did that. It presented that very well." Left unsaid in these responses is the word *slavery.* In fact, despite the focus on slavery offered by the President's House site, only thirty-nine of the eighty-two interviewees mentioned slavery even in passing. The comments of the other forty-three park visitors, though far from identical, were often peppered with words like "interesting" and/or "informative" ("interesting," for example, appears fifty-one times in the transcripts): "It's an interesting site to see," "very informative" and "very interesting, very informative." Two interviewees, part of a joint conversation, responded, "Interesting. Who would have known something like that?" "It's interesting."

In a slightly more specific pattern of responses, visitors indicated that they learned more about history from the President's House installation. The President's House is "really important," explained one visitor, "since it's so much of our history." The site contained "so much information about the history of our country," noted a park guest; "we get the complete history of what happened in America," added another. Visiting the site, then, is an educational experience for these visitors. "Information is right there outside, so, you know, it's . . . a very knowledgeable experience," observed one visitor. As these comments suggest, the visitors within this public were almost assuredly talking about the issue of slavery, but—just as the nation's founders avoided using the word as they talked about it in the U.S. Constitution—visitors used pronouns and terms such as *history, information,* and *knowledge* in so doing.

These general responses indicate that many of the visitors understood the purpose of the site: to communicate the African American story of the eighteenth century, a function made clear by the amount of pictures, video, and text relaying this message. Yet their responses reveal that they had some difficulty deciding how to respond to the interpretive material. One visitor, for instance, said: "The information seems to flow with the start of the house and the way it's laid out. It seems really nice. . . . I think it gives you another opportunity as to your traditional museums and an opportunity to be outside, kind of get a feel, um, it's, it's unique. It's nice." Interestingly, even some African American interviewees who were moved by the site relied on indirect and general references, especially the use of the pronoun *it,* to the interpretive material about slavery: "It was shocking because it's not as widely known. It was definitely, it was not taught in school that I remember"; "I think it's long overdue. . . . It's highly appropriate that it is a part of all of the history."

These reactions, as well as those in the preceding paragraphs, may be due to the awkwardness of the moment (including the fact that the interviewer was a white professor studying responses to the site), the overwhelming nature of the interpretive material, the nation's general reluctance to talk about slavery and its legacy, or any other number of factors. The language, though, reappeared in the comments of visitors interviewed by the *Philadelphia Inquirer* in early 2013. A visitor named Lisa Hightower told the reporter, "You can't water it down as if it didn't happen. It did." Another park guest, Gerald Sweeney, acknowledged the pervasiveness of slaveholding among the nation's founders yet used *it* to reference that fact: "I think they all knew it was against principle." Similarly, Jayme Bullard, whom the *Inquirer* interviewed while he was examining a map depicting slave trade routes, admitted, "It's still hard to see." The stories of the nine enslaved Africans, Vianela Campbell explained, were helpful because "it makes it more human."[109]

Some of the forty-three visitors who did not speak of slavery in their answers to my brief questions instead focused on the design of the installation. The responses of these individuals reflected sentiments similar to those offered by members of the Feel and Re-create publics identified in Chapter 5. Many of these visitors praised the open nature of the installation. "It's very open, very clean, very welcoming," said one park guest. Other visitors commended the site for its "open-air feel," "open, airy" design, and its "modern" quality "because it's open." Another set of visitors enjoyed the site's suggestion of the house, implied by the outline of the structure on the ground and the placement of partial walls and windows in the installation. "I like the concept of the outlay of the building even though the building's not here," observed one visitor. "Rather than build a re-creation over the top of the site, I actually think it's somewhat artistic and leaves more to the imagination," echoed another park guest. "I liked that . . . you can still see the dimensions of the house and stuff, but you can still walk around and it's still like an outside deal," remarked another visitor.

Overall, only about half the interviewees discussed slavery and its implications even minimally, and most of those who did broach the issue seemed to engage the topic as a missing piece of history more than a traumatic memory with political repercussions that continue to linger. That those repercussions were either spoken of without being named or completely ignored by nearly half the interviewees underscores the extraordinary difficulty that contemporary Americans still have in talking about the politics of race and representation—even when squarely confronted with an opportunity to reflect on its historical foundations. Yet these responses are also squarely in line with how visitors to other slavery-related memory places react: by disengaging from the site and distancing themselves from its implications.[110] Erika Doss described conflicted reactions to "public expressions of shame—including memorials that recall the nation's history of slavery and lynching": individuals both look at the difficult memory and look away from its ramifications.[111]

These visitors were certainly unsettled by the heterotopicity of the President's House. On the one hand, they recognized the appropriateness of making the stories of African American history, especially slavery, more public. On the other hand, they did not wholly embrace the telling of the tale nor did their words suggest a strong identification with the narrative or its relevance to the stories told within the park. Instead, they remained at a distance, much like somewhat guilty onlookers, unwilling to experience the site in its entirety (perhaps like those who entered the site and then exited shortly thereafter) but sufficiently aware of the site's importance and relevance to American history.

A Welcomed and Appropriate Exhibit

Individuals in the Welcome public more fully appreciated the President's House for its telling of the long-overdue stories of slavery in U.S. history. Unlike people in the preceding public, these individuals offered responses that directly mentioned slavery *and* that acknowledged the need to present the history of slavery at a public memory site. "It's good that . . . people get a chance to learn about what was going on in slavery because a lot of us just ignore that whole part of history," noted one visitor. "It's very interesting," added another, "especially all the aspects of slavery, and the contradiction between 'All men are created equal' and the fact that the original leaders of our country had slaves." The site's presentation of this contradiction between ideals and practice was also commended by a park guest who noted "the contradiction between the way that people spoke and the way that they lived. . . . It shows how Washington lived, it shows how the, the people who, the slaves, and uh, free slaves were rare, and they were working for him, how they, how they lived and the contrast."

An awareness of these contradictions, affirmed some visitors, is an important step in understanding the nation's past and present. One interviewee, for example, pointed to slavery's influence beyond the southern states: "Slavery . . . really had an effect on, you know, norms that were so far north. And a lot of people think that the slavery was mainly in the south and . . . it did have an effect on [all the colonies]." Another visitor called the site "a must-see" because of "the turmoil that African-Americans went through, to understand how their history applies to their future and how it affects them currently. So I think it's an important stop to realize, I think, what our presidents, what our white presidents have done."

These types of responses, in which untold stories are appreciated, reflect a relatively recent trend in public memorializing: confirmation of the work of those whose efforts had previously been neglected in historical accounts. A couple visiting the President's House expressed appreciation for such recognition.

I thought it was excellent, and I'm really glad to have seen, particularly as a black person, some focus be put on slavery. I think that's really, really great throughout all of the historical pieces here, so I liked that. I think it's great.

Yeah, same here. Also, I think it's also great to feel, you know, more of the focus, on how this country evolved and being objective about laying that out. I think that's a good history lesson.

As another visitor pointed out, this type of public memory work is occurring in other venues around the country: "I see that a lot more information is available about slavery, and it's being incorporated more into America's history, which I appreciate." As these comments, in particular, suggest, individuals in this public found the President's House an entirely appropriate installation both within INHP and within the commemorative landscape generally. They embraced the site's existence more warmly than did the preceding public by directly and clearly talking about the need to discuss slavery in public memory sites, yet their praise generally operated at a cognitive level, indicating that they may not have strongly identified with the stories told at the site. Individuals in the next public, however, both applauded the appropriateness of the installation and demonstrated a strong identification with its interpretation.

A Passionately Embraced Symbol

Individuals in this public argued that the President's House was a powerful and necessary addition to both INHP and the nation's commemorative landscape. "This is a must-go if you are visiting Philadelphia for its history," urged a reviewer on tripadvisor.com. "The president's house tells such a strong tale that this site should not be missed."[112] The power of the President's House story, admitted a Philadelphia resident, may not be easy for some visitors to take, but "I'd even go so far as to partly agree that in telling the story of our nation's birth, we need to have our noses rubbed in the unpleasant past somewhere. Think of all the years where slavery was not even part of the narrative at Mount Vernon, or Monticello, or Ash Lawn [James Monroe's home], or Colonial Williamsburg."[113] In this respect, members of this public shared the same political concerns as the Slavery public discussed in Chapter 5.

Interestingly, I did not discover a single comment that mirrored the concerns of the Insufficient Attention to Slavery public from that chapter. Perhaps, as the *Philadelphia Tribune* writers illustrated earlier in this chapter, the very existence of the *completed* site proved sufficient if not ideal. Coard, for example, has repeatedly praised the finished installation but said, "I didn't get everything I wanted, because if I did it would be called the Nat Turner Revolutionary Center."[114] The content of the site is sufficient, however, if the desire is not to tell every element of a complex story but, instead, to have important chapters in the story acknowledged in the heart of the national park that celebrates the nation's founding. Laurajane Smith's report on what black British visitors to museum displays on slavery desired seems just as relevant here: "what African-Caribbean British visitors were looking for, and often not finding, were indications that they, and their historical and contemporary experiences, were being recognized. This was not only about emotional affirmation, but also political affirmation and social justice."[115]

Smith's comments underscore the distinction between this public and the preceding one. While individuals in the preceding public found the site appropriate, even necessary, on a cognitive level, their appreciation stopped short of emotional and political affirmation. In other words, they did not express the strong feelings of identification with the story that individuals in this public did, nor did they speak as specifically to the site's placement. Many of the individuals in this public shared their experiences online; undoubtedly, the brief, on-site interviews did not occur in a context where such reactions were likely to be shared with a stranger. Only eight of the interviewees, five of whom were African American, expressed their assessment in passionate terms. One visitor found the "very visceral" installation "very moving," and said that she was "staggered" by the experience and "very proud" of the site. Similarly, another visitor told me, "I was pretty emotional when I looked at this site, to realize that people lived and worked there, were held against their own Constitution," while another park guest found the site "shocking because it's not as widely known. It was definitely not taught in school that I remember. I'm, I'm almost thirty years old, and I never learned any of this." One visitor said she was awestruck by the site: "I think it's amazing. I think it's important that, as an African American, our contributions and stories be told. . . . To be here and to see this, I think it's awesome."

A few white visitors were also moved by their experience at the site. One said she found the installation to be "very anti-racist. It makes me feel embarrassed to be a white American." Such a response, added another park guest, is "a good thing" because "it does give you some idea of what transpired here and frankly it's, you get goosebumps when you really think about it." Similarly, another visitor reported that the experience was "heart-wrenching." He said, "I grew up in a basically black neighborhood when I grew up as a kid, and realized what they endured and the way we treated, our own country treated people. It's heart-wrenching. I guess that would be the way to put it."

Visitors in this public spoke powerfully about their experience, often directly engaging the historical and contemporary politics of race as they did so. Individuals who expressed similar sentiments online used, in some cases, even more powerful language to convey their impressions of the installation. Moreover, they spoke more specifically about the appropriateness of telling the story of early Black America *in this place*. Specifically, individuals in this public praised the President's House because it told this story within the home of George Washington and the national park that recounts America's birth and creation. In so doing, many of them referenced the language of *truth* used during the earlier efforts advocating for recognition of the site. "Telling the truth about our enslavement is more important than ANOTHER monument to George Washington. If anything the exhibit doesn't go far enough in showing how it was," wrote Crystal M. Graves of Germantown, Pennsylvania. "The truth must be told," urged an online respondent named Eddy. "Blacks must know that the slaves were not on vacation and this memorial should be upgraded to show the real treatment that the slaves got in slavery." Continuing this theme, Earl Hicks noted, "Slavetrader George Washington was a monster. That's the truth that everyone needs to hear."

Other online posts acknowledged that not everyone would want to hear the truth as it is presented at the President's House, so they emphasized the benefits of telling the stories of the enslaved and of slavery. "The truth must come to light," wrote Kalonji, "and I don't think it takes away anything but enhances the rich, vibrant history that is America." A poster named anylztht emphasized that telling the stories of America's past is not a zero-sum proposition: "Acknowledging the histories of African Americans, takes nothing away from Euro-Americans. It's all American History. And why should the descendants of slaves fear mentioning the enslavement of their ancestors b/c it may offend the sensibilities of someone whose skin is white. It really makes no sense. Tell the truth, accept it, learn from it, and let the chips fall where they may."

Not surprisingly, some of chips fell into the laps of individuals who shared less positive assessments of the President's House. I heard only four visitors express discomfort with the site during my interviews, but a number of people posting online castigated the interpretation at the installation—many of them suggesting that the completed site did not tell the whole truth. For individuals in this public, the President's House was an inappropriate incursion into INHP, one with which they could not identify.

An Inappropriate Account

Some of those who did not like the President's House complained about the installation's design, especially the video monitors and the site's unfinished house appearance. "WHAT A HOT MESS! It's like a bad suburban house!" complained one person using the name Phillyurban8. "Within 25 feet there are THREE flat screen TVs mounted above fake fireplace mantels. Each TV is blaring its own narrative and on top of that there are speakers in some of the knee walls, each with their own recording. . . . It was sheer cacophony! I couldn't get out of there fast enough! Geez, Louise all you need is hard-of-hearing grandpa in his LazyBoy rocker and some plaid couches and the picture is complete!"

Most of the negative responses, however, echoed the concerns of the members of the Insufficient Focus on the Presidency public discussed in Chapter 5; namely, they did not like the focus on slavery and the enslaved within the confines of INHP.[116] Linda Miller complained, "10 times more space devoted to Slavery than to our first two Presidents." And Matt Birnbaum wondered, "What do the Presidents have to do with it anymore?" One subset of this public expressed concern about the absence of other stories within the site, while another subset of individuals argued that the interpretation, in the words of Clint Walker, "re-writes history"; in essence, everyone in this public asserted that, contrary to the claims of its champions, the site did not tell the whole truth.

Some individuals complained about the lack of attention accorded to other residents of the house, such as Adams, Benedict Arnold (who lived there during the Revolutionary War), and its owner, Robert Morris, a signer of the Declaration of Independence and a primary financier of the revolution. "Tell us about General Sir William Howe, tell us about Robert Morris, tell us about John Adams (it was his White House, too)," asserted Joe Smith. Added Daniel Robinson, "The whole property has been turned into a slave memorial, crowding out George Washington and John Adams, not to mention Robert Morris and Benedict Arnold." BenStone, a frequent contributor to the philadelphiaspeaks website, argued that the site could and should have explored a number of issues related to the development of the executive branch:

Take a look at some of the questions that might have been addressed:

What were the major events/challenges of George Washington's presidency?

What were the major events/challenges of John Adams's presidency?

Who were the Cabinet members, and what challenges did they face in their service?

How did the Executive Branch/Presidency evolve/grow over its first 10 years?

How is the Executive Branch/Presidency different now than it was at the beginning?

The heated philosophical debates between Hamilton and Jefferson over what kind of nation the United States should become—agrarian or commercial—took place in the house. Why are they not mentioned/interpreted? Who were the First Ladies and the presidents' families, and what sacrifices did they make?

"Slavery is PART of the history that had to be told at the President's House," he acknowledged, but he lamented, "Instead, slavery has become the only narrative."[117] Ashley Barnes, who described herself as having "a small foot into the museum world," offered a similar assessment: "I think it's deplorable that this site has been exploited for one purpose instead of including ALL relevant history, and such a rich and interesting history at that. Slavery is a huge part of that and should have a prominent place in the translation, but not the only place."

Much as the early advocates for the President's House had pointed out that INHP specifically and the nation's commemorative landscape generally had been telling only part of the nation's history, individuals in this public argued that the President's House interpretation was partial, in both senses of the world; its incompleteness illuminated its politics. "The President's House," argued one person on the IHA website, "is a political statement disguised as a memorial. It is little more than a grievance piece that blames White people for the evils of the world." Other online contributors decried the site as "racially based political maneuvering" designed for "appeasement" and "reparations."[118]

The site's perceived political agenda apparently led some individuals in this public to evaluate the site as a conscious effort to revise the story of the nation's founding—an affront to the long-told stories embedded within the park's domain. One visitor to the site told me: "I think they've tried hard to take away from the mythology of the Founding Fathers, but [they] may have gone a little too far in the other direction." Other individuals reacted even more strongly online. On the IHA website, the interpretation was called "mean-spirited and divisive" (Jerry Hoffman), exhibiting "an anti-white bias" (Brian Dunbar), and "consciously racially-divisive, conceived along the lines of 'You've had your mythology; now it's our turn!'" (Clint Walker). More specifically, some individuals accused the President's House of presenting a *dishonest* account of the people and activities within the house. Sam Smith spoke of his family's visit on July 4, 2012, and noted that "there was nothing patriotic, uplifting, or fair-minded about what we found there. Rather than a celebration of the first two presidents or even an impartial listing of their accomplishments, there was a general negativity bordering on outright dishonesty." David A. Moyer's post offered a more specific version of Smith's concern: "It is dishonest to define Washington's whole presidency by his slaveowning." As a result, bemoaned another park visitor, "this exhibit took away from the true nature of the location, one of the first Presidential Residences of our nation's history."[119]

Just as African Americans have long found the U.S. commemorative landscape lacking in its presentation of their histories, most of the individuals in this public were troubled by the absence of the stories of the white residents of the President's House. In some cases, especially when individuals perceived the site to be politically divisive, Mark McPhail's observations about whites' openness to alternative memories may be relevant. "The vast majority of white people," he wrote, "cannot hear [alternative histories], for to do so would mean becoming something other than who they have been, e(race)ing that mythic public memory that commemorates white innocence and self interest."[120] Indeed, the stories told at the President's House, and the place in which they are told, threaten the long-standing story that the nation has told itself. No wonder, then, that a man named Michael wrote on the IHA website, "How can one feel pride in a country that, according to the exhibit, has so deeply sinned against humanity?"[121]

Michael's lament succinctly summarizes the dilemmas, contradictions, and anxieties packed within the President's House. If we rightfully acknowledge the moral compromises in the nation's founding, how can the ideals of freedom and liberty continue to be celebrated—not just in INHP but throughout the nation? If the nation's founding heroes engaged in the trafficking and enslavement of other human beings, how can we continue to lionize their accomplishments without hypocrisy? If we do not celebrate the founders' morally flawed lives or unabashedly embrace the (un)lived ideal of liberty, what do we celebrate in the commemorative landscape? If the commemorative landscape increasingly adds what Kirk Savage calls "victim memorials,"[122] how will the corresponding cultural guilt and acknowledgment be worked through? The President's House laid bare these questions and revealed an even more fundamental question: Who will we become?

Working through these questions will not be easy. Americans are uncomfortable talking about race in almost any context;[123] doing so within the context of the nation's identity and founding narrative is even more demanding. Perhaps such weight is too much to bear for any place of public memory,[124] but all these issues converged within the site of the President's House. How odd that such vital, consuming, and challenging questions were prompted by a much more innocent query from a tourist visiting INHP: "Where was the White House?"

8

Continuing the Conversation

The Legacy of the President's House

The wide range of reactions to the President's House can be traced to not only the interwoven incongruities among its design and interpretation elements but also the story of its development. From the beginning, advocates for the site imagined its enormous potential. The ironic convergence of slavery and freedom within yards of each other, in the center of Independence Mall no less, generated outsized expectations for what the site could accomplish. As Chapter 4 illustrated, advocates envisioned a powerful and sweeping tale that would expose the nation's tangled and incomplete embrace of liberty in ways that would boldly unearth the long-buried stories of slavery within the national commemorative landscape. Enacting these tantalizing possibilities on a small plot of land, while hewing to the extensive list of themes and cultural values outlined in the RFQ, represented an extraordinary challenge for the installation's would-be designers. Chapter 5 revealed the immense difficulty involved in developing a site that would capture the dreams and wishes of all the publics who were invested in the President's House. At that point, the reality that no single commemorative design could satisfy a diverse population emerged; instead, as with all political debates in democratic societies, compromises produced a concord that proved insufficiently satisfying across the project's constituents. Then the early hopes of the project's advocates were revitalized during the incredibly popular excavation process, as Chapter 6 pointed out. Exposing the foundation remains offered a tangible sign of the site's existence and moved many a Philadelphian to imagine the past in the present as well as the potential power of a completed installation. That hope, as we just saw, was at once dashed and fulfilled during the development of the interpretation that would inhabit the design. The President's House thus offers legacies that speak to disappointment, challenge, and hope.

Disappointment

The symbolic importance of the completed President's House cannot be overstated, but the site seems to have most fully engaged visitors during the excavation. At that time, Michael Coard observed that visitors seemed especially engrossed by the dig: "Comments about race and power, black and white, slavery and freedom, history and identity [were] everywhere in the air. . . . Sometimes it was reasoned dialog and other times it was animated and heated. But that to me was like giving birth—it was painful, it was necessary. From those discussions, from those debates, from those arguments, comes a real movement toward the truth."[1]

Yet, as thoughtful proponents of the site noted in online postings, the completed installation lacks the same power. An individual using the screen name BenStone in the philadelphiaspeaks forum reflected on the experience of the excavation almost two years after the finished site opened:

> I spent a good deal of time on the observation deck during the 2007 archeological dig. What happened there was extraordinary. People would come and spend hours watching the work, but also talking seriously about slavery and race in a protected, non-accusatory environment. I walked by one Sunday morning, and there was a black woman standing there alone, singing gospel hymns to the ruins. I began to get a sense of how enormous an ache Slavery has left, and how powerful the need is to make sense of the past. We were all learning then, and maybe the observation deck experience was unreproducable [sic]. But my hope was for a similar experience at the memorial.

One day after this post, another regular on the philadelphiaspeaks forum responded: "That is why I argued upthread that probably the best thing they could have done was simply build a protective cover over the dig and put up an observation platform with some interpretive panels and a rotating display of objects from the dig. We might have even been able to dispense with the interpretive panels. . . . The dig gave us the space to talk about it in the way it should be talked about."[2] Ashley Hahn, who worked for the NPS as an architectural technician during the excavation, added: "I often stopped by to watch the dig or take pictures. On the observation platform overlooking the site, I overheard strangers engage in real conversations about race and slavery. That was a gift to our city. I don't hear those impromptu dialogues anymore at the President's House, probably because the site itself hasn't ever really worked."[3]

Given comments such as these, one wonders what would have happened if the site had been excavated before the design competition (as one of the semi-finalist designers urged)[4] or if the city and park had decided that the design process needed to begin anew after the power of the excavated remains became clear. Frank Matero, professor of architecture at the University of Pennsylvania, forcefully argued during the summer and fall of 2007 that a new design was needed in order to facilitate the types of visitor experiences generated by the excavation. Instead of using the Kelly/Maiello design, which suggested the ruins of the house, Matero believed that the actual ruins should have formed the basis for the installation. "They should have been the generator of form," he insisted. The vitrine, Matero presciently predicted over a year before the site was completed, would fail to move visitors in the same way as the excavation did: visitors will be "at a safe distance so they don't have to feel anything or be engaged." By sticking with the Kelly/Maiello design, Matero lamented, the park and city missed an opportunity to create a powerful and compelling site. "Philadelphia could have been on the map for this . . . [but] I think we blew it on this. I think we missed it."[5]

A less radical approach was represented by one of the alternatives presented by Kelly/Maiello in the fall of 2007: the creation of an underground room in which the remains would be displayed. Such a room could have offered something similar to the viewing platform experience, and visitors would have remained in close proximity away from the aboveground noise. I suspect that such a design would have encouraged more contemplation and conversation than the current installation permits. The *underground* display of the remains, moreover, would also have provided significant symbolic power to the installation, especially considering the weight carried by the "excavating buried truth" representative anecdote that helped create the site. Unfortunately, as project manager McPherson told me, engineering concerns involving, among other things, the depth of the room and visitor flow scuttled the possibility of including such a room.[6]

As my comments about the benefits of an underground room suggest, I believe that the completed site does not offer the same experiences of *imagination, proximity,* and *contemplation* that the excavation provided. The President's House is so full of stuff—videos, audio, words, pictures, lines on the ground—that visitors experience sensory overload rather than sensory engagement. One cannot imagine Oney Judge's life and escape or Hercules creating culinary masterpieces in the kitchen when contemporary actors are portraying them on a continuous video loop. One cannot imagine the near side-by-side representations of an underground passageway and the first Oval Office when they are overwhelmed with surrounding interpretive material.[7] In working so hard to make the reality of the site vivid, and—significantly— to make a place for the stories of African American history on Independence Mall, the design and interpretation robs visitors of the opportunities to hear and see the past in their own terms. Consider, as an alternative, not just the sparse interpretation during the excavation but the powerful experiences of the Vietnam Veterans Memorial and the Flight 93 Memorial, both of which have been described as "spare"—hardly a word associated with the President's House installation.[8] Sometimes less is more.

In addition, the open nature of the site significantly reduces the opportunities for visitors to congregate, to share in the experience of the site in proximity to others as they can at outdoor sites such as the Vietnam Veterans Memorial or indoor installations such as the U.S. Holocaust Memorial Museum. During the excavation of the President's House site, visitors were confined to a viewing platform along one side of the dig. At the completed installation, the glass-covered remains can be observed from *three* sides—*if* visitors choose to follow one of the many possible paths that lead to the vitrine. The completed site also does not offer a place for contemplation or conversation, nor does its interpretation encourage the same. In fact, Jerry Hoffman, who was quoted in the preceding chapter as finding the site divisive, noted on the IHA website: "My wife and I visited the observation deck for the archeology many times. It was a forum for discussion and a spot where visitors of all colors could stand shoulder to shoulder to actually view the contradictions in our history. There was great value in this—in a small way, it helped to mend the national fabric."

Even with the extensive interpretation at the President's House, the site seems, as a whole, strangely divorced from the remainder of the park. Generally, "a 'productive' memorial must make an impact beyond its enclosed space," argued Kirk Savage. "It must work against the impulse to memorialize itself. . . . It must seek connections to the world outside its own."[9] The stories of the President's House undoubtedly reflect the second half of its formal name, but the interpretation offers few references to other sites in the park and it does not point visitors to other park sites connected to the activities and persons of the President's House. Although the yellow fever epidemic of

1793 is referenced more than once at the President's House, the interpretation never directs visitors to the Deshler-Morris House (Germantown White House), despite noting that Washington and his staff took refuge there during the epidemic. One reference is made to slavery-related trials in nearby Independence Hall, yet the narrative does not underscore the many other ways in which liberty was denied to African Americans within the confines of that structure.[10] While the story of slavery references times and places outside the confines of the house and the 1790s, no mention is made of how the Liberty Bell's inscription inspired abolitionists and only three passing references are made to the LBC itself. The site speaks to the enshrinement of inequality, but no mention is made of the celebration of the U.S. Constitution at the NCC down the mall even though the constitutional compromise is briefly discussed in one paragraph on "The Dirty Business of Slavery" panel. In short, rather than use the President's House to complicate the national narrative of liberty and freedom by talking about that story as insufficiently founded and (still) incompletely enacted, the interpretive material—as Sitarski worried—shapes the President's House as distinct from the remainder of the park.[11]

Two means of shaping the President's House story, in particular, contributed to this condition. First, the interpretation's focus on *recognition* limits the possibility for *acknowledgment*. Nancy Fraser has identified two potential pitfalls when recognition becomes the goal of efforts to re-envision the status quo. First, recognition may displace the problem by focusing attention on tertiary issues. Second, recognition may reify perceived distinctions among groups, perpetuating the separatism that generated the desire for recognition in the first place.[12] To some extent, when the President's House situates many of its stories within Philadelphia and the African diaspora, it displaces the story of slavery within the founding of the United States. In so doing, the nation's reluctant struggle to come to terms with its historical hypocrisy, as well as the dehumanizing legacies of defining black Americans as inferior, becomes tertiary to recognizing the Philadelphia residents of and near the President's House and their common ancestral home in Africa. In addition, reversing both the focus of the story and its implied narrator may be perceived by some visitors as replacing one form of separatism for another.

None of this is to say that the scenes and focus of the President's House stories are inappropriate—as I noted in Chapter 3, the stories of black Americans *should* be present in the nation's commemorative landscape. Instead, I want to underscore the difficulty of telling these stories in ways that both give a distinct presence to the history of African Americans *and* locate that presence within the familiar/white histories of the nation. In cases where giving presence to previously unheard stories challenges established versions of the past, Kenneth Foote argued, "it is an issue not of creating a new tradition but rather of altering existing traditions enough to make room for new meanings. This is of particular relevance to the marking of African American and Native American history in the United States."[13]

Perhaps one means of accomplishing this task was suggested by the strategies embraced by early advocates for recognition of the President's House site: the ironies of liberty. From the outset, the President's House controversy has been backlit by these ironies. Lawler's research undoubtedly received much attention because it highlighted the ironic contrasts among INHP's identity as the cradle of liberty, George Washington's denial of liberty to the nine enslaved persons who worked in the nation's first executive mansion, and the location of Washington's actions on the front porch of the LBC. The notion of *liberty*, Michael McGee emphasized, is a human construction, and its presence in our lives must be felt, not merely understood as an abstraction. "'Slavery,' he asserted, "can exist even in an Anglo-American democracy should we cling so piously to reifications of our 'liberty' that we forget a primary duty to materialize 'the thing itself.'"[14] Appropriately, as Chapter 4 illustrated, the ironic use of liberty accentuated the ways in which the park (and nation) had been forgetting to materialize the idea of liberty; yet the completed installation declines to make liberty the centerpiece of its story.

The President's House storytelling is most definitely ironic, as it reverses the telling of the park's traditional story, but it evokes what Kenneth Burke terms romantic irony ("outside and superior") rather than dialectic irony ("a sense of fundamental kinship").[15] In other words, the romantic ironic reversal of the traditional narrative trades one form of superiority for another, whereas a dialectic ironic narrative would have featured a story in which the term *liberty* was overtly highlighted as a means of illustrating how the nine enslaved Africans (but especially Oney Judge and Hercules) and the free African community of Philadelphia sought to make places in their experience for liberty, just as the nation's white founders promised in their patriotic pronouncements. Instead, the language used in the interpretation more frequently features the term *freedom* (as in Judge and Hercules "escaped to freedom")—even though one interpretive panel quotes Judge as saying, "I knew that if I went back to Virginia [and Mount Vernon], I should never get my liberty."

The distinction between liberty and freedom is, in this context, more than a semantic quibble. As McGee noted, both terms are ideographs, or "an abstraction representing collective commitment to a particular but equivocal and ill-defined normative goal."[16] The abstract nature of ideographs such as freedom and liberty, explained McGee, allows them to be defined in the terms desired by the societies that embrace them. In the United States, freedom has generally been applied to behavior in general (though some behavior, of course, is connected to social and political issues), while liberty has functioned as more of a foundational political philosophy in which one is guaranteed the right to participate in all social and political spaces. In this respect, freedom works well as a counterpart to slavery, in that both reference the ability to act and live without being controlled by others. When freedom is used within the President's House interpretation, it suggests a freedom from white oppression, which points to the existence of a socio-political structure while also symbolically positing the existence of two distinct social places: those where black persons are free and those where they are not. As decades of formal and informal segregation have demonstrated, however, African Americans could be relatively free *in their own places* while still being excluded from other public spaces. In other words, freedom's focus on social behavior deflects attention from liberty's demand for both free behavior *and* unfettered political participation. Moreover, INHP's interpretation has long embraced the idea of liberty more than freedom (hence the park's nickname "the cradle of liberty" rather than, say, "the birthplace of freedom"). Featuring liberty within the President's House would have not only highlighted the ironic juxtaposition between the President's House and the LBC; it would have also framed the site within the core political idea trumpeted throughout the park (and the nation). As a result, the President's House might then have also touched on the legacies of the continued denial of liberty experienced by African Americans as they have sought to make a place in the land of the free. While Jim Crow laws, for example, denied African Americans the freedom to enter many public places, these laws also spoke directly to the failure to enact the nation's political philosophy.[17]

Had the President's House spoken more directly to the political dimensions of irony within the installation, it might also have engaged visitors more fully. As Robert Terrill has insightfully explained, irony typically encourages a distant perspective on the contrasts it highlights. By identifying the previously unseen similarities between seemingly incompatible ideas or activities, such as the heroic quests for freedom enacted by the enslaved and those who enslaved them, we gain a new appreciation for the stories that were not present. Yet, Terrill argued, "audiences may be invited toward insight, but they are not incited to action." Those who use irony with political ends in mind, he continued, should ultimately seek "the collapse of the distances that irony inhabits."[18] Burke's notion of dialectic irony, which pursues "fundamental kinship," promises such a collapse in that it ultimately embraces similarity in difference. For example, the stories of the enslaved and free Africans told at the President's House might have been more fully integrated within the ironies surrounding the nearby Liberty Bell as well as the founders' declarations, uttered in Independence Hall and celebrated in the NCC, about the colonists being treated as slaves by Great Britain. Such interpretation might have afforded a more concrete foundation for addressing the historical and contemporary legacies of slavery within the installation, which, in turn, could have prompted visitors to engage the ongoing politics of race in the United States. As J. Christian Spielvogel pointed out in his critique of contemporary interpretation at three NPS Civil War sites, the Park Service "is not obliged to raise awareness about the current obstacles to racial progress . . . [but] visitors need to recognize that the struggle for racial progress is always ongoing and continuous."[19]

Finally, I believe the President's House should better orient its visitors to the site, its features, and—in a nod to the need for integration of the site within INHP—its spatial relationship to other sites within the park. At the very least, park visitors should be immediately aware of the site's existence within the park. One sign at the entrance of the President's House would do wonders for orienting visitors to the site. Another sign on the exterior wall bordering the mall sidewalk would be even better. Or perhaps the wayside marker parked under the LBC's overhang could be moved next to one of the exterior corners of the site on Market Street so that park guests crossing the street from the Visitor Center could notice it before they enter the home or bypass it along the mall sidewalk. Without such signage, the difficult memories interpreted within the installation will continue to be overlooked by hundreds of thousands of visitors every year.

Once they enter the installation, visitors would be hard-pressed to identify where they were standing in the house. Inset maps on the panels below the video screens identify the room that is represented in that part of the installation, yet the maps always depict the footprint in a south/left to north/right image while the fireplace-mounted screens are located on walls facing all four cardinal directions. The map of the site on the vitrine needs to be rotated ninety degrees so that its directions match the footprint of the house. The other site map, located on the wayside marker near the LBC entrance, does not require rotation, but the wayside faces the LBC rather than the President's House site and—unlike the maps below the video screens—outlines the house in a south/top to north/bottom alignment. In addition, the ground floor rooms are marked with lines, but the site's interpretation does not indicate clearly what functions these lines serve. A series of bronze plaques on the ground of the President's House would orient visitors to their location within the home's footprint, provide a visible set of guides to move to and from, serve as locations where visitors could gather in close proximity, and encourage visitors to imagine the activities of the people who once stood in the same place. For example, a plaque on the floor of the Kitchen could say, "Here is where Hercules prepared meals for the home's residents"; one in the State Dining Room could say, "Here is where Presidents Washington and Adams greeted their guests"; and ones on the ground where the bedrooms were located upstairs could say, "Above this place is where Oney Judge envisioned her liberty." With a stronger sense of place, the foundation remains might also evince more of the power that they displayed during the excavation.

In addition, the site's visual interpretation might benefit from inset displays that indicate where relevant events occurred elsewhere in the park and city (one such map *is* featured on "The Dirty Business of Slavery" panel). The interpretation of the institution of slavery, for example, could point to the Liberty Bell next door as the symbol of abolitionists, and to Independence Hall down the mall as the site where legislative and judicial decisions perpetuated the enslavement of Africans and their descendants. The map embedded in the interpretation of the free African community could offer a visual representation of the *neighborhood* (as opposed to single sites) and its proximity to the President's House. Moreover, the map could also point to the NCC as the excavated area in which free African leader James Dexter's home was located (while noting that the artifacts from that excavation are on display in the park's Independence Archeology Laboratory on nearby Walnut Street).[20] The story of the yellow fever outbreak could encourage guests to visit the Germantown White House, where Washington, his family, and his staff retreated, by pointing out its location relative to the mall.

In so doing, the President's House could have also worked to make Independence Mall less of what Inga Saffron called "an island in the city."[21] Part of the reason for the mall's recent makeover was to integrate it more fully into the surrounding cityscape. Some of these efforts, Saffron argued, worked well, but others failed miserably. In particular, she pointed to the fact that the NCC, the Visitor Center, and the LBC wall off the park on its Sixth Street side. The President's House design, at the corner of Sixth and Market, makes matters worse. The least inviting entrance to the installation is on the Sixth Street side; no interpretation or signage can be found on that side; and the faux walls and fireplaces, while appealing to those who wanted to re-create the impression of the house, impede sight lines and give the impression of a relatively closed space within the already existing "island in the city."

Admittedly, a more abstract design might have dissatisfied the vocal Re-create public, but regardless of the design, orientation might also have been enhanced if visitors felt more drawn to the stories of the house and its residents. As important as the stories told within the current installation are, their volume overwhelms most visitors; park guests do not hear these stories if they do not know where to turn and/or then routinely exit the installation shortly after entering it. The videos are well-intentioned, but they distract from both the historical sense of place that visitors could imagine and the interpretive material that is also on display. The kind of thoughtful contemplation that should occur in difficult places of memory cannot take place in an environment filled with sound and moving images. Perhaps the videos could instead be compiled into a single loop and then displayed on a single screen, with seating, under the shade provided by the roof the LBC. The reduction of distractions could then allow interpretation to place visitors within the rooms of the house and more easily encourage the site's guests to project themselves into the past.

Discerning readers can no doubt identify problems with each of the suggestions that I have proposed. My suggestions reflect not only a particular scholarly point of view—my general interest in place and meaning, for example, drives my desire to envision a President's House with a more place-based design and interpretation—but also the experiences of a white man who has not had to live life on the other side of the color line. In short, my suggestions—any critique, for that matter—reflect the partiality (in both senses of the word) of any perspective. As much as I endeavor to remember and acknowledge the complexity of telling the stories of the President's House, the fact remains that designing and interpreting the site was a monumental challenge.

Challenge

The challenge in presenting difficult memories, and in doing so through the introduction of counter-narratives, lies in balancing the competing demands of directly engaging the past and inviting contemporary visitors to reflect on the imperfections of the past. Too much of an emphasis on the former can lead to didactic installations in which visitors are presented with so much information or material that is hard to endure that they turn away from the site. Too much of an emphasis on the latter can lead to installations in which actions of the past are so indirectly addressed that visitors are comforted and reassured by softened impressions of what happened or by the past's seeming irrelevance to the present. Moreover, as the President's House has demonstrated, different groups of people may find the same installation both insufficiently direct *and* indirect. In other words, disappointments are bound to emerge when *any* site attempts to engage a difficult memory.

My (and likely others') disappointments with the President's House are rooted in outsized expectations. Initially, the delicious irony of the site's location next to the LBC generated so much excitement about symbolic possibilities that *any* physical installation would have seemed insufficient in some ways. Consider, for instance, that the two most popular semi-finalist designs still failed to convince half the members of two of the six invested publics that their designs were worthy of the site. Then, when the excavation promoted powerful conversations about slavery, history, and contemporary racial politics, the site seemed to promise the possibility of racial reconciliation. Here, perhaps, we could finally begin coming to terms, together, with how the nation's embrace of slavery has indelibly marked our understandings of who we are. To ask a single memory place to accomplish such a large task, however, is too large of a demand. Indeed, warned Mark McPhail, "we must be especially careful when advancing the claim that racial history and memory can be reconciled rhetorically. . . . Perhaps our investment in forgetting and the risk of remembering is too great, or our moral amnesia too deeply ingrained."[22]

These unrealistic expectations also stem from the fact that any *single* site, such as the President's House, cannot sufficiently contain all the memories that circulate within and around it. Even with its abundant interpretation, which was extensively edited for length, the site tells incomplete stories about slavery, the nine enslaved Africans, the business of the executive branch, and the domestic experiences of the Washington and Adams families. The stories of some of the home's other inhabitants (Robert Morris, General Sir William Howe, Benedict Arnold) are not present.[23] Thus, like those involved in the development of the installation, I likely want the President's House to accomplish more than is possible.

In addition, sites such as the President's House are bound to generate disappointment because of what A. Susan Owen and Peter Ehrenhaus call our anxiety about how any single representation (or site, in this case) can tell a sufficiently full story about the overwhelming legacies of race and slavery in the United States.[24] Perhaps this anxiety helps explain why visitors to the President's House seemed uncomfortable talking directly about race and politics. Unlike the reports of conversations that occurred on the excavation viewing platform, I did not notice interactions between black and white visitors, nor did I overhear exchanges on the topic of slavery. The comments of one President's House visitor who spoke with me may illustrate the difficulty of sorting through an enormous and difficult topic after experiencing a single site: "Well, it's very interesting and it's good to read about the, uh, history and everything. It's annoying to read about slavery and all of that, but people must learn what happened before to move forward, I guess. It was pretty impressive." Her words indicate an internal contradiction: beginning with a positive response to the inclusivity of the President's House, she then moves on to hint that far from being revealing, talking about slavery can simply be "annoying," before once again moving back to her initial positive reaction. Dropping only a hint of negativity, her decision to both start and end her response on a positive but neutral note—"interesting," "impressive"—could be due to a reluctance to face the contradictions represented by the site head-on.

The President's House is also a challenging place because of the tension between recognizing the untold stories of disenfranchised groups and envisioning the United States as a place where all subscribe to a single national narrative. When the nation's founders embraced the phrase *e pluribus unum* as the nation's unofficial motto, they set in motion in a long-standing expectation that the many peoples of the United States should gather under one story. Yet Americans have never "been comfortable with the pluralistic reality of the American nation," historian Nathan Huggins observed. Instead, "we have tried to fashion a story to serve as the nation's common history—subordinating a great deal of human experience and particularity by the way."[25] When we make places such as the President's House, we struggle to find the elusive perfect balance between envisioning an ongoing *us* while acknowledging the experiences of those who have been treated as *them*. The question then becomes this: "What stories are we prepared to tell, and what stories are we willing to hear, without transforming them into preferred narratives that make no demands on our comforting illusions about the relationship between slavery and freedom in the life of the nation?"[26]

Moreover, when we tell these stories, we are challenged by the ways in which the stories can be told. When places in the South first began to acknowledge the contributions of African American participants in the civil rights movement, Dell Upton noted that the memorials stylistically mirrored those honoring the nation's white leaders: "They celebrated great leaders—always men and usually Martin Luther King, Jr.—and they used the conventions of traditional portrait statuary to do so."[27] As noted earlier, heroic tributes serve noble purposes, but they also indirectly address the social, political, and cultural situations that motivated the heroic actions.

Similarly, Kirt H. Wilson observed that much contemporary talk about remembering the civil rights movement embraces a sentimental style that "invites non-black audiences to reexperience the movement as either sympathetic witnesses or as reformed, enlightened citizens . . . [and] an ideal black audience that always offers whites forgiveness for the wrongs of the past in return for an affective state that diminishes but does not fully remove the pain, anger, hate, and despair so frequently produced by racism."[28] While Wilson acknowledged that such an approach can foster reconciliation, he also warned that it can provide a means of avoiding discussion of "the hard yet essential critiques that resulted from the civil rights movement."[29] Wilson's point helps explain why many commemorations focused on African American history tend to emphasize the heroic acts of black Americans. Recognizing their efforts makes a place for black contributions in the commemorative landscape while offering a view of the past consistent with the nation's preference for stories of triumphant individualism.

A final challenge was more structural: "the thing that is to be built," as Saffron once described the President's House, has never had a concrete identity; it is an outdoor, always open, hybrid memorial/museum. What should such an installation look/feel like? A multitude of answers exist, largely because we have no preconceived frameworks or examples that would help us understand such a site. Memorials suggest permanence both in their materials (i.e., carved stone) and in their minimal verbiage; little needs to be said, memorials suggest, because we all know what is memorialized here. Yet the President's House offers *two* memorials, a traditional stone wall dedicated to the nine enslaved Africans who toiled in the house and a visually busy enclosure honoring all Africans who had been enslaved, *and* provides interpretation reminiscent of a museum experience. Kelly, in fact, incorporated videos into his team's design because they could be changed as new historical knowledge was unearthed, much as a museum maintains the flexibility to change its exhibits. In addition, unlike indoor Holocaust memorial/museum hybrids that mandate paths and enclose their visitors, the President's House—paradoxically, given its content—gives its visitors the freedom to explore, exit, and/or ignore its displays. The slavery memorial enclosure, in particular, suffers from the site's outdoor location. Intended to give visitors the feel of the cramped quarters of the enslaved, the memorial's location at the back of the installation is easily bypassed.

Hope

Given these challenging constraints, the successes of the President's House deserve acknowledgment. Undoubtedly, the President's House serves as a testament to the lives and work of the enslaved and their descendants, and as a commemoration of the oppressive and hypocritical system in which they toiled. As the site's memorial plaque proclaims, the President's House honors the "millions of men, women, and children of African descent . . . [who] endured brutality and mistreatment for over 200 years even as their labor built and enriched the nation." The existence of this statement, and this site, in the park that honors the founding figures, places, and documents of the United States provides immense hope for the possibility of continuing to acknowledge and discuss the difficult public memory of slavery.

As the *Philadelphia Inquirer*'s Stephan Salisbury reported, "The [President's House] controversy compelled sweeping change in the park's narrative and allowed a host of new stories to flood onto the plain of Independence Mall. . . . This change is a monumental revision of America's founding mythology, historians argue—one that has not diminished the sanctity of sacred ground but magnified it."[30] Even those who, like me, share some disappointment in particular elements of the site applaud the President's House for its role in creating an opening to acknowledge the incomplete stories that had been told throughout INHP. An eloquent commentator on the philadelphiaspeaks online forum offered a reminder that accentuated the unique contribution of the President's House: "We have plenty of places we can go to celebrate the genius of the Founders, including the two tourists draws that bracket this memorial, the National Constitution Center and Independence Hall. There aren't that many where we can contemplate the shame that stained that genius. We must never forget that too."[31]

The President's House, retired INHP supervisory ranger Joe Becton noted, "is a great addition [to INHP] for the African American community."[32] When the park's interpretive work over the past ten to fifteen years is considered in comparison with its earlier history, the stories are decidedly more diverse. Becton, for example, pointed out that he developed an Underground Railroad walking tour during his stint working in INHP, while Sitarski sought to integrate untold stories when he managed the park's interpretive efforts. The new long-range interpretive plan unveiled in 2007 suggests that INHP is in the midst of re-envisioning how it tells the stories of the nation's early years. At the same time, as my experiences in the park illustrated, INHP still has room to improve—a belief shared by both Sitarski and Becton. In this respect, INHP is much like the rest of the U.S. commemorative landscape.

The President's House also contributes to the ongoing revision of the nation's commemorative landscape. "Symbolic excavation of slavery," argued Derek Alderman and Rachel Campbell, "requires that individuals and groups engage in the memory work of not only shaping what is said about the enslaved but ensuring that representations of a slave past can be seen, heard, and felt through the landscape."[33] In recent years, the NPS, other government agencies, and private groups have been, as Foote noted earlier, "altering existing traditions enough to make room for new meanings." In Washington,

D.C., for instance, the African American Civil War Memorial was dedicated in 1998 (and control transferred to the NPS in 2004), the Martin Luther King, Jr., Memorial opened in 2011, and the Smithsonian's National Museum of African American History and Culture is scheduled to open in 2015. Each of these places of memory helps reshape the nation's commemorative landscape by making places where the stories and experiences of African Americans can emerge to be seen, heard, and acknowledged.

Yet much remains to be done and more places need to be made. In 2009 and 2011, respectively, the National Parks Conservation Association (NPCA) and the Organization of American Historians (OAH) issued reports, while working in conjunction with the NPS, asserting that the Park Service still had much work to do in making its sites relevant to all Americans. "The National Park Service," Maria Hinojosa bluntly stated in the NPCA document, "must find ways to invite new publics into the parks."[34] In addition, the report urged the Park Service to consider developing new and more diverse sites: "New parks should broaden the diversity of our national narrative and reflect our nation's evolving history."[35] Even though Erika Doss acknowledged that the NPS "has taken a leadership role in commemorating shameful episodes in American history," the OAH report urged the Park Service to rethink its presentation of history within its sites.[36] In particular, it called on the NPS to connect its interpretation to issues outside a historic site's boundaries, embrace stories of conflict and controversy about the past, and highlight the ways in which past understandings of history have changed (and will continue to do so). It also urged the Park Service to listen to professional historians *and* those invested in the telling of history: "We encourage thoughtful efforts to incorporate other voices, perspectives, and 'truths' into conversations about the past and its meaning."[37]

Acknowledging difficult memories is "a sign of openness and honesty—towards the past but also, by association, in the present."[38] In so doing, places such as the President's House carve an opening for discussions about the role of the nation's past in its developing future. More specifically, as we eye the future with an awareness of ongoing demographic changes, we must revisit the challenge of envisioning a national identity in the midst of multiple and complex stories about who *we* are. Marcelo Suarez-Orozco pointedly asked: "How do we then create a narrative of our nation where our shared fate—regardless of generation—now involved folk of very, very different ethnicities, languages, immigration histories, while we continue to emphasize the sheer qualities of what makes us all Americans?"[39]

A good question—and one that we can continue to mull. The imperfections of the President's House point to the difficulty of answering the question yet push us to consider it nonetheless. One of the benefits of an imperfect solution to a difficult memory, Marouf Hasian, Jr., has noted, is that the lack of closure generates continued debate—which, in some ways, is a better result than a widely admired installation.[40] As James E. Young pointed out in his study of public remembrance of the Holocaust in Germany, "Once we assign monumental form to memory, we have to some degree divested ourselves of the obligation to remember."[41] The spate of post–Civil War memorials that sought national harmony by honoring the war's combatants offered a superb representation of Young's idea. When those memorials mourned the dead, they suggested that the divisions that prompted the war had also passed away. The act of mourning, in this case, served to foster reconciliation, but at the expense of directly addressing the underlying causes of division. In other words, accomplishing reconciliation can be less important than honestly questioning the legacies of the difficult memory of slavery.

Mourning, emphasized Joshua Gunn, implies an end rather than ongoing uncertainty. When faced with remembered trauma, he urged, we should resist mourning "by embracing the figure of the specter or *revenant* as a haunting reminder that we can never completely reckon with the past, nor secure the future."[42] Undoubtedly, we will continue to struggle with the specter of slavery's past, just as we will continue to wrestle with defining the nation in the increasingly multicultural future. In this respect, the President's House serves the nation well. As it sits firmly planted on the doorstep of the home of the Liberty Bell, it functions as a haunting reminder of the founders' unfulfilled promises. While Independence National Historical Park has loudly extolled the virtues of the American experiment, the whispers of absent stories have always wafted through the stately arches, columns, and doorways of its venerable structures. Today those whispers are amplified and emphatically echo within the walls of the President's House. "The stories of the people who inhabited this place, especially those held against their will," noted the historian Charlene Mires, "provide a starting point for understanding desperate struggles for freedom at many levels—for individuals, communities, and the nation, in the past and in the present."[43]

Acknowledgments

L ike the President's House itself, this book has evolved over a period of
several years. Earlier versions of portions of Chapters 2, 4, and 5, for
example, were previously published as, respectively, Roger C. Aden, Min
Wha Han, Stephanie Norander, Michael E. Pfahl, Timothy P. Pollock, Jr.,
and Stephanie L. Young, "Re-collection: A Proposal for Refining the Study
of Collective Memory and Its Places," *Communication Theory* 19 (2009):
311–336 (reprinted by permission of John Wiley and Sons Inc.); Roger C.
Aden, "Re-defining the 'Cradle of Liberty': The President's House Controversy in Independence National Historical Park," *Rhetoric & Public Affairs*
13 (2010): 251–280; and Roger C. Aden, "When Memories and Discourses
Collide: The President's House and Places of Public Memory," *Communication Monographs* 79 (2012): 72–92 (reprinted by permission of Taylor and
Francis [http://www.tandfonline.com]). I owe special thanks to Min Wha
Han, Stephanie Norander, Michael E. Pfahl, Timothy P. Pollock, Jr., and
Stephanie L. Young, my co-authors on the article that provided the basis
for Chapter 2. An earlier version of a portion of Chapter 6 was presented at
the 2011 National Communication Association conference: Roger C. Aden,
"The Story of a Hole: Aristotle's Phantasia, Visual Rhetoric, and Haunting
Voices in Places of Public Memory," National Communication Association,
2011. Portions of the material that formed the basis of Chapter 7 were initially presented at two conferences: Roger C. Aden, "Difficult Reflections: The

President's House Site, Heterotopia, and Public Memories," National Communication Association, 2012; and Roger C. Aden and Allison Hight, "The Elephant on the Mall: Politics, Public Memory, and the President's House in Independence National Historical Park," Central States Communication Association, 2012.

As these journal articles and conference papers changed shape and took the form of book chapters, I gained invaluable expertise, perspective, and wisdom from current and retired staff members of Independence National Historical Park, advocates seeking recognition of the President's House and its inhabitants, scholars working in relevant fields, and visitors to the site. I also took advantage of some wonderful online resources—especially the marvelous website maintained by the late Doug Heller of the Independence Hall Association—that allowed me to listen and learn about the battle over the site. I am particularly grateful for the assistance of several individuals who helped me understand the stakes, context, and implications embedded in the story of the President's House: Davis Buckley, Michael Coard, Ken Finkel, Ken Foote, Doug Heller, Jeff Howard, Emanuel Kelly, Ed Lawler, Rosalyn McPherson, Gary Nash, Dwight Pitcaithley, and Inga Saffron. In addition, I leaned heavily on a number of individuals who worked with the National Park Service in Independence National Historical Park: Joe Becton, Christian Higgins, Mary Jenkins, Jed Levin, Steve Sitarski, Karen Stevens, and Anna Coxe Toogood provided perspective, information, and advice, while Andrea Ashby, Jane Cowley, Adam Duncan, Frank Eidmann, and Doris Fanelli offered logistical assistance as I wrote about a site in Philadelphia while working in Athens, Ohio. All these individuals gladly visited with me, answered my questions, or helped direct me to valuable information during my research, and a number of them graciously agreed to read drafts of chapters as well. I owe a special thank-you to those who read my work in progress: Ken Finkel, Ken Foote, Mary Jenkins, Ed Lawler, Jed Levin, Gary Nash, Inga Saffron, and Steve Sitarski. To Ed and Gary, in particular, I owe a debt of gratitude for their instrumental expertise and support.

Throughout this process, I have benefited from support provided by Ohio University's School of Communication Studies, Scripps College of Communication, Honors Tutorial College, and Vice President's Office for Research. Wonderful colleagues working in these offices provided both financial and personnel assistance. I am particularly grateful for the research assistance provided by Ohio University undergraduate students Gail Clendinin and Allison Hight, who devoted a summer each to help me research Chapters 5 and 7, respectively. Ohio University graduate students Anna Wiederhold and Abbey Wojno also provided valuable assistance.

I could not have completed this book without the encouragement of my family. My wife, Christie Beck, offered unflagging support, while my daughters, Britti, Chelsea, Emmy, and Ellie, understood both when I needed to work and when I needed to take a break from work. Throughout the intensive investments of time and energy required to write this book, their understanding kept me both balanced and focused.

Finally, I thank Micah Kleit and the staff at Temple University Press. Micah's enthusiastic support for this book was especially gratifying, and his title suggestion was brilliant. I am delighted that I have been able to work with him and the other fine members of the team at Temple University Press.

Notes

PREFACE

1. In Nathaniel Lee, "Slavery Memorial Marks First Anniversary," *Philadelphia Tribune*, December 16, 2011, available at http://www.ushistory.org/presidentshouse/news/pt121611.htm.

2. See Edward Lawler, Jr., "The President's House in Philadelphia: The Rediscovery of a Lost Landmark," *Pennsylvania Magazine of History and Biography* 126 (2002): 5–96, and "The President's House Revisited," *Pennsylvania Magazine of History and Biography* 129 (2005): 371–410.

CHAPTER 1

1. Edward Lawler, Jr., in discussion with the author, May 24, 2007. Lawler's guests were, of course, referring not to the White House itself but to the nation's first executive mansion.

2. The house was closed for renovations in much of 2011. In May 2010, for example, the Deshler-Morris House was the twenty-third (out of twenty-six) most popular site to visit, according to park figures (see http://www.nps.gov/inde/parkmgmt/upload/May-2011.pdf).

3. For an account of Lawler's extensive efforts, see Stephan Salisbury, "A Visitor's Innocent Query Spurs Historical Revelations," *Philadelphia Inquirer*, July 3, 2002, available at http://www.ushistory.org/presidentshouse/news/inq070302a.htm.

4. See Edward Lawler, Jr., "The President's House in Philadelphia: The Rediscovery of a Lost Landmark," *Pennsylvania Magazine of History and Biography* 126 (2002): 5–96, and "The President's House Revisited," *Pennsylvania Magazine of History and Biography* 129 (2005): 371–410.

5. Lawler, "President's House in Philadelphia," 27–28.

6. Pennsylvania outlawed slavery in 1780 but implemented grandfather clauses that ultimately allowed many residents to keep enslaved persons until the 1840s. The law also granted freedom to any enslaved person—not affected by the grandfathering—who resided in the state for more than six months, which would include those individuals Washington brought from Virginia. See Lawler's more detailed explanation, including excerpts from correspondence on the subject between Washington and his chief secretary, at http://www.ushistory.org/presidentshouse/slaves/washingtonand8.htm.

7. Jill Ogline, "'Creating Dissonance for the Visitor': The Heart of the Liberty Bell Controversy," *The Public Historian* 26, no. 3 (2004): 50.

8. Nash, a UCLA historian, was in town to promote in his most recent book on Philadelphia's history. He reviewed Lawler's work and pointed out its significance during his visit with Marty Moss-Coane on WHYY's *Radio Times* program on March 13, 2002.

9. Phil Sheridan and Cara Schneider, "America's Liberty Bell Moves to a New Home," September 8, 2003, news release from INHP and Greater Philadelphia Tourism Marketing Group, available at http://view.officeapps.live.com/op/view.aspx?src=http%3A%2F%2Fwww.nsf.gov%2Fnews%2Fspecial_reports%2Fliberty%2Fpress%2Fliberty_bell_lead.doc.

10. Gary B. Nash, *The Liberty Bell* (New Haven, CT: Yale University Press, 2010), x.

11. Ogline, "Creating Dissonance," 54

12. Ibid., 50.

13. Kenneth E. Foote, *Shadowed Ground: America's Landscapes of Violence and Tragedy* (Austin: University of Texas Press, 1997), 33.

14. Henry Tudor, *Political Myth* (New York: Praeger, 1972), 65.

15. David Lowenthal, "Fabricating Heritage," *History & Memory* 10 (1998): 8.

16. Laurajane Smith, *Uses of Heritage* (London: Routledge, 2006), 29.

17. Kristen Hoerl, "Selective Amnesia and Racial Transcendence in News Coverage of President Obama's Inauguration," *Quarterly Journal of Speech* 98 (2012): 180.

18. Ogline, "Creating Dissonance," 50.

19. Derek H. Alderman, "Surrogation and the Politics of Remembering Slavery in Savannah, Georgia," *Journal of Historical Geography* 36 (2010): 91.

20. Eric Foner, *Who Owns History? Rethinking the Past in a Changing World* (New York: Hill and Wang, 2002), 153.

21. Kirt H. Wilson, *The Reconstruction Desegregation Debate: The Politics of Equality and the Rhetoric of Place, 1870–1875* (East Lansing: Michigan State University Press, 2002).

22. I thank Kenneth Foote for this idea.

23. Gary Nash, *Forging Freedom: The Formation of Philadelphia's Black Community, 1720–1840* (Cambridge, MA: Harvard University Press, 1988), 2.

24. W. E. B. DuBois, *The Philadelphia Negro: A Social Study* (Oxford, UK: Oxford University Press, 2007).

25. Dana H. Taplin, Suzanne Scheld, and Setha M. Low, "Rapid Ethnographic Assessment in Urban Parks: A Case Study of Independence National Historical Park," *Human Organization* 61 (2002): 90.

26. This phrasing is not to suggest that African Americans living in Philadelphia have not made places of their own in different ways and in different parts of the city. See Marcus Anthony Hunter's *Black Citymakers: How the Philadelphia Negro Changed Urban America* (Oxford, UK: Oxford University Press, 2013) for a thorough historical analysis of how black Philadelphians have crafted communities across the city while shaping the development of the city as a whole.

27. See http://www.census.gov/newsroom/releases/archives/population/cb12–90.html.

28. In Carol Morello and Ted Mellnik, "Whites' Deaths Outnumber Births for First

Time," *Washington Post,* June 13, 2013, available at http://articles.washingtonpost.com/2013-06-13/local/39934184_1_non-hispanic-whites-demographer-census-figures.

29. Erika Doss, *Memorial Mania: Public Feeling in America* (Chicago: University of Chicago Press, 2012), 31.

30. Foner, *Who Owns History?*

31. James Oliver Horton and Lois E. Horton, "Introduction," in *Slavery and Public History: The Tough Stuff of American Memory,* ed. James Oliver Horton and Lois E. Horton (New York: New Press, 2006), xi.

32. In his book *Defining Reality: Definitions and the Politics of Meaning* (Carbondale: Southern Illinois University Press, 2003), Edward Schiappa argued "that definitional disputes should be treated less as philosophical or scientific questions of 'is' and more as sociopolitical and pragmatic questions of 'ought'" (3).

33. Smith, *Uses of Heritage,* 306.

34. Nathan Glazer, *We Are All Multiculturalists Now* (Cambridge, MA: Harvard University Press, 1997), 147.

35. Clarence Lusane, *The Black History of the White House* (San Francisco: City Lights Books, 2011), 21.

36. Seth Bruggeman, "'The President's House: Freedom and Slavery in the Making of a New Nation,' Independence National Historical Park, Philadelphia, Pa.," exhibit review in *The Journal of American History* 100 (2013): 155–156.

37. Ira Berlin, Marc Favreau, and Steven F. Miller, *Remembering Slavery: African Americans Talk about Their Personal Experiences of Slavery and Freedom* (New York: New Press, 1996), xlvi.

CHAPTER 2

1. Maya Lin, "Maya Lin," in *Grounds for Remembering: Monuments, Memorials, Texts,* by Maya Lin, Andrew Barshay, Stephen Greenblatt, Thomas Laqueur, and Stanley Saitowitz (Berkeley, CA: Doreen B. Townsend Center for the Humanities, 1995), 13.

2. Carole Blair and Neil Michel, "Commemorating in the Theme Park Zone: Reading the Astronauts Memorial," in *At the Intersection: Cultural Studies and Rhetorical Studies,* ed. Thomas Rosteck (New York: Guilford Press, 1999), 38–39.

3. Ibid., 46.

4. Ibid., 47.

5. Ibid., 48.

6. Ibid., 67.

7. Barry Brummett argues that rhetorical criticism, at its best, teaches us more about how symbols shape our experiences and understanding of the world around us. In "Rhetorical Theory as Heuristic and Moral: A Pedagogical Justification," *Communication Education* 33 (1984): 97–107.

8. Blair and Michel, "Commemorating," 68.

9. Ibid., 55.

10. Ibid., 67.

11. Carroll C. Arnold, "Johnstone's 'Wedge' Theory of Rhetoric," *Philosophy & Rhetoric* 20 (1987): 125; emphasis original. See also Henry Johnstone, *The Problem of the Self* (University Park: Pennsylvania State University Press, 1970).

12. See, for example, Wolfgang Iser, *The Implied Reader* (Baltimore: Johns Hopkins University Press, 1974), and Jane P. Tompkins (ed.), *Reader-Response Criticism: From Formalism to Post-structuralism* (Baltimore: Johns Hopkins University Press, 1980).

13. Edward Schiappa, *Beyond Representational Correctness: Rethinking Criticism of Popular Media* (Albany: State University of New York Press, 2008); Jennifer Stromer-Galley and Edward Schiappa, "The Argumentative Burdens of Audience Conjectures: Audience Research in Popular Culture Criticism," *Communication Theory* 8 (1998): 27–62.

14. Michael K. Middleton, Samantha Senda-Cook, and Danielle Endres, "Articulating Rhetorical Field Methods: Challenges and Tensions," *Western Journal of Communication* 75 (2011): 386–406. They describe rhetorical field methods as "a practical and theoretical synthesis of CR [critical rhetoric], performance studies, and ethnography that function as an orientation that utilizes methodological tools from (but is not bound by) these subdisciplines in order to understand 'live' rhetorics" (388). They continue: "Rhetorical field methods offer a productive articulation of the careful textual analyses characteristic of CR with the provocative insights uncovered by in situ research common in ethnography and performance studies. Specifically, we argue that influences from ethnography and performance studies ought to be more effectively pressed into the service of rhetorical criticism, especially insofar as the insights offered by these approaches can help shape the constitutive, strategic, politically motivated, and social justice–oriented readings of domination and freedom made by critical rhetoricians" (388).

15. I borrow and adapt this phrase from Edward Casey (*Getting Back into Place: Toward a Renewed Understanding of the Place-World* [Bloomington: Indiana University Press, 1993]), who writes, "Instead of thinking of places as *causing* people to have certain individual and social characteristics, or simply the reverse, we should concentrate instead on the single complex unit, 'persons-in-places'" (305). I add "with" to Casey's phrase in order to emphasize the interaction of persons with *and* in places of memory.

16. Roger C. Aden, Min Wha Han, Stephanie Norander, Michael E. Pfahl, Timothy P. Pollock, Jr., and Stephanie L. Young, "Re-collection: A Proposal for Refining the Study of Collective Memory and Its Places," *Communication Theory* 19 (2009): 311–336.

17. Richard Rabinowitz, "The Devil in the (Liberty Bell's) Belfry: The Transformation of Cultural Practice," address at the MARCH [Mid-Atlantic Regional Center for the Humanities] Forum on the President's House Controversy, May 16, 2003, available at http://www.americanhistoryworkshop.com/news/devil_in_the_belfry.htm.

18. Carole Blair, Greg Dickinson, and Brian Ott, "Introduction: Rhetoric/Memory/Place," in *Places of Public Memory: The Rhetoric of Museums and Memorials*, ed. Greg Dickinson, Carole Blair, and Brian L. Ott (Tuscaloosa: University of Alabama Press, 2010), 1–54. See also Catherine M. Cameron and John B. Gatewood, "Seeking Numinous Experiences in the Unremembered Past," *Ethnology* 42 (2003): 55–71.

19. See, for example, Carole Blair, "Reflections on Criticism and Bodies: Parables from Public Places," *Western Journal of Communication* 65 (2001): 271–294; Marouf Hasian, Jr., "Remembering and Forgetting the 'Final Solution': A Rhetorical Pilgrimage through the U.S. Holocaust Memorial Museum," *Critical Studies in Media Communication* 21 (2004): 64–92; Theodore O. Prosise, "Prejudiced, Historical Witness, and Responsible: Collective Memory and Liminality in the Beit Hashoah Museum of Tolerance," *Communication Quarterly* 51 (2003): 351–366.

20. See, for example, Carole Blair, Marsha S. Jeppeson, and Enrico Pucci, Jr., "Public Memorializing in Postmodernity: The Vietnam Veterans Memorial as Prototype," *Quarterly Journal of Speech* 77 (1991): 263–288; A. Cheree Carlson and John E. Hocking, "Strategies of Redemption at the Vietnam Veterans' Memorial," *Western Journal of Speech Communication* 52 (1988): 203–215; Peter Ehrenhaus, "Silence and Symbolic Expression," *Communication Monographs* 55 (1988): 41–57; Sonja K. Foss, "Ambiguity as Persuasion: The Vietnam Veterans Memorial," *Communication Quarterly* 34 (1986): 326–340; Harry W. Haines, "'What

Kind of War?' An Analysis of the Vietnam Veterans Memorial," *Critical Studies in Mass Communication* 3 (1986): 1–20; Marita Sturken, *Tangled Memories: The Vietnam War, the AIDS Epidemic, and the Politics of Remembering* (Los Angeles: University of California Press, 1997); Robin Wagner-Pacifici and Barry Schwartz, "The Vietnam Veterans Memorial: Commemorating a Difficult Past," *American Journal of Sociology* 97 (1991): 376–420.

21. Stephen Manning, "Vietnam Memorial Still Gets Offerings 25 Years Later," *USA Today*, November 11, 2007, available at http://www.usatoday.com/news/nation/2007-11-10-viet nammemorial_N.htm?loc=interstitialskip.

22. Barbie Zelizer, "Reading the Past against the Grain: The Shape of Memory Studies," *Critical Studies in Mass Communication* 12 (1995): 219 and 218. Other scholars working in this area, of course, have referred to processes of refiguring and/or recollecting; see, for example, Carole Blair, "Collective Memory," in *Communication as . . . : Perspectives on Theory*, ed. Gregory J. Shepherd, Jeff St. John, and Ted Striphas (Thousand Oaks, CA: Sage, 2006), 51–59; Robert J. Cox, "Memory, Critical Theory and the Argument from History," *Argumentation & Advocacy* 27 (1990): 1–13; Nathan Stormer, "To Remember, to Act, to Forget: Tracing Collective Remembrance through 'A Jury of Her Peers,'" *Communication Studies* 54 (2003): 510–529.

23. Maurice Halbwachs, *The Collective Memory*, trans. Francis J. Ditter, Jr., and Vida Y. Ditter (New York: Harper and Row, 1980), 140, 156–157. Original work published in French, 1950.

24. In this respect, I am "odd" compared with many rhetorical scholars: "Most contemporary rhetoricians take discourses to be definitively symbolic—containers of meanings that attract or secure the adherence of an audience" (Blair and Michel, "Commemorating," 30).

25. Blair and Michel, "Commemorating," 38.

26. Ibid.

27. See, for example, Wagner-Pacifici and Schwartz, "Vietnam Veterans Memorial"; Barry Schwartz and Todd Bayma, "Commemoration and the Politics of Recognition," *American Behavioral Scientist* 42 (1999): 946–967.

28. Marita Sturken, "The Wall, the Screen and the Image: The Vietnam Veterans Memorial," *Representations* 35 (1991): 118–142.

29. "A failure to represent a particular content publicly is not a necessary, or even provisional sign of forgetting," argued Blair, Dickinson, and Ott, in "Introduction," 18.

30. Zelizer, "Reading the Past," 224.

31. Ibid., 217; my emphasis.

32. E. V. Walter, *Placeways: A Theory of Human Environment* (Chapel Hill: University of North Carolina Press, 1988), 205.

33. The French theorist Henri Lefebvre referred to this practice in the translated phrase *spaces of representation*—that is, the everyday places through which we travel and pause and are shaped by the decisions of governmental and private entities (e.g., political boundaries, zoning, covenants). In *The Production of Space*, trans. Donald Nicholson-Smith (Oxford, UK: Blackwell, 1991; original work published 1974).

34. Michel de Certeau, *The Practice of Everyday Life* (Berkeley: University of California Press, 1984).

35. Blair, Dickinson, and Ott, "Introduction," 28.

36. See, for example, Stephen C. Bitgood, "Environmental Psychology in Museums, Zoos, and Other Exhibition Centers," in *Handbook of Environmental Psychology*, ed. Robert B. Bechtel and Arza Churchman (Hoboken, NJ: John Wiley and Sons, 2002), 461–480; David Blight, *Race and Reunion: The Civil War in American Memory* (Cambridge, MA: Harvard University Press, 2001); Erika Doss, *Memorial Mania: Public Feeling in America* (Chicago:

University of Chicago Press, 2012); Kenneth E. Foote, *Shadowed Ground: America's Landscapes of Violence and Tragedy* (Austin: University of Texas Press, 1997); Jeffrey K. Olick, "Collective Memory: The Two Cultures," *Sociological Theory* 17 (1999): 333–348; Kirk Savage, *Monument Wars: Washington, D.C., the National Mall, and the Transformation of the Memorial Landscape* (Berkeley: University of California Press, 2009).

37. Hasian, "Remembering and Forgetting"; Carole Blair and Neil Michel, "The AIDS Memorial Quilt and the Contemporary Culture of Public Commemoration," *Rhetoric & Public Affairs* 10 (2007): 595–626; V. William V. Balthrop, Carole Blair, and Neil Michel, "The Presence of the Present: Hijacking 'The Good War'?" *Western Journal of Communication* 74 (2010): 170–207; Theodore O. Prosise, "The Collective Memory of the Atomic Bombings Misrecognized as Objective History: The Case of the Public Opposition to the National Air and Space Museum's Atomic Bomb Exhibit," *Western Journal of Communication* 62 (1998): 316–347; Gregory Clark, "Rhetorical Experience and the National Jazz Museum in Harlem," in *Places of Public Memory: The Rhetoric of Museums and Memorials,* ed. Greg Dickinson, Carole Blair, and Brian L. Ott (Tuscaloosa: University of Alabama Press, 2010), 113–135; Rebecca M. Kennerly, "Getting Messy: In the Field and at the Crossroads with Roadside Shrines," *Text & Performance Quarterly* 22 (2002): 229–260; Beth A. Messner and Mark T. Vail, "A 'City at War': Commemorating Dr. Martin Luther King, Jr.," *Communication Studies* 60 (2009): 17–31.

38. Blair and Michel, "Commemorating," 69.

39. John Ackerman, "The Space for Rhetoric in Everyday Life," in *Towards a Rhetoric of Everyday Life: New Directions in Research on Writing, Text, and Discourse,* ed. Martin Nystrand and John Duffy (Madison: University of Wisconsin Press, 2003), 86 and 91.

40. Michel Foucault, "Of Other Spaces," trans. Jay Miskowiec, *diacritics* 16 (1986): 23.

41. Edward S. Casey, "How to Get from Space to Place in a Fairly Short Stretch of Time: Phenomenological Prolegomena," in *Senses of Place,* ed. Steven Feld and Keith H. Basso (Santa Fe, NM: School of American Research Press, 1996), 24.

42. Walter, *Placeways,* 205.

43. Mikhail M. Bakhtin, *The Dialogic Imagination: Four Essays,* trans. Caryl Emerson and Michael Holquist, ed. Michael Holquist (Austin: University of Texas Press, 1981). See also James Jasinski, "Heteroglossia, Polyphony, and *The Federalist Papers,*" *Rhetoric Society Quarterly* 27 (1997): 23–46; Linda M. Park-Fuller, "Voices: Bakhtin's Heteroglossia and Polyphony, and the Performance of Narrative Literature," *Literature in Performance* 7 (1986): 1–12.

44. Ackerman, "Space for Rhetoric," 97.

45. Greg Dickinson, Brian L. Ott, and Eric Aoki, "Spaces of Remembering and Forgetting: The Reverent Eye/I at the Plains Indian Museum," *Communication and Critical Cultural Studies* 3 (2006): 30.

46. Ibid., 29.

47. Wagner-Pacifici and Schwartz, "Vietnam Veterans Memorial." See also Savage (*Monument Wars*) for a thorough discussion of how the landscape of the mall was altered throughout the history of Washington, D.C.

48. Sharon Macdonald, *Difficult Heritage: Negotiating the Nazi Past in Nuremberg and Beyond* (New York: Routledge, 2009), 186.

49. Blair, Dickinson, and Ott, "Introduction," 30.

50. Scott A. Sandage, "A Marble House Divided: The Lincoln Memorial, the Civil Rights Movement, and the Politics of Memory, 1939–1963," *Journal of American History* 80 (1993): 135–167.

51. Owen J. Dwyer, "Symbolic Accretion and Commemoration," *Social & Cultural Geography* 5 (2004): 425.

52. D. W. Meinig, "The Beholding Eye: Ten Versions of the Same Scene," *Landscape Architecture* 66 (January 1976): 47. Meinig described ten ways in which we make sense of landscape as nature, habitat, artifact, system, problem, wealth, ideology, history, place, aesthetic (47–54).

53. Joy Sather-Wagstaff, *Heritage That Hurts: Tourists in the Memoryscapes of September 11* (Walnut Creek, CA: Left Coast Press, 2011), 78.

54. Wulf Kansteiner, "Finding Meaning in Memory: A Methodological Critique of Collective Memory Studies," *History and Theory: Studies in the Philosophy of History* 41 (2002): 180.

55. Samuel L. Becker, "Rhetorical Studies for the Contemporary World," in *The Prospect of Rhetoric,* ed. Lloyd F. Bitzer and Edwin Black (Englewood Cliffs, NJ: Prentice-Hall, 1971), 33.

56. See, for example, Barbara A. Biesecker, "Remembering World War II: The Rhetoric and Politics of National Commemoration at the Turn of the 21st Century," *Quarterly Journal of Speech* 88 (2002): 393–409; Marouf Hasian, Jr., and A. Cheree Carlson, "Revisionism and Collective Memory: The Struggle for Meaning in the Amistad Affair," *Communication Monographs* 67 (2000): 42–62; and Alan L. Mintz, *Popular Culture and the Shaping of Holocaust Memory in America* (Seattle: University of Washington Press, 2001).

57. Eric Gable and Richard Handler, "Public History, Private Memory: Notes from the Ethnography of Colonial Williamsburg, Virginia, USA," *Ethnos* 65 (2000): 249–250.

58. Michael C. McGee, "Text, Context, and the Fragmentation of Contemporary Culture," *Western Journal of Speech Communication* 54 (1990): 288.

59. Jean Nienkamp, *Internal Rhetorics: Toward a History and Theory of Self-Persuasion,* (Carbondale: Southern Illinois University Press, 2001), 130.

60. Ibid.

61. Ibid., 131.

62. Halbwachs, *Collective Memory*, 48.

63. John R. Gillis noted: "Everyone belongs simultaneously to several different groups, each with its own collective memory." "Memory and Identity: The History of a Relationship," in *Commemorations: The Politics of National Identity,* ed. John R. Gillis (Princeton, NJ: Princeton University Press, 1994), 15.

64. Walter, *Placeways,* 21.

65. See, for example, Roger M. Downs and David Stea, *Maps in Mind: Reflections on Cognitive Mapping* (New York: Harper and Row, 1977), and Francis T. McAndrew, *Environmental Psychology* (Pacific Grove, CA: Brooks/Cole, 1993).

66. Edward Relph, *Place and Placelessness* (London: Pion, 1976), 43.

67. Roy Rosenzweig and David Thelen, *The Presence of the Past: Popular Uses of History in American Life* (New York: Columbia University Press, 1998), 115–116.

68. Gable and Handler, "Public History."

69. Blair, Dickinson, and Ott, "Introduction," 26.

70. "The discourse is silenced, dismissed and forgotten, if it seems uninteresting or irrelevant," argued McGee ("Text," 281).

71. Savage, *Monument Wars,* 21.

72. Blair, "Reflections," 286–287.

73. See http://www.nps.gov/flni/planyourvisit/design-and-construction.htm.

74. See http://www.oklahomacitynationalmemorial.org/.

75. John B. Gatewood and Catherine M. Cameron, "Battlefield Pilgrims at Gettysburg National Military Park," *Ethnology* 43 (2004): 206.

76. Catherine M. Cameron and John B. Gatewood, "Excursions into the Un-remem-

bered Past: What People Want from Visits to Historical Sites," *Public Historian* 22, no. 1 (2000): 107–127; Cameron and Gatewood, "Seeking Numinous Experiences."

77. Sather-Wagstaff (*Heritage That Hurts,* 80–81) discussed this process of using photographs or other visual displays as portals.

78. Savage, *Monument Wars,* 14 and 4; emphasis original. The experience of emotion or affect is now so prominent a part of public memory places that scholars such as Erika Doss (*Memorial Mania*) have suggested that "much of today's memorial making is excessive, frenzied, and extreme" (13).

79. As sociologists, in particular, have illustrated, the making of collective memories is an interactional process. See, for example, Aaron Beim, "The Cognitive Aspects of Collective Memory," *Symbolic Interaction* 30 (2007): 7–26; Per Gustafson, "Meanings of Place: Everyday Experience and Theoretical Conceptualizations," *Journal of Environmental Psychology* 21 (2001): 5–16; Melinda J. Milligan, "Buildings as History: The Place of Collective Memory in the Study of Historic Preservation," *Symbolic Interaction* 30 (2007): 105–123; and Melinda J. Milligan, "Interactional Past and Potential: The Social Construction of Place Attachment," *Symbolic Interaction* 21 (1998): 1–33.

80. Blair, Dickinson, and Ott, "Introduction," 16.

81. Keith Basso, *Wisdom Sits in Places: Landscape and Language among the Western Apache* (Albuquerque: University of New Mexico Press, 1996), 62.

82. My argument here is rooted in Stuart Hall's explanation of the processes of encoding and decoding. In short, Hall argued that the same message may be interpreted differently based on the political leanings of the interpreter. "Encoding/Decoding," in *Culture, Media, Language: Working Papers in Cultural Studies, 1972–79,* ed. Stuart Hall, Dorothy Hobson, Andrew Lowe, and Paul Willis (London: Hutchinson, 1980), 128–140.

83. Referring to a display of traditional agricultural implements and the ways in which the museum tour guides attached biblical stories to the tools, Katriel observed that Arab audiences found the practice "an act of cultural appropriation, even of symbolic violence" (Tamar Katriel, "Sites of Memory: Discourses of the Past in Israeli Pioneering Settlement Museums," *Quarterly Journal of Speech* 80 [1994]: 14). Bryan Hubbard and Marouf A. Hasian, Jr., "Atomic Memories of the Enola Gay: Strategies of Remembrance of the National Air and Space Museum," *Rhetoric & Public Affairs* 1 (1998): 363–385.

84. Richard C. Prentice, Stephen F. Witt, and Claire Hamer, "Tourism as Experience: The Case of Heritage Parks," *Annals of Tourism Research* 25 (1998): 15.

85. Michael Warner, "Publics and Counterpublics (abbreviated version)," *Quarterly Journal of Speech* 88 (2002): 415 and 416.

86. Whether these distinct interpretations are the product of polysemy or polyvalence is not of interest to me (on polysemy, see, for example, Leah Ceccarelli, "Polysemy: Multiple Meanings in Rhetorical Criticism," *Quarterly Journal of Speech* 84 [1998]: 395–415, and John Fiske, "Television: Polysemy and Popularity," *Critical Studies in Mass Communication* 3 [1986]: 391–408; on polyvalence, see Celeste Condit, "The Rhetorical Limits of Polysemy," *Critical Studies in Mass Communication* 6 [1989]: 103–122). I suspect, in fact, that most interpretations reflect a bit of both in that individuals' beliefs color their interpretations but their interpretations are also influenced by the symbols the individuals encounter. Additionally, I assume that shared interpretations *may* be informed by shared demographic characteristics, but I do not *expect* demographics to account for shared interpretations.

87. Michael Warner, *Publics and Counterpublics* (New York: Zone Books, 2002), 106.

88. My use of *Native American* is not intended to treat all Indian Nations as part of a single, essentialized collective. Indeed, Doss (*Memorial Mania*) pointed out that some individuals "oppose the inclusion of references to Arikara and Crow scouts who sided with the

7th Cavalry, or the use of the term 'Sioux' rather than 'Lakota' in the memorial's reference panels and publicity materials" (354).

89. Yaniv Poria, Avital Biran, and Arie Reichel, "Visitors' Preferences for Interpretation at Heritage Sites," *Journal of Travel Research* 48 (2009): 102. Written from the perspective of tourism studies, the authors identify a range of motivations, expectations, and experiences for visiting heritage sites.

90. Paul A. Shackel, *Memory in Black and White: Race, Commemoration, and the Post-bellum Landscape* (Walnut Creek, CA: Alta Mira Press, 2003), 173. Shackel also noted, "While all blacks were American citizens from the time of the Reconstruction Amendments, it was close to a hundred years before they could gain inclusion in the collective memory of the United States" (173).

91. Derek H. Alderman, "Surrogation and the Politics of Remembering Slavery in Savannah, Georgia," *Journal of Historical Geography* 36 (2010): 94.

92. This famous phrase was coined by Tom Carhart in the controversy during the memorial's design: "Insulting Vietnam Vets," *The New York Times*, October 24, 1981, page 23, section 1, late city final edition.

93. "Each position occupies a distinctive historical relationship to anxieties about white supremacist race violence and its resulting race trauma, and each employs distinctive rhetorical strategies for engaging representations and discourses about this nation's racial contract" (A. Susan Owen and Peter Ehrenhaus, "Communities of Memory, Entanglements, and Claims of the Past on the Present: Reading Race Trauma through *The Green Mile*," *Critical Studies in Media Communication* 27 [2010]: 132).

94. Stephen P. Hanna, "A Slavery Museum? Race, Memory, and Landscape in Fredericksburg, Virginia," *Southeastern Geographer* 48 (2008): 328–333.

95. Cameron and Gatewood, "Excursions"; Cameron and Gatewood, "Seeking Numinous Experiences"; Gable and Handler, "Public History"; Gatewood and Cameron, "Battlefield Pilgrims"; Gustafson, "Meanings of Place"; Myriam Jansen-Verbeke and Johan van Rekom, "Scanning Museum Visitors: Urban Tourism Marketing," *Annals of Tourism Research* 23 (1996): 364–375; Marjorie Kelly, "Enshrining History: The Visitor Experience at Pearl Harbor's USS Arizona Memorial," *Museum Anthropology* 20, no. 3 (1996): 45–57; Reuben A. Buford May, "Race Talk and Local Collective Memory among African American Men in a Neighborhood Tavern," *Qualitative Sociology* 23 (2000): 201–214; Alison J. McIntosh and Richard C. Prentice, "Affirming Authenticity: Consuming Cultural Heritage," *Annals of Tourism Research* 26 (1999): 589–612; Milligan, "Interactional Past and Potential"; Milligan, "Buildings as History"; Prentice, Witt, and Hamer, "Tourism as Experience"; Anna L. Tota, "Ethnographying Public Memory: The Commemorative Genre for the Victims of Terrorism in Italy," *Qualitative Research* 4 (2004): 131–159; Martin Young, "The Social Construction of Tourist Places," *Australian Geographer* 30 (1999): 373–389.

96. S. Elizabeth Bird, "It Makes Sense to Us: Cultural Identity in Local Legends of Place," *Journal of Contemporary Ethnography* 31 (2002): 519–547.

97. James J. Ponzetti, Jr., "Growing Old in Rural Communities: A Visual Methodology for Studying Place Attachment," *Journal of Rural Community Psychology* E6, no. 1 (2003), available at http://www.marshall.edu/jrcp/E6one_Ponzetti.htm.

98. Sather-Wagstaff, *Heritage That Hurts*.

99. See, for example, Gable and Handler, "Public History"; Carlson and Hocking, "Strategies of Redemption."

100. My assumption is rooted in Kenneth Burke's idea of *equipment for living,* or the notion that we use rhetoric to negotiate, understand, and cope with everyday life. See, for example, Kenneth Burke, *The Philosophy of Literary Form: Studies in Symbolic Action,* 3rd ed.,

(Berkeley: University of California Press, 1973), and Barry Brummett, "Electric Literature as Equipment for Living: Haunted House Films," *Critical Studies in Mass Communication* 2 (1985): 247–261. In terms more specific to our encounters with the remembered past, Rosenzweig and Thelen's (*Presence of the Past*) description of how individuals report using the past in general no doubt applies to their experiences at sites of memory as well: "They assemble their experiences into patterns, narratives that allow them to make sense of the past. . . . By using these narratives to mark change and continuity, they chart the course of their lives" (12).

CHAPTER 3

1. Gary B. Nash, *The Liberty Bell* (New Haven, CT: Yale University Press, 2010), 11.

2. Ibid., 34. Nash's book provides a full and authoritative story of the Liberty Bell's birth, near death (arrangements to haul it away as scrap metal in 1828 were stopped, Nash wrote, only because the cost of lowering the bell from the fourth floor of Independence Hall was more than it would bring in scrap), and its resurrection as an American icon.

3. Deirdre Gibson, Mary Whelchel Konieczny, Kathy Schlegel, and Anna Coxe Toogood, *Cultural Landscape Report, Independence Mall* (Washington, DC: U.S. Department of the Interior, 1994), 92. This report provides an extensive history of the development of the park and the mall.

4. Attendance data are available at https://irma.nps.gov/Stats/Reports/Park. Independence Visitor Center attracted 2.4 million people during 2012, roughly four hundred thousand more than the LBC.

5. See https://irma.nps.gov/Stats/Reports/Park.

6. In *1994 Statement for Interpretation*, National Park Service, Independence National Historical Park Archives, Interpretation and Visitor Services Records, 1852–2011, undated (bulk dates: 1948–2010), Catalog Number: INDE 74045, Box 78, Folder 6. I thank Abbey Wojno for her assistance in gathering some of the archived material cited in this chapter.

7. Charlene Mires, *Independence Hall in American Memory* (Philadelphia: University of Pennsylvania Press, 2002), xiii.

8. *Draft General Management Plan Environmental Impact Statement,* Independence National Historical Park (Washington, DC: U.S. Department of the Interior, 1995), 3; my emphasis.

9. Nathan Irvin Huggins, *Revelations: American History, American Myths,* ed. Brenda Smith Huggins (New York: Oxford University Press, 1995), 178.

10. Robert N. Bellah, "Civil Religion in America," *Daedalus* 96 (Winter 1967): 1–21.

11. Michael B. Chornesky, "Visceral History: Interpreting Independence National Historical Park," *Hindsight Graduate History Journal* 2 (Spring 2008), available at http://www.fresnostate.edu/socialsciences/historydept/organizations/hindsight/spring2008.html.

12. Richard B. Morris, *Independence National Historical Park* (Washington, DC: U.S. Government Printing Office, 1979), National Park Service, Independence National Historical Park Archives, Interpretation and Visitor Services Records, 1852–2011, undated (bulk dates: 1948–2010), Catalog Number: INDE 74045, Box 91, Folder 25.

13. *Unlocking the Past,* National Park Service, Independence National Historical Park Archives, Interpretation and Visitor Services Records, 1852–2011, undated (bulk dates: 1948–2010), Catalog Number: INDE 74045, Box 92, Folder 13.

14. *Abbreviated Final General Management Plan Environmental Impact Statement, Independence National Historical Park* (Washington, DC: Department of the Interior, 1997), 1:18, 1:18, 1:13, 1:29 (the document contains four separately paginated sections; the first number listed refers to the section).

15. *Independence National Historical Park* (Washington, DC: U.S. Government Printing Office, 1965).

16. *Final Interpretive Plan, National Constitution Center* (March 2001), National Park Service, Independence National Historical Park Archives, Interpretation and Visitor Services Records, 1852–2011, undated (bulk dates: 1948–2010), Catalog Number: INDE 74045, Box 156, Folder 14, 13.

17. Minutes of the Independence National Historical Park Advisory Commission, March 26, 1968, National Park Service, Independence National Historical Park Archives, Interpretation and Visitor Services Records, 1852–2011, undated (bulk dates: 1948–2010), Catalog Number: INDE 74045, Box 71, Folder 3.

18. *FY91 Statement for Interpretation,* National Park Service, Independence National Historical Park Archives, Interpretation and Visitor Services Records, 1852–2011, undated (bulk dates: 1948–2010), Catalog Number: INDE 74045, Box 146, Folder 10. Congress met in Philadelphia, for instance, between 1778 and 1783.

19. *Annual Narrative for 1991—Interpretation and Visitor Services for Independence National Historical Park and Edgar Allan Poe National Historic Site,* National Park Service, Independence National Historical Park Archives, Interpretation and Visitor Services Records, 1852–2011, undated (bulk dates: 1948–2010), Catalog Number: INDE 74045, Box 73, Folder 15.

20. In discussion with the author, April 12, 2012. Jenkins added later in our conversation that the park's superintendent at the time, Hobie Cawood, encouraged the celebrations of two-hundred-year anniversaries throughout the park.

21. *1994 Statement for Interpretation,* Independence National Historical Park, 7.

22. *Abbreviated Final General Management Plan,* 1:26–31. The explanations of the themes are quite lengthy; the abridged quotations here provide synopses.

23. *Final General Management Plan, Independence National Historical Park,* March 10, 1996, 3.

24. See http://www.tripadvisor.com/Attraction_Review-g60795-d147134-Reviews-Independence_National_Historical_Park-Philadelphia_Pennsylvania.html#REVIEWS.

25. Mary Jenkins, INHP retired interpretive services specialist, in discussion with the author, April 12, 2012.

26. Jill Ogline, "'Creating Dissonance for the Visitor': The Heart of the Liberty Bell Controversy," *Public Historian* 26, no. 3 (2004): 50.

27. Anna Coxe Toogood, INHP historian, in discussion with the author, August 21, 2013. She has not yet researched the extent to which the New England signers enslaved Africans.

28. Morris, *Independence National Historical Park.*

29. *Interpretation Statement 1979–80,* National Park Service, Independence National Historical Park Archives, Interpretation and Visitor Services Records, 1852–2011, undated (bulk dates: 1948–2010), Catalog Number: INDE 74045, Box 77, Folder 27.

30. *FY91 Statement for Interpretation,* 55 and 12.

31. In discussion with the author, October 11, 2012.

32. *INHP Annual Narrative,* 1993, National Park Service, Independence National Historical Park Archives, Interpretation and Visitor Services Records, 1852–2011, undated (bulk dates: 1948–2010), Catalog Number: INDE 74045, Box 153, Folder 11, 12.

33. *INHP Annual Narrative,* 1995, National Park Service, Independence National Historical Park Archives, Interpretation and Visitor Services Records, 1852–2011, undated (bulk dates: 1948–2010), Catalog Number: INDE 74045, Box 153, Folder 11, n.p.

34. *Abbreviated Final General Management Plan,* 1:10.

35. Gary Nash, *First City: Philadelphia and the Forging of Historical Memory* (Philadelphia: University of Pennsylvania Press, 2002), 7.

36. Gibson, Konieczny, Schlegel, and Toogood, *Cultural Landscape Report*.

37. Yen Le, Eleonora Papadogiannaki, Nancy C. Holmes, James Gramman, and Steven J. Hollenhorst, *Independence National Historical Park Visitor Survey Study* (Washington, DC: U.S. Department of the Interior, 2007), 28 and 81. This study was completed by the University of Idaho's Park Studies Unit in conjunction with the National Park Service.

38. Edward S. Casey, *Remembering: A Phenomenological Study*, 2nd ed. (Bloomington: Indiana University Press, 2000), 247.

39. Roy Rosenzweig and David Thelen, *The Presence of the Past: Popular Uses of History in American Life* (New York: Columbia University Press, 1998), 106.

40. In *Draft General Management Plan*, 245.

41. John Bodnar, *Remaking America: Public Memory, Commemoration, and Patriotism in the Twentieth Century* (Princeton, NJ: Princeton University Press, 1992), 169–170.

42. Gibson, Konieczny, Schlegel, and Toogood, *Cultural Landscape Report*, 59.

43. The city owns Independence Hall, the Liberty Bell, Congress Hall, and Old City Hall. On pages 28–29 of the park's 2007 long-range interpretive plan, the city of Philadelphia is listed as the first entity under the heading of "Partnerships" maintained by INHP. The concluding paragraph of this section notes, "The park works closely with various tourism organizations in the city such as The Greater Philadelphia Tourism Marketing Corporation (GPTMC) and the Philadelphia Convention and Visitors Bureau" (*Independence National Historical Park Long-Range Interpretive Plan*, prepared by Independence National Historical Park Interpretation and Visitor Services, December 2007, available at http://www.nps.gov/history/history/online_books/inde/inde_interpretive_plan.pdf).

44. *Draft General Management Plan*, 244.

45. *GMP Press Briefing, Prepared Remarks by Ann Marie DiSerafino*, September 6, 1996, National Park Service, Independence National Historical Park Archives, Interpretation and Visitor Services Records, 1852–2011, undated (bulk dates: 1948–2010), Catalog Number: INDE 74045, Box 149, Folder 17.

46. *Abbreviated Final General Management Plan*, 1:1–2; my emphasis.

47. Bodnar, *Remaking America*, 177. Toogood suggested that Chatelain's strategy may also have been motivated by a desire to lift sagging spirits during the Depression (in discussion with the author, August 21, 2013).

48. Ogline, "Creating Dissonance," 55.

49. Dwight T. Pitcaithley, "'A Cosmic Threat': The National Park Service Addresses the Causes of the American Civil War," in *Slavery and Public History: The Tough Stuff of American Memory*, ed. James Oliver Horton and Lois E. Horton (New York: New Press, 2006), 172.

50. Ogline, "Creating Dissonance," 54.

51. In discussion with the author, April 12, 2012.

52. In discussion with the author, October 11, 2012.

53. *Report on Site Review of Interpretive Programs by the Organization of American Historians*, 5, available at http://www.nps.gov/inde/upload/OAH%20Report%20Summary%20May%202005.pdf.

54. Ibid., 7.

55. Ibid., Gary Nash, 7. The report contains unique sections written by each of the reviewers.

56. In discussion with the author, April 12, 2012.

57. *Report on Site Review*, J. Ritchie Garrison, 2.

58. James W. Loewen, *Lies across America: What Our Historic Sites Get Wrong* (New York: New Press, 1999), 358.

59. Jenkins told me that Aikens, much to the dismay of the interpretive guides, eliminated the use of guides (except with tour groups) at the new LBC because she wanted visitors to enjoy the view of the bell, with Independence Hall in the background, as a moment of reflection. Instead, I discovered (and others have confirmed) that most visitors to the LBC move quickly to the bell, take a picture, and then exit the building.

60. Carole Blair, Greg Dickinson, and Brian Ott, "Introduction: Rhetoric/Memory/ Place," in *Places of Public Memory: The Rhetoric of Museums and Memorials,* ed. Greg Dickinson, Carole Blair, and Brian L. Ott (Tuscaloosa: University of Alabama Press, 2010), 6.

61. Gibson, Konieczny, Schlegel, and Toogood, *Cultural Landscape Report,* 45.

62. Ibid., 58.

63. Charlene Mires, "In the Shadow of Independence Hall: Vernacular Activities and the Meanings of Historic Places," *The Public Historian* 21, no. 2 (Spring 1999): 64.

64. Le, Papadogiannaki, Holmes, Gramman, and Hollenhorst, *Independence National Historical Park,* 14 and 20.

65. In discussion with the author, October 18, 2012.

66. Blair, Dickinson, and Ott, "Introduction," 6.

67. Nash, *First City,* 118.

68. Mires, *Independence Hall,* 89.

69. Mires, "In the Shadow," 57.

70. Mires, *Independence Hall,* 93.

71. Dana H. Taplin, Suzanne Scheld, and Setha M. Low, "Rapid Ethnographic Assessment in Urban Parks: A Case Study of Independence National Historical Park," *Human Organization* 61 (2002): 83. Kirk Savage (*Monument Wars: Washington, D.C., the National Mall, and the Transformation of the Memorial Landscape* [Berkeley: University of California Press, 2009]) noted that a similar process occurred in the early twentieth century as the Washington Mall was expanded. Both black and white residents were dislodged as the designers "displaced not only inconvenient histories but actual people." The result, he wrote, "was a white space, undisturbed by minority voices" (171).

72. Audrey Peterman and Frank Peterman, *Legacy on the Land: A Black Couple Discovers Our National Inheritance and Tells Why Every American Should Care* (Atlanta: Earthwise Productions, 2009), 48.

73. Ibid.

74. Ibid., 192.

75. See "Letters," *National Parks* 68, nos. 10/11 (1994): 6.

76. Peggy McIntosh, "White Privilege: Unpacking the Invisible Knapsack," *Independent School* 49.2 (1990): 31–36.

77. Patricia Davis, "Memoryscapes in Transition: Black History Museums, New South Narratives, and Urban Regeneration," *Southern Communication Journal* 78 (2013): 111.

78. See James W. Loewen, *Sundown Towns: A Hidden Dimension of American Racism* (New York: New Press, 2005). The phrase "sundown towns" refers to non-southern towns where African Americans were made to feel unwelcome either formally or informally. The phrase itself references the idea that African Americans should not still be in town when the sun went down. The measures used to enforce this type of racial exclusion included "ordinances, restrictive covenants, acts of private violence, police harassment, white flight, NIMBY zoning, and other mechanisms" (342). These practices have perpetuated "a certain wariness in African American culture, leading to a persistence of caution that in turn helps maintain sundown towns today" (342).

79. G. Mitchell Reyes, "Introduction: Public Memory, Race, and Ethnicity," in *Public*

Memory, Race, and Ethnicity, ed. G. Mitchell Reyes (Newcastle upon Tyne, UK: Cambridge Scholars Publishing, 2010), 2.

80. Mark McPhail, "Stones the Builders Rejected: Freedom Summer, Kent State, and the Politics of Public Amnesia," in *Public Memory, Race, and Ethnicity,* ed. G. Mitchell Reyes (Newcastle upon Tyne, UK: Cambridge Scholars Publishing, 2010), 103.

81. Nathan Irvin Huggins, *Black Odyssey: The African-American Ordeal in Slavery* (New York: Vintage Books, 1990), xlv.

82. Ibid., xi.

83. Paul Connerton, "Seven Types of Forgetting," *Memory Studies* 1 (2008): 67.

84. See McPhail, "Stones," as well as Kristen Hoerl, "Selective Amnesia and Racial Transcendence in News Coverage of President Obama's Inauguration," *Quarterly Journal of Speech* 98 (2012): 178–202.

85. Huggins, *Black Odyssey,* xi.

86. Stephen H. Browne, "Remembering Crispus Attucks: Race, Rhetoric, and the Politics of Commemoration," *Quarterly Journal of Speech* 85 (1999): 172.

87. Margot Minardi, *Making Slavery History: Abolitionism and the Politics of Memory in Massachusetts* (Oxford, UK: Oxford University Press, 2010), 44.

88. Nash (*First City*) noted: "To exclude their black neighbors from public celebrations may have intensified white patriotism [in Philadelphia]. . . . After their Revolution, white Americans set about constructing a common memory of the struggle for independence and renewal" (118).

89. Kenneth Burke, *Language as Symbolic Action: Essays on Life, Literature, and Method* (Berkley: University of California Press, 1966), 9–11.

90. Eric Foner, *Who Owns History? Rethinking the Past in a Changing World* (New York: Hill and Wang, 2002), 152.

91. In discussion with the author, October 18, 2012.

92. Kirk Savage, *Standing Soldiers, Kneeling Slaves: Race, War and Monument in Nineteenth-Century America* (Princeton, NJ: Princeton University Press, 1997), 4 and 5.

93. David Blight, *Race and Reunion: The Civil War in American Memory* (Cambridge, MA: Harvard University Press, 2001); James Oliver and Lois E. Horton (eds.), *Slavery and Public History: The Tough Stuff of American Memory* (New York: New Press, 2006); Savage, *Standing Soldiers.*

94. Savage, *Standing Soldiers,* 192. In the pages that follow this reference, Savage tells the story of the exceptional monument, a commemoration of Colonel Robert Gould Shaw and the 54th Massachusetts Regiment, "the first regiment of black troops mustered in the North" (194). The white Shaw and the black troops under his command were later depicted in the 1989 film *Glory.*

95. Blight, *Race,* 5.

96. Browne, "Remembering," 170.

97. Doss, *Memorial Mania,* 213.

98. Steven Hoelscher, "The White-Pillared Past: Landscapes of Memory and Race in the American South," in *Landscape and Race in the United States,* ed. Richard H. Schein (New York: Routledge, 2006), 46–47.

99. Ron Eyerman, *Cultural Trauma: Slavery and the Formation of African American Identity* (Cambridge, UK: Cambridge University Press, 2001), 5.

100. Samuel F. Dennis, Jr., "Seeing Hampton Plantation: Race and Gender in a South Carolina Heritage Landscape," in *Landscape and Race in the United States,* ed. Richard H. Schein (New York: Routledge, 2006), 84. For a similar analysis of the same site, see Christine N. Buzinde and Carla Almeida Santos, "Representations of Slavery," *Annals of Tourism Research* 35 (2008): 469–488.

101. Loewen, *Lies*, 273–278.

102. Mark Auslander, "We've Come a Long Way from the Effort to Memorialize the Slave Mammy," *History News Network*, available at http://hnn.us/articles/10-3-11/weve-come-a-long-way-from-memorializing-the-slave-mammy.html. See also Micki McElya, *Clinging to Mammy: The Faithful Slave in Twentieth-Century America* (Cambridge, MA: Harvard University Press, 2007), and Kimberly Wallace Sanders, *Mammy: A Century of Race, Gender, and Southern Memory* (Ann Arbor: University of Michigan Press, 2009).

103. See http://abagond.wordpress.com/2010/07/23/uncle-jack-the-good-darky/. I thank Mansa Bantu for providing me with the information in this paragraph.

104. Bruce Levine, "In Search of a Usable Past: Neo-Confederates and Black Confederates," in *Slavery and Public History: The Tough Stuff of American Memory*, ed. James Oliver Horton and Lois E. Horton (New York: New Press, 2006), 191.

105. Stephen P. Hanna, "A Slavery Museum? Race, Memory, and Landscape in Fredericksburg, Virginia," *Southeastern Geographer* 48 (2008): 320.

106. Owen J. Dwyer, "Symbolic Accretion and Commemoration," *Social & Cultural Geography* 5 (2004): 420.

107. James Oliver Horton, "Slavery in American History: An Uncomfortable National Dialogue," in *Slavery and Public History: The Tough Stuff of American Memory*, ed. James Oliver Horton and Lois E. Horton (New York: New Press, 2006), 48.

108. Jennifer L. Eichstedt and Stephen Small, *Representations of Slavery: Race and Ideology in Southern Plantation Museums* (Washington, DC: Smithsonian Institution Press, 2002), 257. Seventy-nine percent of the tours occurred at privately owned sites; 4 percent were operated by the federal government. "In general," they noted, "public sites are more likely to incorporate a greater amount of substantive information on slavery than privately organized sites" (61).

109. Dwight T. Pitcaithley, "Public Education and the National Park Service: Interpreting the Civil War," *Perspectives on History* 45.8 (2007), available at http://www.historians.org/perspectives/issues/2007/0711/0711pro2.cfm.

110. Report is available at http://www.nps.gov/history/history/categrs/mili2/high_ground_1998.pdf.

111. Pitcaithley, "Public Education."

112. Pitcaithley, "Cosmic Threat," 175. Thanks to the efforts of Pitcaithley and other NPS officials, the interpretation at Civil War sites operated by the federal government now discusses slavery as the cause of the war.

113. Pitcaithley, "Public Education."

114. Clarence Lusane, *The Black History of the White House* (San Francisco: City Lights Books, 2011), 459. Oddly, the Georgia proclamation pointedly honors the efforts of "many Jews who saw action in the Confederate armed forces as well as in governmental service" (see http://confederateheritagemonth.com/heritage/2009/proclamations/georgia.pdf).

115. Eric Gable, Richard Handler, and Anna Lawson, "On the Uses of Relativism: Fact, Conjecture, and Black and White Histories at Colonial Williamsburg," *American Ethnologist* 19 (1992): 791–805.

116. Derek H. Alderman, "Surrogation and the Politics of Remembering Slavery in Savannah, Georgia," *Journal of Historical Geography* 36 (2010): 92.

117. See ibid.; Bettina M. Carbonell, "The Syntax of Objects and the Representation of History: Speaking of *Slavery in New York*," *History and Theory* 47 (2009): 122–137; Davis, "Memoryscapes"; and Doss, *Memorial Mania*.

118. *Independence National Historical Park Long-Range Interpretive Plan* (2007): 14–15.

119. Doss, *Memorial Mania*, 256.

120. David W. Blight, "If You Don't Tell It Like It Was, It Can Never Be as It Ought

to Be," in *Slavery and Public History: The Tough Stuff of American Memory*, ed. James Oliver Horton and Lois E. Horton (New York: New Press, 2006), 30.

121. Ira Berlin, "Coming to Terms with Slavery in Twenty-First-Century America," in *Slavery and Public History: The Tough Stuff of American Memory*, ed. James Oliver Horton and Lois E. Horton (New York: New Press, 2006), 7.

122. Loewen, *Lies*, 208. Alderman, "Surrogation," also pointed to "the range of ideologies and discourses flowing through the African American community about the legacy of slavery" (98).

123. Rosenzweig and Thelen, *Presence*, 159.

124. John Michael Vlach, "The Last Great Taboo Subject: Exhibiting Slavery at the Library of Congress," in *Slavery and Public History: The Tough Stuff of American Memory*, ed. James Oliver Horton and Lois E. Horton (New York: New Press, 2006), 58.

125. Doss (*Memorial Mania*) quoted the mission of the National Underground Railroad Freedom Center in Cincinnati, for example, as telling "'stories about freedom's heroes, past and present, challenging and inspiring everyone to take courageous steps for freedom today'" (295). Foote (*Shadowed Ground*) noted that commemorative work about African Americans takes an "oblique" approach that features heroic stories while "downplaying divisive issues" (324). In his study of a proposed U.S. slavery museum in Fredericksburg, Virginia, Hanna ("Slavery Museum?") pointed out that "adding Civil Rights and segregation-era black history memorials to the landscape did not threaten the dominant memories of Fredericksburg's Colonial and Civil War eras" (326).

126. Rosenzweig and Thelen, *Presence*, 150.

127. Reuben A. Buford May, "Race Talk and Local Collective Memory among African American Men in a Neighborhood Tavern," *Qualitative Sociology* 23 (2000): 201–214.

128. Hoerl, "Selective Amnesia," 196.

129. James Oliver Horton and Lois E. Horton, *Hard Road to Freedom: The Story of African America* (New Brunswick, NJ: Rutgers University Press, 2001), 1.

130. In discussion with the author, October 18, 2012.

131. Christine Chivallon, "Bristol and the Eruption of Memory: Making the Slave-Trading Past Visible," *Social & Cultural Geography* 2 (2001): 349.

132. In discussion with the author, October 18, 2012.

CHAPTER 4

1. Ed Lawler, "Letter: Washington Slept Here, and That House Ought to Be Rebuilt," *Philadelphia Inquirer*, October 13, 1996, available at http://www.ushistory.org/presidents house/news/inq101396.htm. Lawler had suggested that the park locate the proposed Independence Park Institute, a building designed to provide educational programming about and within the park, within a reconstructed President's House. Lawler noted that his suggestion was motivated by the architect Robert Venturi's conceptual plan for redesigning the mall, in which Venturi proposed to reconstruct a couple of buildings on Chestnut Street as a means of strengthening the colonial feel of the central park area.

2. *Abbreviated Final General Management Plan Environmental Impact Statement, Independence National Historical Park* (Washington, DC: Department of the Interior, 1997), 4:172. The park had also encountered a fair share of controversy when it earlier considered the possibility of reconstructing colonial era sites. It built a replica of the Graff House, where Thomas Jefferson wrote the Declaration of Independence, but declined to create a similar structure at the site of Ben Franklin's former home, opting instead for a "ghost structure" in which the house was suggested by an architectural installation. See Barry Mackintosh,

"National Park Service Reconstruction Policy and Practice," in *The Reconstructed Past: Reconstructions in the Public Interpretation of Archaeology and History*, ed. John H. Jameson, Jr. (Walnut Creek, CA: Alta Mira Press, 2004), 69.

3. Inga Saffron, "Street: Let Pavilion Work Proceed," *Philadelphia Inquirer*, March 26, 2002, available at http://www.ushistory.org/presidentshouse/news/inq032602.htm.

4. In discussion with the author (via e-mail), May 4, 2013.

5. Martha Aikens, "Park Tells the Story of Slavery," *Philadelphia Inquirer*, April 7, 2002, available at http://www.ushistory.org/presidentshouse/news/inq040702.htm. Aikens's letter response to IHA chair Nancy Gilboy ("Park Superintendent Martha B. Aikens Reply to IHA Letter") is available at http://www.ushistory.org/presidentshouse/controversy/aikens1.htm.

6. See http://www.ushistory.org/presidentshouse/controversy/iha1.htm.

7. See http://www.ushistory.org/presidentshouse/controversy/iha2.htm.

8. Stephan Salisbury and Inga Saffron, "Echoes of Slavery at Liberty Bell Site," *Philadelphia Inquirer*, March 24, 2002, available at http://www.ushistory.org/presidentshouse/news/inq032402.htm.

9. See http://www.whyy.org/91FM/philaslaves.html.

10. See http://www.ushistory.org/presidentshouse/controversy/controversyoverview.htm. To be fair, no one has been allowed to touch the Liberty Bell since a man attacked it with a hammer in 2001.

11. Aikens, "Aikens Reply"; Aikens, "Park Tells the Story."

12. Gary B. Nash, "For Whom Will the Liberty Bell Toll? From Controversy to Cooperation," in *Slavery and Public History: The Tough Stuff of American Memory*, ed. James Oliver Horton and Lois E. Horton (New York: New Press, 2006), 80.

13. Stephan Salisbury, "Slave Discovery Roils Mall Issue," *Philadelphia Inquirer*, July 4, 2004, available at http://www.ushistory.org/presidentshouse/news/inq070404.htm.

14. Aikens, "Park Tells the Story."

15. According to Lawler, the enslaved Africans Giles and Paris definitely slept in the building and Austin may have as well. The white indentured coachman Arthur Dunn also stayed in the addition. Oney Judge and Moll slept over the kitchen, while Hercules, Richmond, and Christopher were quartered in the attic. See http://www.ushistory.org/presidentshouse/slaves/slavequartersfaq.htm.

16. Stephan Salisbury, "Proposed Wording on Slave Quarters Draws Fire," *Philadelphia Inquirer*, October 31, 2002, available at http://www.ushistory.org/presidentshouse/news/inq103102.htm.

17. Ibid. INHP spokesperson Phil Sheridan asserted in the same article that "primary documents call [the rear of the President's House] the servants' hall," while also noting that "there's no question slaves existed on the site. But we're standing with what Washington called it, and we are standing with the fact that no one knows if slaves slept there or if slaves didn't sleep there." After historians pointed out that "servant" was a frequently used euphemism for "slave" in the eighteenth century, the INHP website pulled the page with the inaccurate wording.

18. See http://www.ushistory.org/presidentshouse/controversy/questions.htm.

19. On July 4, 2004, *Philadelphia Inquirer* reporter Stephan Salisbury ("Slave Discovery") noted that "there is still no mention, no marker, no sign acknowledging the fact that Washington's slaves were housed near the Liberty Bell Center entrance."

20. *Final Report to the United States Congress by the Philadelphia National Shrines Park Commission*, 8 vols. (Philadelphia, 1947), 1:xii.

21. Ibid., 1:257, 259, 260, 267–268.

22. Ibid., 1:269.

23. Ernest Howard Yardley, "To the Editor of the Evening Bulletin," [Philadelphia] *Evening Bulletin*, January 9, 1952, available at http://www.ushistory.org/presidentshouse/news/eb010952.htm. A note on the IHA website reads, "This article was written for the Evening Bulletin. We have not been able to verify that it was published."

24. James R. George, "Bulldozers Trample Where Washington Slept," *Philadelphia Inquirer*, February 22, 1952, available at http://www.ushistory.org/presidentshouse/news/inq02221952.htm.

25. *Final Report*, 1:266.

26. John Bodnar, *Remaking America: Public Memory, Commemoration, and Patriotism in the Twentieth Century* (Princeton, NJ: Princeton University Press, 1992). Vernacular discourse is defined in slightly different ways by others; see, for example, Lisa A. Flores and Marouf Hasian, "Returning to Aztlán and La Raza: Political Communication and the Vernacular Construction of Chicana/o Nationalism," in *Politics, Communication and Culture*, ed. Alberto González and Dolores V. Tanno (Thousand Oaks, CA: Sage, 1997), 186–203; Gerard Hauser, *Vernacular Voices: The Rhetoric of Publics and Public Spheres* (Columbia: University of South Carolina Press, 1999); Michelle A. Holling, "Forming Oppositional and Social Concord to California's Proposition 187 and Squelching Social Discord in the Vernacular Space of CHICLE," *Communication and Critical/Cultural Studies* 3 (2006): 202–222; Kent A. Ono and John M. Sloop, "The Critique of Vernacular Discourse," *Communication Monographs* 62 (1995): 19–46; and Erin M. Reser, "Strategies of Negotiation in Mainstream Media: Vernacular Discourse and Masculinity in *The Full Monty*," *Popular Communication* 3 (2005): 217–237.

27. Ono and Sloop, "Critique"; Holling, "Forming Oppositional and Social Concord." The results of this positioning are not always agreed on by those who study vernacular discourses. Hauser (*Vernacular Voices*), for instance, seems optimistic about the ability of vernacular discourse to alter political and cultural landscapes, while Bodnar (*Remaking America*)—despite his identification of cases in which vernacular discourse produced notable changes in those landscapes—ultimately concludes that "the dialogic activity examined here almost always stressed the desirability of maintaining the social order and existing structures" (246).

28. As Michael Peters and Colin Lankshear explain, such counter-narratives tell the stories "of those individuals and groups whose knowledge and histories have been marginalized, excluded, subjugated or forgotten in the telling of official narratives." In "Postmodern Counternarratives," in *Counternarratives: Cultural Studies and Critical Pedagogies in Postmodern Spaces*, ed. Henry Giroux, Colin Lankshear, and Michael Peters (New York: Routledge, 1996), 2.

29. Stephen Legg, "Sites of Counter-memory: The Refusal to Forget and the Nationalist Struggle in Colonial Delhi," *Historical Geography* 33 (2005): 181.

30. Kenneth E. Foote, *Shadowed Ground: America's Landscapes of Violence and Tragedy* (Austin: University of Texas Press, 1997), 231–232.

31. Owen J. Dwyer, "Symbolic Accretion and Commemoration," *Social & Cultural Geography* 5 (2004): 421.

32. Stacy A. Teicher and Walter H. Robinson, "The Other Side of Liberty," *Christian Science Monitor*, July 3, 2003.

33. Linn Washington, Jr., "Park Service Burying a Shameful Fact," *Philadelphia Tribune*, April 2, 2002.

34. Ibid.

35. Ibid.

36. In Stephan Salisbury, "Planners Rethink Slavery, Liberty Project," *Philadelphia Inquirer*, December 25, 2002.

37. Karen Warrington, "African American History Must Be Taught," *Philadelphia Inquirer,* June 14, 2005, available at http://www.ushistory.org/presidentshouse/news/inq 061405.htm.

38. Ray Raphael, *Founding Myths: Stories That Hide Our Patriotic Past* (New York: New Press, 2004), 185.

39. Eugene Kane, "Reparations Don't Have to Cost a Dime," *Milwaukee Journal Sentinel,* May 21, 2002.

40. Mike Toner, "Digs Unearth Slave Plantations in North," *Atlanta Journal-Constitution,* March 2, 2003.

41. Edward Lawler, Jr., "How Much Do We Really Know about Slavery?" *Philadelphia Inquirer,* April 2, 2007.

42. In Teicher and Robinson, "Other Side."

43. Scott A. Sandage, "A Marble House Divided: The Lincoln Memorial, the Civil Rights Movement, and the Politics of Memory, 1939–1963," *Journal of American History* 80 (1993): 135–167.

44. Jacqueline Bacon, "Taking Liberty, Taking Literacy: Signifying in the Rhetoric of African-American Abolitionists," *Southern Communication Journal* 64 (1999): 271.

45. Jack P. Geise, "The Rhetoric and Politics of Liberty," *Social Science Quarterly* 79 (1989): 836–850.

46. Bacon, "Taking Liberty," 272.

47. Elizabethada A. Wright, "'Joking Isn't Safe': Fanny Fern, Irony, and Signifyin(g)," *Rhetoric Society Quarterly* 31 (2001): 92; see also Mark K. Burns, "'A Slave in Form but Not in Fact': Subversive Humor and the Rhetoric of Irony in *Narrative of the Life of Frederick Douglass,*" *Studies in American Humor* 3:12 (2005): 83–96.

48. Robert E. Terrill, "Irony, Silence, and Time: Frederick Douglass on the Fifth of July," *Quarterly Journal of Speech* 89 (2003): 216–234.

49. Morris had letters to the editor published in the *Philadelphia Inquirer* on June 21, 2002, and October 11, 2005; in the *Philadelphia Daily News* on October 20, 2005; and in *The Bulletin* on July 16, 2008. The quotation is from the most recent letter, available at http://www.ushistory.org/presidentshouse/news/pb071608.htm.

50. Bryan J. McCann, "Genocide as Representative Anecdote: Crack Cocaine, the CIA, and the Nation of Islam in Gary Webb's 'Dark Alliance,'" *Western Journal of Communication* 74 (2010): 399. In *A Grammar of Motives* (New York: Prentice-Hall, 1945), Kenneth Burke introduces the idea of representative anecdotes, explaining that they are summations that at once represent and reduce what they are summarizing (60). See also Barry Brummett, "The Representative Anecdote as a Burkean Method, Applied to Evangelical Rhetoric," *Southern Communication Journal* 50 (1984): 1–23, and "Burke's Representative Anecdote as Method in Media Criticism," *Critical Studies in Mass Communication* 1 (1984): 161–176.

51. Derek H. Alderman and Rachel M. Campbell, "Symbolic Excavation and the Artifact Politics of Remembering Slavery in the American South: Observations from Walterboro, South Carolina," *Southeastern Geographer* 48 (2008): 340.

52. Mary Douglas, *Purity and Danger: An Analysis of Concepts of Pollution and Taboo* (New York: Praeger, 1966), 2; Kenneth Burke, *Permanence and Change: An Anatomy of Purpose,* 3rd ed. (Berkeley: University of California Press, 1984), 274–294. See also Daniel A. Grano and Kenneth S. Zagacki, "Cleansing the Superdome: The Paradox of Purity and Post-Katrina Guilt," *Quarterly Journal of Speech* 97 (2011): 201–223.

53. Bradford Vivian, "The Veil and the Visible," *Western Journal of Communication* 63 (1999): 117.

54. McCann, "Genocide," 397–398.

55. In William C. Kashatus, "Burying Slave Past Is a Travesty," *Philadelphia Daily News,* April 15, 2002, available at http://www.ushistory.org/presidentshouse/news/pdn041502.htm.

56. Gary B. Nash and Randall M. Miller, "Don't Bury the Past," *Philadelphia Inquirer,* March 31, 2002, available at http://www.ushistory.org/presidentshouse/news/inq033102a.htm.

57. Ibid.

58. All comments were posted on http://www.ushistory.org/presidentshouse/controversy/write.htm. The names cited are those offered on the web page.

59. Michael Z. Muhammad, "Philadelphia's Dirty Secret to Be Told," Finalcall.com, February 16, 2003.

60. Stephan Salisbury, "Liberty Bell's Symbolism Rings Hollow for Some," *Philadelphia Inquirer,* May 26, 2002, available at http://www.ushistory.org/presidentshouse/news/inq052502.htm.

61. Deborah Bolling, "Don't Tread on Me," *Philadelphia CityPaper,* July 10–16, 2003, available at http://www.ushistory.org/presidentshouse/news/cp071003.htm. The rumors, of course, were not true; the site of the National Constitution Center, for example, underwent an extensive excavation that unearthed many pieces of evidence from colonial times but no slave remains.

62. Joe Becton, in discussion with the author, October 1, 2013. Becton worked in INHP from 1986 to 1989 and 1992 to 2009, serving as supervisory ranger from 2001 until his retirement in 2009.

63. Stephan Salisbury, "Beneath Independence Mall, Story of Early Free Black America," *Philadelphia Inquirer,* July 2, 2008, available at http://www.ushistory.org/presidentshouse/news/inq070208.htm. Interestingly, the NPS trumpets this episode as a successful example of its Civic Engagement Initiative. As the Park Service notes on its website: "Initially NPS managers were reluctant to change their position on non-excavation for several reasons. However, the force and legitimacy of the group's argument led NPS to view the issue in a fresh light and ultimately to reverse its decision" (see http://www.nps.gov/civic/casestudies/INDEDexter10-18.pdf).

64. In Stephan Salisbury, "Remaking History," *Philadelphia Inquirer,* June 30, 2008, available at http://www.ushistory.org/presidentshouse/news/inq063008.htm.

65. Bolling, "Don't Tread on Me"; Spencer P. M. Harrington, "Bones and Bureaucrats," *Archaeology,* March/April 1993, available at http://archive.archaeology.org/online/features/afrburial/.

66. Acel Moore, "Whole Story of Slavery, Liberty Bell Still Untold," *Philadelphia Inquirer,* May 16, 2002, available at http://www.ushistory.org/presidentshouse/news/inq051602.htm.

67. In Mary Mitchell, "Making Sure Liberty Bell Keeps It Real," *Chicago Sun-Times,* October 9, 2007, available at http://www.ushistory.org/presidentshouse/news/cst100907.htm.

68. In Stephan Salisbury, "Forum Furthers Memorial to Slaves," *Philadelphia Inquirer,* November 7, 2004, available at http://www.ushistory.org/presidentshouse/news/inq110704.htm.

69. In Salisbury, "Planners Rethink Slavery."

70. In Bruce Schimmel, "All the President's Men," *Philadelphia City Paper,* July 7–13, 2005, available at http://www.ushistory.org/presidentshouse/news/cp071305.htm.

71. Letter from Pitcaithley to Aikens, quoted by Nash ("For Whom")—with permission from Pitcaithley—on pages 87 and 86, respectively.

72. Nash, "For Whom," 85.

73. Ibid., 91.

74. Ibid., 88. Nash's chapter provides both a more thorough account of the meeting and a compelling insider's account of the early efforts to convince INHP staffers of the need to acknowledge the President's House site.

75. Ibid., 90.

76. See http://legislation.phila.gov/attachments/8242.pdf.

77. See http://www.legis.state.pa.us/CFDOCS/Legis/PN/Public/btCheck.cfm?txtType=HTM&sessYr=2001&sessInd=0&billBody=H&billTyp=R&billNbr=0490&pn=3509.

78. See http://www.ushistory.org/presidentshouse/controversy/houserpt.htm.

79. The IHA website, http://www.ushistory.org/presidentshouse/controversy/write/htm, accepted 1,119 entries between March 31, 2002, and May 1, 2002. The ATAC website, http://avengingtheancestors.com/info/index.htm, did not provide dates for its "continuing petition drive" but claimed to have collected more than fifteen thousand signatures (accessed June 30, 2008).

80. Michael Coard, "Letter: Mayor Honors Memory of Slaves," *Philadelphia Inquirer,* October 17, 2003, available at http://www.ushistory.org/presidentshouse/news/inql101703.htm. The full text of Street's letter to Coard is available at http://www.ushistory.org/presidentshouse/controversy/street.htm.

81. See, for example, Kendall R. Phillips, "A Rhetoric of Controversy," *Western Journal of Communication* 63 (1999): 499.

82. Joseph Slobodzian, "Independence Mall Slavery Memorial Gets Federal Funding," *Philadelphia Inquirer,* September 6, 2005, available at http://www.ushistory.org/presidentshouse/news/inq090605.htm.

83. Doris Devine Fanelli, "History, Commemoration, and an Interdisciplinary Approach to Interpreting the President's House Site," *Pennsylvania Magazine of History and Biography* 129 (2005): 453.

84. Michael Coard, "The 'Black' Eye on George Washington's 'White' House," *Pennsylvania Magazine of History and Biography* 129 (2005): 464.

85. INHP and NPS officials met with designers and community representatives (including Lawler, Coard, Karen Warrington, and Harry Harrison) on October 31, 2002, to brainstorm and develop interpretive themes; see http://www.ushistory.org/presidentshouse/plans/jan2003/image02.htm and http://www.ushistory.org/presidentshouse/plans/jan2003/image03.htm. Becton later told me that interim superintendent Reidenbach told him that he did not need to attend the January 15, 2003, gathering in which the plans would be revealed because it would be noncontroversial. In discussion with the author, October 1, 2013.

86. In Stephan Salisbury, "Design of Liberty Bell Site Criticized," *Philadelphia Inquirer,* January 16, 2003, available at http://www.ushistory.org/presidentshouse/news/inq011603.htm.

87. Inga Saffron, "A Historic Site That Has Defied Designers" [blog], September 8, 2006, available at http://www.ushistory.org/presidentshouse/news/inq090806.htm.

CHAPTER 5

1. Inga Saffron, "Try This in One High-Profile Memorial: Honor America's First White House, Acknowledge the Stain of Slavery," *Changing Skyline,* August 24, 2006, available at http://www.ushistory.org/presidentshouse/news/so082406.htm.

2. See *The President's House: Freedom and Slavery in Making a New Nation,* RFQ for a professional services contract for the city of Philadelphia, available at http://www.ushistory.org/presidentshouse/images/rfq.presidentshouse.final2.pdf, accessed August 21, 2009. The first five themes also appeared in the preliminary design offered by the Olin Partnership and Vincent Ciulla Design in their January 15, 2003, proposal; see http://www.ushistory.org/presidentshouse/plans/jan2003/image03.htm.

3. James E. Young, *At Memory's Edge: After-Images of the Holocaust in Contemporary Art and Architecture* (New Haven, CT: Yale University Press, 2000), 7.

4. All quotations in the paragraphs that describe the designs were provided by the design team and retrieved from the city of Philadelphia's website: http://www.phila.gov/presidents house/design.htm.

5. The first item (overall impression of the models) had the following response options: I love it; I like it, with some reservations; I'm neutral; I don't like it. The second item (how well does each model commemorate the lives of *all* the people who inhabited the President's House?) had the following response options: exceptionally well; well; adequately; not well at all.

6. The PDF files are available at http://www.phila.gov/presidentshouse/comments.htm.

7. Sara Ahmed, "Affective Economies," *Social Text* 22, no. 2 (2004): 117–139.

8. Carole Blair, Greg Dickinson, and Brian Ott, "Introduction: Rhetoric/Memory/ Place," in *Places of Public Memory: The Rhetoric of Museums and Memorials*, ed. Greg Dickinson, Carole Blair, and Brian L. Ott (Tuscaloosa: University of Alabama Press, 2010), 18.

9. A. Susan Owen and Peter Ehrenhaus, "Communities of Memory, Entanglements, and Claims of the Past on the Present: Reading Race Trauma through *The Green Mile*," *Critical Studies in Media Communication* 27 (2010): 133.

10. Marita Sturken, *Tangled Memories: The Vietnam War, the AIDS Epidemic, and the Politics of Remembering* (Los Angeles: University of California Press, 1997), 182.

11. This conceptualization of publics differs from Hauser's definition of a public as the conglomeration of all those groups "who hold different opinions about a mutual problem" in that each group that holds a different opinion is theorized here as a distinct public. Gerard Hauser, *Vernacular Voices: The Rhetoric of Publics and Public Spheres* (Columbia: University of South Carolina Press, 1999), 32.

12. Blair, Dickinson, and Ott, "Introduction," 15. Their recognition that these groups of individuals are shaped by and through discourse seems to share much of Michael Warner's widely accepted definition of publics (*Publics and Counterpublics* [New York: Zone Books, 2002]). That said, one could call these groups by different appellations as well, such as *communities of memory* (see Owen and Ehrenhaus, "Communities of Memory"), but I prefer the more widely recognized and less cumbersome term *public*.

13. As Daniel Brouwer and Robert Asen remind us, "We are well-served by recognizing that precedents, habits, norms, sedimented articulations, and myriad institutions shape the constitution of publics" ("Introduction: Public Modalities, or the Metaphors We Theorize By," in *Public Modalities: Rhetoric, Culture, Media, and the Shape of Public Life*, ed. Daniel C. Brouwer and Robert Asen [Tuscaloosa: University of Alabama Press, 2010], 9). In similar terms, Peter Dahlgren argued that "civic culture" contributes to the activities of public spheres: "civic culture points to those features of the socio-cultural world—dispositions, practices, processes—that constitute pre-conditions for people's actual participation in the public sphere" ("Reconfiguring Civic Culture in the New Media Milieu," in *Media and the Restyling of Politics: Consumerism, Celebrity and Cynicism*, ed. John Corner and Dick Pels [London: Sage, 2003], 154).

14. Kendall R. Phillips, "A Rhetoric of Controversy," *Western Journal of Communication* 63 (1999): 507.

15. Public spheres inevitably contain traces of previous debates and controversies; see, for example, Brouwer and Asen, "Introduction," and Swantje Lingenberg, "The Citizen Audience and European Transcultural Public Spheres: Exploring Civic Engagement in European Political Communication," *Communications: The European Journal of Communication Research* 34 (2009): 45–72.

16. Celeste M. Condit, "Hegemony in a Mass-Mediated Society: Concordance about Reproductive Technologies," *Critical Studies in Mass Communication* 11 (1994): 205–230. Dana

Cloud took issue with Condit's conceptualization of *concordance* as the result of public debate and argued that Condit minimized the role that material power differences play in policymaking ("Hegemony or Concordance? The Rhetoric of Tokenism in 'Oprah' Winfrey's Rags-to-Riches Biography," *Critical Studies in Mass Communication* 13 [1996]: 115–137). Their exchange continued in Celeste Condit, "Hegemony, Concordance and Capitalism: Reply to Cloud," *Critical Studies in Mass Communication* 13 (1996): 382–384, and Dana Cloud, "Concordance, Complexity, and Conservatism: Rejoinder to Condit," *Critical Studies in Mass Communication* 14 (1997): 193–197.

17. Hauser, *Vernacular Voices*, 275–276.

18. Mark Porrovecchio, "Lost in the WTO Shuffle: Publics, Counterpublics, and the Individual," *Western Journal of Communication* 71 (2007): 235–256.

19. My investigation at once tries to honor these ideas, and falls short of so doing. Although I analyzed the entire population of comment cards to highlight, rather than obscure, individuals' participation in definable publics, my analysis nonetheless erases the existence of individuals who did not readily fit within the publics identified here. Among those whose participation was neglected were those I identified as members of the publics whose discourse was not examined, those whose comments could not be coded using one or more of the initial themes, those whose evaluations did not contain comments (214 voters), and those who did not choose to complete an evaluation but held opinions about the design models.

20. To identify distinct publics, each with a unique affective investment in how the designs remembered the site, I conducted an inductive, thematic analysis of the 780 cards with comments while following Richard E. Boyatzis's five steps for developing an inductive code: reducing the raw information, identifying themes within the subsamples, comparing themes across subsamples, developing a code, and determining the reliability of the code (*Transforming Qualitative Information: Thematic Analysis and Code Development* [Thousand Oaks, CA: Sage, 1998]). I closely examined each of the 780 cards with comments, but I reviewed no more than three batches (or subsamples) of the eleven groups of cards at any one sitting. As similar types of comments recurred within a single batch of cards, I listed the topics on the last evaluation card posted in that batch. I then compiled a list of all the topics (a total of 83) noted on the last card of each of the eleven groups. I reduced the list of 83 by initially noting duplicate topics, then combining topics that seemed to share an underlying theme, and finally, checking for distinctness among the themes. For example, in the second step of reduction, topics such as "open," "simple," "powerful," and "interactive" all dealt with the imagined experience or "feel" of the design model. In the third step of reduction, for instance, I separated comments that praised the inclusion of slavery in the designs from comments that suggested either that the treatment of slavery was insufficient or that it overwhelmed the rest of the design. As a result of this three-step process of reduction, some evaluation cards were not labeled (this group includes the 214 cards without comments and the cards with comments that did not fit any of the themes), and some evaluation cards were labeled with multiple themes. I found as many as four themes in eleven cards, and I discovered fifty different combinations of themes in the population of cards.

After completing the first four steps of this process, I had identified seven distinct themes. I determined the reliability of these themes by having a graduate student research assistant verify the reliability of my initial coding. I trained the research assistant by first working through a set of coded evaluation cards that would not be used to determine reliability. I explained the coding scheme and how I made decisions to code comments as belonging to none of the themes, one of the themes, or more than one of the themes. The research assistant then practiced by coding a set of ten cards and discussing the results with me. After completing this training, the research assistant independently coded ten of the first cards with comments from each of the eleven groups of evaluation cards (a total of 110 cards), using one or more of the seven themes or leaving the card blank (no themes detected). Given the eight possible choices for each card, 880 possible coding decisions were made by the research assistant. We agreed on 795 of the 880 decisions, for a 90.3 percent agreement rate—a figure well above the 70 percent standard that Boyatzis (*Transforming Qualitative Information*) identified for this type of intercoder reliability check.

21. Undoubtedly, African American voters significantly populated the Slavery and Insufficient Attention to Slavery publics, but I would caution against conceptualizing these two publics as the only ones in which African Americans were present or as occupied by only African Americans. Comment cards did not contain demographic information, and, as noted in Chapter 3, no single perspective on how slavery should be publicly remembered can be identified among the nation's African American population.

22. "To residents [of Philadelphia]," noted Taplin, Scheld, and Low in their ethnographic analysis of the park and its relationship to the city, "the park is symbolically and functionally part of the larger landscape of the city" (Dana H. Taplin, Suzanne Scheld, and Setha M. Low, "Rapid Ethnographic Assessment in Urban Parks: A Case Study of Independence National Historical Park," *Human Organization* 61 [2002]: 91).

23. Significant portions of the material presented in the next two sections of the chapter ("Aesthetics-Driven Publics" and "Politics-Driven Publics") originally appeared in Roger C. Aden, "When Memories and Discourses Collide: The President's House and Places of Public Memory," *Communication Monographs* 79 (2012): 72–92. I use the material here with the permission of the publisher of that article, Taylor and Francis.

24. See comments posted in July 2007, in particular, available at http://www.ushistory .org/presidentshouse/guests.asp.

25. James R. George, "Bulldozers Trample Where Washington Slept," *Philadelphia Inquirer,* February 22, 1952, available at http://www.ushistory.org/presidentshouse/news/ inq02221952.htm.

26. Alison J. McIntosh and Richard C. Prentice, "Affirming Authenticity: Consuming Cultural Heritage," *Annals of Tourism Research* 26 (1999): 589–612.

27. See comments on the TripAdvisor website, http://www.tripadvisor.com/Attrac tion_Review-g58313-d102549-Reviews-Colonial_Williamsburg-Williamsburg_Virginia .html#REVIEWS.

28. All quotations are taken verbatim from the comment cards posted online at the city of Philadelphia's website: http://www.phila.gov/presidentshouse/comments.htm. If a person did not put a name on the evaluation card, he or she was listed as "Anonymous" on the card. If a person provided his or her name on the card, but asked that the name not be made public, the name space on the card was marked by a blank line.

29. In Deirdre Gibson, Mary Whelchel Konieczny, Kathy Schlegel, and Anna Coxe Toogood, *Cultural Landscape Report, Independence Mall* (Washington, DC: U.S. Department of the Interior, 1994), 81.

30. See, for example, Kirk Savage, *Monument Wars: Washington, D.C., the National Mall, and the Transformation of the Memorial Landscape* (Berkeley: University of California Press, 2009), for a discussion of how the idea of feeling was behind the many iterations of the commemorative landscape in Washington, D.C. In urban areas in particular, the influence of the City Beautiful Movement in the late 1800s and early 1900s also contributed to cities' desire to offer pleasant and uplifting landscapes for their residents. In addition, Erika Doss (*Memorial Mania: Public Feeling in America* [Chicago: University of Chicago Press, 2012]) catalogued a number of contemporary memory sites in which emotions played an integral role in the design of the site.

31. See http://www.oklahomacitynationalmemorial.org/secondary.php?section=2&ca tid=29.

32. David Glassberg, *Sense of History: The Place of the Past in American Life* (Amherst: University of Massachusetts Press, 2001), 7.

33. See, for example, Eric Aoki, Greg Dickinson, and Brian L. Ott, "The Master Naturalist Imagined: Directed Movement and Simulations at the Draper Museum of Natural History," in *Places of Public Memory: The Rhetoric of Museums and Memorials,* ed. Greg Dickinson, Carole Blair, and Brian L. Ott (Tuscaloosa: University of Alabama Press, 2010), 238–265, and Carole Blair and Neil Michel, "Commemorating in the Theme Park Zone: Reading the Astronauts Memorial," in *At the Intersection: Cultural Studies and Rhetorical Studies,* ed. Thomas Rosteck (New York: Guilford Press, 1999).

34. Steven Conn, *Metropolitan Philadelphia: Living with the Presence of the Past* (Philadelphia: University of Pennsylvania Press, 2006), 72.

35. *General Management Plan, Independence National Historical Park* (Washington, DC: Department of the Interior, 1997), 30.

36. Gibson, Konieczny, Schlegel, and Toogood, *Cultural Landscape Report,* 133.

37. See http://phlvisitorcenter.com/must-see#History.

38. Two designs earned exactly 50 percent approval in only one category. Davis Buckley received 50 percent in *Overall Impression* and 37.5 percent in *All Inhabitants,* while Ewing-Cole received 36 percent in *Overall Impression* and 50 percent in *All Inhabitants.*

39. Gibson, Konieczny, Schlegel, and Toogood, *Cultural Landscape Report,* 18, 134. In addition, each of the mall's major renovations has sought, in some way, to generate a sense of harmony among the structures and landscape of the area.

40. Blair, Dickinson, and Ott, "Introduction," 29.

41. Carole Blair and Neil Michel, "The AIDS Memorial Quilt and the Contemporary Culture of Public Commemoration," *Rhetoric & Public Affairs* 10 (2007): 595–626.

42. John Bodnar, *Remaking America: Public Memory, Commemoration, and Patriotism in the Twentieth Century* (Princeton, NJ: Princeton University Press, 1992).

43. Blair and Michel, "AIDS Memorial Quilt," 615.

44. Kenneth E. Foote, *Shadowed Ground: America's Landscapes of Violence and Tragedy* (Austin: University of Texas Press, 1997), 324.

45. Disappointment with indirect accounts of past atrocities is bound to occur because, by their very definition, atrocities contain unspeakable horrors perpetrated by human beings on other human beings. See, for example, Owen and Ehrenhaus's and Hasian's accounts of reactions to *The Green Mile* and the U.S. Holocaust Memorial Museum, respectively (Owen and Ehrenhaus, "Communities of Memory," 135; Marouf Hasian, Jr., "Remembering and Forgetting the 'Final Solution': A Rhetorical Pilgrimage through the U.S. Holocaust Memorial Museum," *Critical Studies in Media Communication* 21 [2004]: 86).

46. Blair and Michel, "AIDS Memorial Quilt," 620.

47. Kirk Savage, "Trauma, Healing, and the Therapeutic Monument," in *Terror, Culture, Politics: Rethinking 9/11,* ed. Daniel J. Sherman and Terry Nardin (Bloomington: Indiana University Press, 2006), 106.

48. Deborah Posel, "History as Confession: The Case of the South African Truth and Reconciliation Commission," *Public Culture* 20 (2008): 119–141.

49. Erik Doxtader, "The Faith and Struggle of Beginning (with) Words: On the Turn between Reconciliation and Recognition," *Philosophy & Rhetoric* 40 (2007): 119–146.

50. Laurajane Smith discovered similar concerns about black British visitors to museum displays about slavery: "Negative engagement tended to manifest itself in criticisms of the exhibitions/museums they were visiting for failing to offer fuller recognition, or offering

what were considered sanitized views of the history" ("Affect and Registers of Engagement: Navigating Emotional Responses to Dissonant Heritages," in *Representing Enslavement and Abolition in Museums: Ambiguous Engagements,* ed. Laurajane Smith, Geoffrey Cubitt, Ross Wilson, and Kalliopi Fouseki [New York: Routledge, 2011], 271).

51. Nathan K. Austin, "Managing Heritage Attractions: Marketing Challenges at Sensitive Historical Sites," *International Journal of Tourism Research* 4 (2002): 453.

52. Derek H. Alderman, "Surrogation and the Politics of Remembering Slavery in Savannah, Georgia," *Journal of Historical Geography* 36 (2010): 94; Ron Eyerman, *Cultural Trauma: Slavery and the Formation of African American Identity* (Cambridge, UK: Cambridge University Press, 2001), 16; James Oliver Horton, "Slavery in American History: An Uncomfortable National Dialogue," in *Slavery and Public History: The Tough Stuff of American Memory,* ed. James Oliver Horton and Lois E. Horton (New York: New Press, 2006), 49–53; Roy Rosenzweig and David Thelen, *The Presence of the Past: Popular Uses of History in American Life* (New York: Columbia University Press, 1998), 10.

53. Foote, *Shadowed Ground,* 8.

54. Thomas Carlyle, *On Heroes, Hero-Worship, and the Heroic in History: Six Lectures; Reported, with Emendations and Additions* (New York: D. Appleton, 1841).

55. Stephan Salisbury, "Remaking History," *Philadelphia Inquirer,* June 30, 2008, available at http://www.ushistory.org/presidentshouse/news/inq063008.htm.

56. *General Management Plan,* INHP, 1997, 26, 28, 310.

57. David G. McCullough, *John Adams* (New York: Simon and Schuster, 2001), and *1776* (New York: Simon and Schuster, 2005).

58. Inga Saffron, "A Historic Site That Has Defied Designers," *Changing Skyline,* September 8, 2006, available at http://www.ushistory.org/presidentshouse/news/inq090806.htm.

59. Condit, "Hegemony in a Mass-Mediated Society," 211–212.

60. To determine which designs were most popular among the voting population, I conducted a frequencies analysis of each response in the first two items (Overall Impression and Reflects All Inhabitants) on all 994 cards. I assigned a 1–4 numerical scale, in which "1" was the most positive response category, in place of the verbal categories so that a mean score could be calculated for each item on every design. In addition, I counted the number of positive evaluations (1's or 2's) for each design model in items one and two.

61. All quotes are from letters dated November 7, 2006, and sent to the three design teams by Richard Tustin, director of the city of Philadelphia's Capital Program Office. Tustin also alerted each of the three teams to changes in the park's security procedures for entering the LBC; according to Tustin's letter, those changes meant "that nearly every visitor to the Liberty Bell Center will pass through at least a portion of the President's House commemoration." Letters obtained on appeal of a FOIA request submitted to the NPS and Department of the Interior.

62. Two members of the Oversight Committee told me that committee members agreed to keep their preferences to themselves. Nevertheless, I discovered that, in e-mail exchanges during this time period, two members of the committee shared their preferences in that venue. One ranked Kelly/Maiello first, Davis Buckley second, and Howard+Revis third; the other had Davis Buckley first, Howard+Revis second, and Kelly/Maiello third. I have no way of knowing if these preferences were reflected in those members' final evaluations.

63. Ted Qualli, "Finalist Team for President's House Selected: Joint Press Release from the City of Philadelphia and Independence National Historical Park," February 27, 2007, available at http://www.ushistory.org/presidentshouse/news/pr022707.htm.

64. Cloud, "Hegemony or Concordance?" 118.

65. Marcus Anthony Hunter, *Black Citymakers: How the Philadelphia Negro Changed Urban America* (Oxford: Oxford University Press, 2013), 8.

66. In Cynthia Burton, "Street Touts His Record on Rights; He Reminded an NAACP Gathering of High-Ranking Positions Held by Minorities in His Administration," *Philadelphia Inquirer,* April 14, 2013, available at LexisNexis, accessed October 1, 2013.

67. See http://www.ushistory.org/presidentshouse/controversy/october_30_2004_report .htm.

68. See http://avengingtheancestors.com/releases/r2.htm.

69. In Kenny Waters, "Memorial Hearing Offers Lessons," *Philadelphia Tribune,* June 6, 2006, available at http://www.ushistory.org/presidentshouse/news/pt061206.htm.

70. *Philadelphia Inquirer* columnist Tom Ferrick, Jr., analyzed five years' worth of city construction jobs and discovered that the union laborers on those projects were 80 percent white and 70 percent of them lived outside the city ("Why the Unions Won't Share," *Philadelphia Inquirer,* January 6, 2008, C5). Mayor Street's successor used the phrase "economic apartheid" to refer to these conditions when he spoke at a union hall on December 18, 2007; Mayor Michael Nutter pushed City Council to demand more diverse representation among unions that worked on city-funded projects (in Jane M. Von Bergen, "Leaders Rally for Diversity of Labor," *Philadelphia Inquirer,* December 19, 2007, available at http://articles.philly .com/2007-12-19/news/25226830_1_project-labor-agreement-union-hall-diversity-plans).

71. In Linn Washington, Jr., "Op-Ed: Black Architects Face a Wall of Exclusion," *Philadelphia Tribune,* November 4, 2003, available at http://www.ushistory.org/presidentshouse/ news/pt110403.htm.

72. Ibid.

73. An audio recording of the meeting is available at http://www.ushistory.org/presidents house/news/ph060506.htm.

74. In discussion with the author, via e-mail, May 22, 2013.

75. Letter dated July 27, 2006, from Alice A. Dommert, Stuart Appel, and Thomas W. Nason III to Mayor John Street, James Lowe (of the city of Philadelphia's Capital Program Office), and the members of the Oversight Committee, obtained on appeal of a FOIA request submitted to the NPS and Department of the Interior.

76. Condit, "Hegemony in a Mass-Mediated Society," 210.

CHAPTER 6

1. Jed Levin, in discussion with the author, January 23, 2014.

2. See http://www.ushistory.org/presidentshouse/inhp_cached/lbe02.htm, which contains an undated INHP briefing paper on the President's House and LBC.

3. See http://www.phila.gov/presidentshouse/pdfs/PHS%20Archeology%20Brief ing%20Paper.pdf.

4. Stephan Salisbury, "Should President's House Findings Stay on View? Should Memorial Proceed?" *Philadelphia Inquirer,* June 3, 2007, available at http://www.ushistory.org/ presidentshouse/news/inq060307.htm; "First Finds from Archeological Dig of the President's House," INHP and City of Philadelphia press release, May 2, 2007, available at http://www .ushistory.org/presidentshouse/news/pr050207.htm.

5. See a story written by the AP's Rubina Madan as it appeared in the *Washington Post* on June 7, 2007 ("Slave Passage Found at Washington House"), available at http://www .washingtonpost.com/wp-dyn/content/article/2007/06/07/AR2007060701655.html. The second paragraph of the story features the incorrect statement that the passageway "was

designed so Washington's guests would not see slaves as they slipped in and out of the main house." The passageway's existence likely predated Washington's stay, given that the home's previous tenants would also have used servant and/or slave labor and such passageways were fairly common in larger homes of the time. Nonetheless, its symbolic power was immense: "[The passageway] seemed to suggest that a man whose name is synonymous with probity was trying to deceive both his neighbors and history about his deep involvement with the peculiar institution of slavery" (Philip Kennicott, "Plain as Dirt: History without Gimmickry," *Washington Post,* July 4, 2007, available at http://www.ushistory.org/presidentshouse/news/wp070407.htm).

6. Inga Saffron, "Let's Not Throw Dirt on the City's History," *Philadelphia Inquirer,* May 25, 2007, available at http://www.ushistory.org/presidentshouse/news/inq052507.htm.

7. In discussion with the author, July 3, 2013.

8. The excavated area covered only a portion of the footprint of the house. According to the brief written, largely by Levin, in advance of the excavation, the excavation site was selected to minimize problems in a number of areas (see http://www.ushistory.org/presidents house/plans/arch.htm):

> The area delineated was drawn to maximize the research potential of the study while minimizing disruption and possible damage to critical existing infrastructure. The area that encompasses the main house, as well as the north end of the yard to the east, has been excluded from the recommended study area. In the discussion, above, the research potential of possible foundations of the main house was found to be minimal. In addition, excavation of the northern portion of this area would require excavation under the existing Market Street sidewalk. This would necessitate closing most or all of the width of the sidewalk to pedestrian traffic during the period of excavation and site restoration.
>
> The southern end of the President's House site is excluded from the study area because it is situated under or directly adjacent to the LBC buildings or its exterior piers. Excavation of these areas would impede access to the LBC and might compromise the structural integrity of the building. An engineering study will be needed in order to determine with certainty how close excavation can safely come to the building; the southern boundary of the possible study area might have to be adjusted accordingly.
>
> The area within the recommended study area includes approximately 45% of the previously unexcavated yard areas which are believed to have existed on the President's House site. The former yard areas are the locations within which there is the highest potential to uncover shaft features dating to the President's House period. In addition, this area includes the location of the bath house. As noted above, this is the only building extension which seems at all likely to have had a basement and corresponding foundation which might have survived twentieth century construction activities.

9. Gavin Lucas, "Destruction and the Rhetoric of Excavation," *Norwegian Archaeological Review* 34 (2001): 40.

10. In discussion with the author, January 23, 2014.

11. Regan Toomer, "Digging Begins on Mall," *Philadelphia Tribune,* March 23, 2007, available at http://www.ushistory.org/presidentshouse/news/pt032307.htm.

12. Cheryl LaRoche, "Public History at Sites of Protest: Citizenship on the President's House Viewing Platform," *Cross Ties/Mid-Atlantic Regional Center for the Humanities,* Fall 2007, available at http://www.ushistory.org/presidentshouse/news/ctfall07.htm.

13. All are quoted in Niko Koppel, "A Country's Past Is Unearthed, and Comes into Focus," *The New York Times,* July 4, 2007, available at http://www.ushistory.org/presidents house/news/nyt070407.htm.

14. Unless otherwise noted, quotes from visitors are culled from the IHA website: http://www.ushistory.org/presidentshouse/guests.asp (hereafter cited as IHA website).

15. The allure of the excavation exemplifies Rosenzweig and Thelen's discovery that Americans have a "desire for unmediated experience" of the past (Roy Rosenzweig and David Thelen, *The Presence of the Past: Popular Uses of History in American Life* [New York: Columbia University Press, 1998], 22).

16. James E. Young, *The Texture of Memory: Holocaust Memorials and Meaning* (New Haven, CT: Yale University Press, 1993), 119.

17. Michael Mayerfeld Bell, "The Ghosts of Place," *Theory and Society* 26 (1997): 813.

18. Ibid., 815.

19. Benjamin Hannavy Cousen, "Memory, Power and Place: Where Is *Guernica?*" *Journal of Romance Studies* 9 (2009): 59.

20. Sonja Kuftinec, "[Walking through a] Ghost Town: Cultural Hauntologie in Mostar, Bosnia-Herzegovina or Mostar: A Performance Review," *Text & Performance Quarterly* 18 (1998): 83.

21. Erika Doss (*Memorial Mania: Public Feeling in America* [Chicago: University of Chicago Press, 2012]) observed: "The 'presence' of absence is a dominant metaphor in memorial mania" (143). Moreover, the phrase "absent presence" is used frequently by scholars who talk about the lingering sensations, memories, and traces of the past in our daily lives. See, for example, Avery F. Gordon, *Ghostly Matters: Haunting and the Sociological Imagination* (Minneapolis: University of Minnesota Press, 1997); Tim Edensor, "Mundane Hauntings: Commuting through the Phantasmagoric Working-Class Spaces of Manchester, England," *Cultural Geographies* 15 (2008): 313–333; Brian L. Ott, Eric Aoki, and Greg Dickinson, "Ways of (Not) Seeing Guns: Presence and Absence at the Cody Firearms Museum," *Communication and Critical/Cultural Studies* 8 (2011): 215–239; Caroline Chung Simpson, *An Absent Presence: Japanese Americans in Postwar American Culture, 1945–1960* (Durham, NC: Duke University Press, 2001); and Marita Sturken, "Absent Images of Memory: Remembering and Reenacting the Japanese Internment," *positions* 5 (1997): 687–707.

22. Edensor, "Mundane Hauntings," 330.

23. Jacques Derrida, *Specters of Marx: The State of the Debt, the Work of Mourning, and the New International,* trans. Peggy Kamuf (New York: Routledge, 1994).

24. Warren Montag, "Spirits Armed and Unarmed: Derrida's *Specters of Marx,*" in *Ghostly Demarcations: A Symposium on Jacques Derrida's* Specters of Marx, ed. Michael Sprinkler (London: Verso, 2008), 71. See also, in the same book, Jacques Derrida, "Marx & Sons," 213–269. First version published 1999 by Verso.

25. Simpson, *Absent Presence,* 11. Haunting is by no means a new way of describing the idea of absent presences. See, for example, Edensor, "Mundane Hauntings"; Karen A. Foss and Kathy L. Domenici, "Haunting Argentina: Synecdoche in the Protests of the Mothers of the Plaza de Mayo," *Quarterly Journal of Speech* 87 (2001): 237–258; Gordon, *Ghostly Matters;* Joshua Gunn, "Review Essay: Mourning Humanism, or, the Idiom of Haunting," *Quarterly Journal of Speech* 92 (2006): 77–102; Joshua Gunn, "Mourning Speech: Haunting and the Spectral Voices of Nine-Eleven," *Text & Performance Quarterly* 24 (2004): 91–114; Gabriele Schwab, *Haunting Legacies: Violent Histories and Transgenerational Trauma* (New York: Columbia University Press, 2010); and Kevin T. Jones, Kenneth S. Zagacki, and Todd V. Lewis, "Communication, Liminality, and Hope: The September 11th Missing Person Posters," *Communication Studies* 58 (2007): 105–121.

26. Michele Kennerly, "Getting Carried Away: How Rhetorical Transport Gets Judgment Going," *Rhetoric Society Quarterly* 40 (2010): 269.

27. Ned O'Gorman, "Aristotle's *Phantasia* in the *Rhetoric: Lexis*, Appearance, and the Epideictic Function of Discourse," *Philosophy & Rhetoric* 38 (2005): 17.

28. Martha C. Nussbaum, *Aristotle's* De Motu Animalium (Princeton, NJ: Princeton University Press, 1978), 244.

29. Kennerly ("Getting Carried Away") writes about Quintilian's version of phantasia; a discussion of Longinus's version can be found in Shadi Bartsch, "'Wait a Moment, Phantasia': Ekphrastic Interference in Seneca and Epictetus," *Classical Philology* 102 (2007): 83–95.

30. Nussbaum, *Aristotle's* De Motu Animalium, 222.

31. See, for example, Victor Caston, "Why Aristotle Needs Imagination," *Phronesis* 41 (1996) 20–55; Dan Flory, "Stoic Psychology, Classical Rhetoric, and Theories of Imagination in Western Philosophy," *Philosophy & Rhetoric* 29 (1996): 147–167; José M. González, "The Meaning and Function of Phantasia in Aristotle's *Rhetoric* III.1," *Transactions of the American Philological Association* 136 (2006): 99–131; and O'Gorman, "Aristotle's *Phantasia*."

32. Chaim Perelman and Lucie Olbrechts-Tyteca, *The New Rhetoric: A Treatise on Argumentation*, trans. John Wilkinson and Purcell Weaver (Notre Dame, IN: University of Notre Dame Press, 1969).

33. Robert E. Tucker, "Figure, Ground and Presence: A Phenomenology of Meaning in Rhetoric," *Quarterly Journal of Speech* 87 (2001): 397. See also Alan G. Gross, "Presence as Argument in the Public Sphere," *Rhetoric Society Quarterly* 35, no. 2 (2005): 5–21.

34. See, for example, Gross, "Presence as Argument," 7.

35. John Brinkerhoff Jackson, *The Necessity for Ruins and Other Topics* (Amherst: University of Massachusetts Press, 1980), 91.

36. Saffron, "Let's Not Throw Dirt."

37. Louise A. Karon, "Presence in *The New Rhetoric*," *Philosophy & Rhetoric* 9 (1976): 107.

38. Carole Blair, Greg Dickinson, and Brian Ott, "Introduction: Rhetoric/Memory/Place," in *Places of Public Memory: The Rhetoric of Museums and Memorials*, ed. Greg Dickinson, Carole Blair, and Brian L. Ott (Tuscaloosa: University of Alabama Press, 2010); see also Michael S. Bowman, "Tracing Mary Queen of Scots," in *Places of Public Memory: The Rhetoric of Museums and Memorials*, ed. Greg Dickinson, Carole Blair, and Brian L. Ott (Tuscaloosa: University of Alabama Press, 2010), 191–215.

39. See, for example, Bernard J. Armada, "Memorial Agon: An Interpretive Tour of the National Civil Rights Museum," *Southern Communication Journal* 63 (1998): 235–243; Greg Dickinson, Brian L. Ott, and Eric Aoki, "Memory and Myth at the Buffalo Bill Museum," *Western Journal of Communication* 69 (2005): 85–108; and Marouf Hasian, Jr., "Remembering and Forgetting the 'Final Solution': A Rhetorical Pilgrimage through the U.S. Holocaust Memorial Museum," *Critical Studies in Media Communication* 21 (2004): 64–92.

40. Catherine M. Cameron and John B. Gatewood, "Excursions into the Un-remembered Past: What People Want from Visits to Historical Sites," *Public Historian* 22, no. 1 (2000): 123.

41. IHA website.

42. Ibid.

43. Inga Saffron, "Cover Up at the President's House," *Skyline Online,* July 25, 2007, available at http://www.ushistory.org/presidentshouse/news/so072507.htm.

44. IHA website.

45. Ibid.

46. Karon, "Presence," 97.

47. Henry Home, Lord Kames, *Elements of Criticism,* 6th ed., ed. Peter Jones (Indianapolis: Liberty Fund, 2005), vol. 1. First published 1762 by A. Millar, A. Kincaid, and J. Bell.

48. Ibid.

49. Eric Rothstein argued that Kames's position outlined how audiences participated in "an imaginative expansion of the text . . . [that] was by no means exclusively visual" ("'Ideal Presence' and the 'Non Finito' in Eighteenth-Century Aesthetics," *Eighteenth-Century Studies* 9 [1976]: 310). Similarly, Victor Caston suggested that phantasia possesses auditory dimensions because it works as an imaginative echo. "Phantasia," he wrote, "is, in effect, an echoing of the initial stimulation in the sense organs" ("Why Aristotle Needs Imagination," 47).

50. Rothstein, "Ideal Presence," 312. See also Nussbaum, *Aristotle's* De Motu Animalium.

51. Catherine M. Cameron and John B. Gatewood, "Seeking Numinous Experiences in the Unremembered Past," *Ethnology* 42 (2003): 55–71.

52. John B. Gatewood and Catherine M. Cameron, "Battlefield Pilgrims at Gettysburg National Military Park," *Ethnology* 43 (2004): 208. Alison J. McIntosh and Richard C. Prentice ("Affirming Authenticity: Consuming Cultural Heritage," *Annals of Tourism Research* 26 [1999]: 589–612) also discovered through interviews that "tourists at heritage attractions assist in the production of their own experiences through their imaginations, emotions, and thought processes" (607).

53. Rosenzweig and Thelen, *Presence,* 12.

54. Ibid., 106.

55. My linking of phantasia with imagination is more closely connected with a Stoic interpretation of phantasia, although it is not inconsistent with Aristotle's treatment of the concept. Flory ("Stoic Psychology") offered a thoughtful account of the Stoics' conceptualization of phantasia, perhaps best summarized in this line: "Phantasia, in other words, can produce what the senses have never experienced, but the mind has conceived" (150). In the case of the President's House foundation remains, viewers experienced the sight of the remains and imagined the activities that occurred within the structure.

56. In Julie Shaw, "Historic Dig Drawing a Crowd," *Philadelphia Daily News,* May 4, 2007, available at http://www.ushistory.org/presidentshouse/news/dn050407.htm; my emphasis.

57. IHA website.

58. Gerald D. Klein, "Letter: Live the History," *Philadelphia Inquirer,* May 24, 2007, available at http://www.ushistory.org/presidentshouse/news/inq2052407.htm.

59. Ibid.

60. See, for example, Armada, "Memorial Agon"; Hasian, "Remembering and Forgetting."

61. In Annette John-Hall, "Slavery in Phila. Is Her Obsession," *Philadelphia Inquirer,* June 1, 2007, available at http://www.ushistory.org/presidentshouse/news/inq060107.htm; my emphasis.

62. In Shaw, "Historic Dig."

63. At one point, Hercules was thought to have escaped from the President's House. Later research concluded that he escaped from Mount Vernon—on Washington's sixty-fifth birthday. See Edward Lawler, Jr., "Hercules," available at http://www.ushistory.org/presidentshouse/slaves/hercules.htm.

64. IHA website.

65. Ibid.

66. Ibid.

67. In Stephan Salisbury, "Slavery Laid Bare: A Historic Platform for Dialogue on Race," *Philadelphia Inquirer,* May 20, 2007, available at http://www.ushistory.org/presidentshouse/news/inq052007.htm.

68. Robert Miles, "The Eye of Power: Ideal Presence and Gothic Romance," *Gothic Studies* 1 (1999): 15.

69. Kimberly Wedeven Segall, "Pursuing Ghosts: The Traumatic Sublime in J. M. Coetzee's *Disgrace,*" *Research in African Literatures* 36, no. 4 (2005): 41.

70. Ibid. 42.

71. Elizabethada A. Wright, "Rhetorical Spaces in Memory Places: The Cemetery as a Rhetorical Memory Place/Space," *Rhetoric Society Quarterly* 35, no. 4 (2005): 70.

72. I borrow this idea from Robert Hariman and John Louis Lucaites, "Public Identity and Collective Memory in U.S. Iconic Photography: The Image of 'Accidental Napalm,'" *Critical Studies in Media Communication* 20 (2003): 55.

73. In Salisbury, "Slavery Laid Bare."

74. Ronnie Polaneczky, "Trying to Get It Right, the 'Philly' Way," *Philadelphia Daily News,* July 3, 2007, available at http://www.ushistory.org/presidentshouse/news/dn070307.htm.

75. In Valerie Russ, "At President's House Dig, 'We Get a Lot of Tears,'" *Philadelphia Daily News,* July 31, 2007, available at http://www.ushistory.org/presidentshouse/news/dn073107.htm.

76. Segall, "Pursuing Ghosts," 42. In addition, Schwab (*Haunting Legacies*) observed that "most cultures share a tendency to silence traumatic histories. Traumatic amnesia seems to become inscribed as cultural practice. Yet trauma can never be completely silenced since its effects continue to operate unconsciously" (79).

77. Dylan Trigg, *The Memory of Place: A Phenomenology of the Uncanny* (Athens: Ohio University Press, 2012), 270.

78. Segall, "Pursuing Ghosts," 51.

79. Ibid.

80. IHA website.

81. Ibid.

82. Ibid.

83. Saffron, "Cover Up."

84. See Armada, "Memorial Agon."

85. Victoria J. Gallagher and Kenneth S. Zagacki, "Visibility and Rhetoric: Epiphanies and Transformations in the *Life* Photographs of the Selma Marches of 1965," *Rhetoric Society Quarterly* 37 (2007): 113–135; Christine Harold and Kevin Michael DeLuca, "Behold the Corpse: Violent Images and the Case of Emmett Till," *Rhetoric & Public Affairs* 8 (2005): 263–286.

86. Hariman and Lucaites, "Public Identity," 60.

87. IHA website.

88. In Salisbury, "Slavery Laid Bare."

89. Michael J. Hyde, "Acknowledgement, Conscience, Rhetoric, and Teaching: The Case of *Tuesdays with Morrie,*" *Rhetoric Society Quarterly* 35, no. 2 (2005): 26.

90. Ibid., 26.

91. In discussion with the author, October 11, 2012.

92. In discussion with the author, March 7, 2011.

93. In discussion with the author, October 1, 2013.

94. LaRoche, "Public History."

95. See, for example, Carole Blair and Neil Michel, "The AIDS Memorial Quilt and the

Contemporary Culture of Public Commemoration," *Rhetoric & Public Affairs* 10 (2007): 595–626, and Barry Schwartz and Todd Bayma, "Commemoration and the Politics of Recognition," *American Behavioral Scientist* 42 (1999): 946–967

96. Schwartz and Bayma, "Commemoration," 949.

97. See, for example, Cheryl R. Jorgenson-Earp and Lori A. Lanzilotti, "Public Memory and Private Grief: The Construction of Shrines at the Sites of Public Tragedy," *Quarterly Journal of Speech* 84 (1998): 150–170.

98. See, for example, Jack E. Davis, "A Struggle for Public History: Black and White Claims to Natchez's Past," *The Public Historian* 22, no. 1 (2000): 45–63; Greg Dickinson, Brian L. Ott, and Eric Aoki, "Spaces of Remembering and Forgetting: The Reverent Eye/I at the Plains Indian Museum," *Communication and Critical Cultural Studies* 3 (2006): 27–47; Kenneth E. Foote, *Shadowed Ground: America's Landscapes of Violence and Tragedy* (Austin: University of Texas Press, 1997); and Roseann M. Mandziuk, "Commemorating Sojourner Truth: Negotiating the Politics of Race and Gender in Spaces of Public Memory," *Western Journal of Communication* 67 (2003): 271–291.

99. Segall, "Pursuing Ghosts," 42.

100. Hariman and Lucaites, "Public Identity," 62.

101. In Koppel, "Country's Past."

102. Roger I. Simon, "A Shock to Thought: Curatorial Judgment and the Public Exhibition of 'Difficult Knowledge,'" *Memory Studies* 9. Prepublished February 21, 2011, available at http://mss.sagepub.com/content/early/2011/02/18/1750698011398170.full.pdf.

103. IHA website.

104. In Koppel, "Country's Past."

105. See http://www.philly.com/philly/news/special_packages/inquirer/Tell_us__What_should_be_done_with_the_President_s_House_site_.html.

106. Jeffrey K. Olick, "Collective Memory: The Two Cultures," *Sociological Theory* 17 (1999): 345.

107. Steven Conn, *Metropolitan Philadelphia: Living with the Presence of the Past* (Philadelphia: University of Pennsylvania Press, 2006), 114.

108. "Ad Hoc Historians' Letter to the Mayor and to the Superintendent of INHP," June 27, 2007, available at http://www.ushistory.org/presidentshouse/controversy/adhocs_062707.htm.

109. IHA website.

110. See http://www.philly.com/philly/news/special_packages/inquirer/Tell_us__What_should_be_done_with_the_President_s_House_site_.html.

111. In "The President's House: Freedom and Slavery in the Making of a New Nation," available at http://www.youtube.com/watch?feature=player_embedded&v =ZPxu2z2 GEcc.

112. Rosalyn McPherson, project manager for the President's House installation, in discussion with the author, July 3, 2013. McPherson told me that architects, like artists, feel attached to their original visions and are reluctant to alter them.

113. "Meeting Minutes—PRIORITY Oversight Committee Meeting," minutes dated June 14, 2007 (meeting occurred on June 5, 2007). Made available through a FOIA request submitted to the NPS and Department of the Interior.

114. *Evaluation of Alternatives for Incorporating Archaeological Fragments in the Design*, November 7, 2007, proposal developed by Kelly/Maiello; received by the author through a FOIA request submitted to the NPS and Department of the Interior.

115. "A Fitting and Conflicted Memorial," *Philadelphia Inquirer,* December 19, 2007, available at http://www.ushistory.org/presidentshouse/news/inq121907.htm.

116. "A fundraising event held in September 2008 yielded $200,000 in grants from Bank of America, PECO and PNC Bank and pledges from a number of private donors, including Bernard Smalley, Christopher Lewis, Denise Smyler, Manuel Stamatakis and William Sasso" ("Governor Rendell Recommends DRPA Funding for Completion of President's House Site," available at http://www.ushistory.org/presidentshouse/news/pa012109.htm).

117. Paul Nussbaum, "DRPA OKs $11 Million for Six Projects," *Philadelphia Inquirer*, February 19, 2009, available at http://www.ushistory.org/presidentshouse/news/inq021909.htm.

CHAPTER 7

1. A copy of the letter is available at http://www.ushistory.org/presidentshouse/controversy/iha3.htm.

2. Stephan Salisbury, "President's House Design Criticized," *Philadelphia Inquirer*, August 20, 2009, available at http://www.ushistory.org/presidentshouse/news/inq082009.htm.

3. Michael Coard, "President's House Must Be Practical, Too," *Philadelphia Inquirer*, August 31, 2009, available at http://www.ushistory.org/presidentshouse/news/inq083109.htm.

4. E-mails between Cynthia MacLeod and Rosalyn McPherson on August 17, September 25, and September 28, 2009, obtained through a FOIA request submitted to the NPS and Department of the Interior.

5. "President's House Oversight Committee Meets to Resolve Design Controversy," September 21, 2009, available at http://www.ushistory.org/presidentshouse/news/pr092109.htm. Despite the title of the release, individuals in addition to the Oversight Committee were present at the meeting.

6. In Carolyn Davis, "Opening of President's House Pushed Back," *Philadelphia Inquirer*, December 25, 2009, available at http://www.ushistory.org/presidentshouse/news/inq122509.htm.

7. Eric Mayes, "How to Tell the Story?" *Philadelphia Tribune*, November 21, 2009, available at http://www.ushistory.org/presidentshouse/news/pt112109.htm.

8. In discussion with the author, September 5, 2013. According to Nash, Rabinowitz "selected a board of advisors, convened them once, then never showed them the deeply flawed interpretive script he developed."

9. Minutes of the Oversight Committee meeting of December 12, 2008, obtained through a FOIA request submitted to the NPS and Department of the Interior.

10. In discussion with the author, October 11, 2012. According to the minutes of Oversight Committee meetings obtained through a FOIA request submitted to the NPS and Department of the Interior, Sitarski also encouraged the committee to recognize inhabitants of the house before its use as the executive mansion.

11. Project manager Rosalyn McPherson, in discussion with the author, July 3, 2013.

12. In discussion with the author, July 9, 2013.

13. Minutes of the Oversight Committee meetings of December 11 and December 18, 2009, obtained through a FOIA request submitted to the NPS and Department of the Interior.

14. Derek H. Alderman, "Surrogation and the Politics of Remembering Slavery in Savannah, Georgia," *Journal of Historical Geography* 36 (2010): 100.

15. Eisterhold Associates received glowing reviews from those I talked with about the project.

16. Stephan Salisbury, "Critics Denounce Plans for President's House," *Philadelphia Inquirer*, May 8, 2010, available at http://www.ushistory.org/presidentshouse/news/inq050810.htm.

17. In Linn Washington, Jr., "Facing Facts from Timbuktu to Center City," *Philadelphia Tribune*, May 11, 2010, available at http://www.ushistory.org/presidentshouse/news/

pt051110.htm. Blockson later argued in his book *The President's House Revisited behind the Scenes: The Samuel Fraunces Story* (Eubank, KY: Still Publications, 2013): "From the conception, I emphasized that I had no interest in the House of Bondage and that my interest pertained to creating a memorial to our African ancestors that displayed dignity, inspiration, the terror of slavery, and the rebellions against it" (220).

18. Rob Morris, "Come on Down to ~~Independence~~ Slavery Mall," *American Thinker,* May 25, 2010, available at http://www.ushistory.org/presidentshouse/news/at052510.htm.

19. Both Mary Jenkins and Steve Sitarski told me that they championed the use of concise interpretive material but were rebuffed.

20. Ken Finkel, "Smothered in Words," *Redbricker* blog, April 29, 2010, available at http://www.ushistory.org/presidentshouse/news/kf042910.htm.

21. E-mail to Ed Lawler, July 22, 2009, provided by the NPS and Department of the Interior through a FOIA request submitted to the NPS and Department of the Interior.

22. Rosalyn McPherson told me that her contract expired at the end of the year and that appropriations for the installation also were required to be spent by the end of 2010. In discussion with the author, July 3, 2013.

23. In discussion with the author, July 9, 2013.

24. Rosalyn McPherson, in discussion with the author, July 3, 2013.

25. INHP staff were largely tasked with editing during this period. Anna Coxe Toogood, INHP historian, in discussion with the author, August 21, 2013.

26. Mary Jenkins (April 12, 2012) and Rosalyn McPherson (July 3, 2013), in discussion with the author. Given that this "was a period of time with no sketches of people of color," McPherson noted, those working on the interpretation relied on descriptions of the enslaved found in letters. An African American artist working with Eisterhold Associates created the images of the enslaved featured on the glass panels. Geoffrey Cubitt, Laurajane Smith, and Ross Wilson identify "the persistent tendency of abolitionist imagery to cast the enslaved African as a passive victim—a submissive figure, imploring a freedom he or she can only receive through the benevolence of others" ("Introduction: Anxiety and Ambiguity in the Representation of Dissonant History," in *Representing Enslavement and Abolition in Museums: Ambiguous Engagements,* ed. Laurajane Smith, Geoffrey Cubitt, Ross Wilson, and Kalliopi Fouseki [New York: Routledge, 2011], 7). Kirk Savage (*Monument Wars: Washington, D.C., the National Mall, and the Transformation of the Memorial Landscape* [Berkeley: University of California Press, 2009]), provides a thorough account of perhaps the most well known of these kinds of images in the United States: the Freedmen's Memorial to Abraham Lincoln in Washington, D.C., which features "Lincoln standing with outstretched hand above a crouching slave whose chains have just been broken" (82).

27. Gary Nash, in discussion with the author, September 5, 2013. Nash, who was instrumental in the development of the glass panels, noted that "we created them as 'moments in time' in the 1790s that would bring alive the incredible tumult of the 1790s in the midst of the French and Haitian revolutions, the Whiskey Rebellion, the Alien and Sedition Acts, the Quasi War with France, Jay's Treaty, etc."

28. *Annual Report FY 2010,* Independence National Historical Park, Philadelphia, 18, available at http://www.nps.gov/inde/parkmgmt/upload/2010-Annual-Report.pdf.

29. Stephan Salisbury, "President's House—with Memorial to Enslaved Africans—Opens on Independence Mall," *Philadelphia Inquirer,* December 16, 2010, available at http://www.ushistory.org/presidentshouse/news/inq121610.htm, and Gary B. Nash, in discussion with the author, September 5, 2013.

30. In Salisbury, "President's House."

31. See http://avengingtheancestors.com/releases/coardspeech_121501.htm.

32. The video screens were all being replaced at the time of this writing. See Stephan Salisbury, "Faulty Video Screens at President's House Being Replaced," *Philadelphia Inquirer,* February 29, 2012, available at http://www.ushistory.org/presidentshouse/news/inq022912 .htm.

33. Michael J. Lewis, "Trashing the President's House," *Commentary,* April 2011, 62. The concerns among Oversight Committee members were raised in a November 6, 2008, meeting, according to the minutes from the meeting, obtained through a FOIA request submitted to the NPS and Department of the Interior.

34. Mary Jenkins, in discussion with the author, April 12, 2012.

35. See Lawler's biography of Judge, available at http://www.ushistory.org/presidents house/slaves/oney.htm.

36. The video scripts were written by Lorene Cary, author of several novels that feature the experiences of historical and contemporary African Americans. The videos were pro-duced by Philadelphia documentarian Louis Massiah.

37. Similarly, a photographic display of the excavation inside the Visitor Center noted, more than five months after the site was dedicated, "The National Park Service and the City of Philadelphia *plan to build* a permanent commemoration" across the street (my emphasis).

38. Minutes of the Oversight Committee meeting of August 28, 2007, obtained through a FOIA request submitted to the NPS and Department of the Interior.

39. In discussion with the author, July 9, 2013.

40. Steve Sitarski, who retired before the design process was complete, expressed surprise that no sign existed. He also told me that INHP was concerned that brochures on site would lead to litter and waste problems in the park. In addition, the park told stakeholders during the design process that it did not have the funding to staff the site.

41. Seth Bruggeman, "'The President's House: Freedom and Slavery in the Making of a New Nation,' Independence National Historical Park, Philadelphia, Pa.," exhibit review in *Journal of American History* 100 (2013): 157.

42. Posted by *Disappointed* on March 17, 2011, at http://www.ushistory.org/presidents house/guests.asp.

43. Lewis, "Trashing," 61.

44. See http://www.philadelphiaspeaks.com/forum/architecture-urban-planning/18773-presidents-house-independence-mall-4.html.

45. In discussion with the author, September 5, 2013.

46. In discussion with the author, July 3, 2013.

47. The park now offers a smartphone app with several interactive features.

48. After several unsuccessful attempts to visit with individuals within the site and in line for the LBC, I developed a more productive strategy: I purchased a lanyard at a nearby gift store, slid my university ID into it, and stood near the wayside marker so that I could watch people enter the site and see how much of the installation they perused before I ap-proached them with a request for "two minutes [an accurate approximation of the average in-terview's length] to answer a few questions for some research I am doing about the President's House site." I used the following protocol to select potential interviewees: first, individuals with children were not approached unless another adult in the group was watching the chil-dren; second, individuals were not approached until they had started to exit the site; third, individuals whose mannerisms or conversation with fellow travelers indicated that they were in a rush—typically to join the LBC line—were not approached; fourth, individuals were not approached unless they had moved through at least half the site, reaching the vitrine in the center, *and* had spent some time at another part of the site as well. I asked each interviewee three questions: (1) What was your impression of the site? (2) How well does the site fit with the rest of the park? (3) How would you describe the site to someone who hasn't been here?

Visitors were not asked for their names and thus remained anonymous. I did not mention the interpretation or design of the site except in occasional follow-up questions that sought to clarify the visitor's comments about either or both subjects. This interview procedure, including asking visitors if their remarks could be recorded, was approved by both my university's Institutional Review Board (IRB 10E-278) and the staff at INHP (Permit #INDE-12-10).

49. According to INHP park ranger Adam Duncan, of the park's Public Affairs Office (e-mail on July 8, 2011), 10,402 people visited the LBC on Saturday, May 28, and 12,345 people visited on Sunday, May 29.

50. Marita Sturken, "Absent Images of Memory: Remembering and Reenacting the Japanese Internment," *positions* 5 (1997): 703.

51. In Erika Doss, *Memorial Mania: Public Feeling in America* (Chicago: University of Chicago Press, 2012), 285.

52. Bruggeman, "President's House," 156.

53. Inga Saffron, "Brick Pile's Colliding Tales," *Changing Skyline,* December 17, 2010, available at http://www.ushistory.org/presidentshouse/news/inq121710.htm.

54. Edward Rothstein, "The President's House in Philadelphia," *The New York Times,* December 14, 2010, available at http://www.ushistory.org/presidentshouse/news/nyt121410.htm, and "Identity Museums Challenge History's Received Truths," *The New York Times,* December 28, 2010, available at http://www.ushistory.org/presidentshouse/news/nyt122810.htm.

55. Lewis, "Trashing," 61, 63, and 63.

56. Julia M. Klein, "President's House, Philadelphia: All the President's Men," *The Wall Street Journal,* January 4, 2011, available at http://www.ushistory.org/presidentshouse/news/wsj010411.htm.

57. Thom Nickels, "The Last Word," *Icon,* February 2011, available at http://www.ushistory.org/presidentshouse/news/icon0211.htm.

58. Chris Satullo, "President's House—A Redress of Grievances," December 17, 2010, available at http://www.newsworks.org/index.php/local/centre-square/9471 presidents-house-a-redress-of-grievances.

59. A. Bruce Crawley, "Crawley: President's House Project Just a First Step," *Philadelphia Tribune,* January 8, 2011, available at http://www.ushistory.org/presidentshouse/news/pt010811.htm.

60. "President's House: A Powerful Symbol," *Philadelphia Tribune,* December 16, 2010, available at http://www.ushistory.org/presidentshouse/news/pt121610a.htm.

61. Doss, *Memorial Mania.*

62. In discussion with the author, October 1, 2013.

63. Michel Foucault, "Of Other Spaces," trans. Jay Miskowiec, *diacritics* 16 (1986): 24.

64. Ibid.

65. Kevin Hetherington, *The Badlands of Modernity: Heterotopia and Social Ordering* (Routledge: London, 1997), 49.

66. Hetherington, *Badlands,* viii, 42, 42, 50, and 50. Some scholars have noted that heterotopia also may discipline or constrain the possibility of alternative orders while suggesting the possible enactment of those orders. See, for example, Andrew F. Wood, "Managing the Lady Managers: The Shaping of Heterotopian Spaces in the 1893 Chicago Exposition's Woman's Building," *Southern Communication Journal* 69 (2004): 289–302.

67. Brent Allen Saindon also used the notion of heterotopia in his analysis of a difficult memory site: the Jewish Museum Berlin: "A Doubled Heterotopia: Shifting Spatial and Visual Symbolism in the Jewish Museum Berlin's Development," *Quarterly Journal of Speech* 98 (2012): 24–48. See also Elizabethada A. Wright, "Rhetorical Spaces in Memory Places:

The Cemetery as a Rhetorical Memory Place/Space," *Rhetoric Society Quarterly* 35, no. 4 (2005): 51–81.

68. Foucault, "Of Other Spaces," 25.

69. Ibid., 26.

70. See Carole Blair, Marsha S. Jeppeson, and Enrico Pucci, Jr., "Public Memorializing in Postmodernity: The Vietnam Veterans Memorial as Prototype," *Quarterly Journal of Speech* 77 (1991): 263–288, for example.

71. Hetherington, *Badlands,* ix.

72. Ibid., 50.

73. Kenneth Burke, *Permanence and Change: An Anatomy of Purpose,* 3rd ed. (Berkeley: University of California Press, 1984), lv.

74. Ibid., 76.

75. Naomi R. Rockler, "'It's Just Entertainment'—Perspective by Incongruity as Strategy for Media Literacy," *Journal of Popular Film and Television* 30, no. 1 (2002): 16–22.

76. In discussion with the author, October 1, 2013.

77. Maoz Azaryahu and Kenneth Foote explore "the spatial configuration of history—the way historical stories are arranged to be told in space to produce what we term 'spatial narratives' of history" (180). The President's House comes closest to their *hybrid* category, but their focus on stories told about events does not mesh well with the more topic-oriented interpretation at the President's House. See "Historical Space as Narrative Medium: On the Configuration of Spatial Narratives of Time at Historical Sites," *GeoJournal* 73 (2008): 179–194.

As I demonstrate how juxtapositions take shape within the site of the President's House, I rely on nineteen hours of fieldwork completed over Memorial Day weekend in 2011. During this time, I observed thousands of visitors to the park who encountered the site, interviewed eighty-two visitors who spent a significant amount of time within the installation, studied the design and interpretation of the site from a rhetorical perspective, and documented the audio and visual dimensions of the site through digital recording and photography, respectively.

78. Derek H. Alderman and Rachel M. Campbell ("Symbolic Excavation and the Artifact Politics of Remembering Slavery in the American South: Observations from Walterboro, South Carolina," *Southeastern Geographer* 48 [2008]: 338–355) also address the importance of control or ownership of what is represented in a memory site devoted to a discussion of slavery. Elsewhere Alderman ("Surrogation") explains that such sites perform *surrogation,* which occurs when "societies create commemorative surrogates to fill the voids in memory and identity left open by slavery" (91).

79. All panel titles are reported as they appear at the site, even when the grammar is inconsistent with traditional usage and usage in other panel titles.

80. Gary Nash, who was involved in the writing of the panels, argued that Adams lost his bid for reelection because his policies divided the nation. In discussion with the author, September 5, 2013.

81. Jennifer L. Eichstedt and Stephen Small, *Representations of Slavery: Race and Ideology in Southern Plantation Museums* (Washington, DC: Smithsonian Institution Press, 2002), 266.

82. Doris Devine Fanelli, *Consensus Document from the President's House Roundtable,* available at http://www.ushistory.org/presidentshouse/controversy/consensus.htm.

83. *President's House Civic Engagement Forum,* available at http://www.ushistory.org/presidentshouse/controversy/october_30_2004_report.htm.

84. Doris Devine Fanelli, "History, Commemoration, and an Interdisciplinary Approach to Interpreting the President's House Site," *Pennsylvania Magazine of History and Biography* 129 (2005): 453 and 455.

85. "Narratives," asserted Gareth Hoskins, "should be examined for the work they do as well as what they represent" (260). See "A Secret Reservoir of Values: The Narrative Economy of Angel Island Immigration Station," *Cultural Geographies* 17 (2010): 259–275.

86. Roy Rosenzweig and David Thelen (*The Presence of the Past: Popular Uses of History in American Life* [New York: Columbia University Press, 1998]) discovered, in fact, that African Americans "sometimes use [their] collective pasts to construct the sort of progressive narratives—history with a capital 'H'—that seem harder to find among white Americans" (149). Dana Cloud ("Hegemony or Concordance? The Rhetoric of Tokenism in 'Oprah' Winfrey's Rags-to-Riches Biography," *Critical Studies in Mass Communication* 13 [1996]: 115–137) argues, however, that narratives of individual accomplishment—what she calls "the rhetoric of tokenism" (her subject was Oprah Winfrey)—contribute to the continuing neglect of the structural impediments to widespread progress (119).

87. Doss, *Memorial Mania,* 294–295.

88. The John Brown Museum in Harpers Ferry National Historical Park also contains a timeline of slavery in the United States.

89. See Gary Nash's *First City: Philadelphia and the Forging of Historical Memory* (Philadelphia: University of Pennsylvania Press, 2002) and *Forging Freedom: The Formation of Philadelphia's Black Community, 1720–1840* (Cambridge, MA: Harvard University Press, 1988) for extensive discussions of African American history in Philadelphia.

90. Ron Eyerman, *Cultural Trauma: Slavery and the Formation of African American Identity* (Cambridge, UK: Cambridge University Press, 2001), 16.

91. See http://www.nps.gov/inde/second-bank.htm.

92. See http://www.nps.gov/inde/congress-hall.htm.

93. See http://www.nps.gov/inde/parknews/germantown-white-house-to-open-for-commemoration-of-the-battle-of-germantown.htm.

94. Even the high-traffic Visitor Center has a large alcove area in which museum-like displays are offered.

95. Stephan Salisbury, "Problems Still Plague Philadelphia's President's House Memorial," *Philadelphia Inquirer,* August 20, 2012, available at http://articles.philly.com/2012-08-20/news/33273307_1_maiello-architects-planners-memorial-site-ancestors-coalition.

96. In a November 7, 2006, letter to Emanuel Kelly, the director of the city of Philadelphia's Capital Program Office, Richard Tustin, wrote, "There is a concern that much of the subtlety of your audio interpretation could be lost in the street noise of the location." Letter obtained on appeal of a FOIA request submitted to the NPS and Department of the Interior.

97. Savage (*Monument Wars*) noted that contemporary monuments are expected to be "spaces of reflection and psychological engagement" (12).

98. Michael Leff, "Letter: Where's the Quiet Contemplation?" *Philadelphia Inquirer,* March 5, 2012, available at http://www.ushistory.org/presidentshouse/news/inq030512.htm.

99. Jennifer Bonnell and Roger I. Simon, "'Difficult' Exhibitions and Intimate Encounters," *Museum and Society* 5, no. 2 (2007): 67.

100. Hetherington, *Badlands,* 51.

101. Kenneth Burke, *A Rhetoric of Motives* (New York: Prentice Hall, 1950), 20–22.

102. Yaniv Poria, Avital Biran, and Arie Reichel, "Visitors' Preferences for Interpretation at Heritage Sites," *Journal of Travel Research* 48 (2009): 101.

103. Victoria J. Gallagher, "Remembering Together: Rhetorical Integration and the Case of the Martin Luther King, Jr., Memorial," *Southern Communication Journal* 60 (1995): 109–119.

104. Saindon, "Doubled Heterotopia."

105. See, for example, John Poulakos, "Toward a Sophistic Definition of Rhetoric," *Phi-*

losophy & Rhetoric 16 (1983): 35–48; Phillip Sipiora and James S. Baumlin (eds.), *Rhetoric and Kairos: Essays in History, Theory, and Praxis* (Albany: State University of New York Press, 2002).

106. Wright, "Rhetorical Spaces," 53. See also Jerry Blitefield, "*Kairos* and the Rhetorical Place," *Professing Rhetoric: Selected Papers from the 2000 Rhetoric Society of America Conference*, ed. Frederick J. Antczak, Cinda Coggins, and Geoffrey D. Klinger (Mahwah, N.J: Lawrence Erlbaum Associates, 2002), 69–76.

107. Wright, "Rhetorical Spaces," 55.

108. Kirt H. Wilson, *The Reconstruction Desegregation Debate: The Politics of Equality and the Rhetoric of Place, 1870–1875* (East Lansing: Michigan State University Press, 2002), 12.

109. Maddie Hanna, "Visitors to President's House Grapple with Reality of Slavery," *Philadelphia Inquirer*, February 18, 2013, available at http://articles.philly.com/2013-02-18/news/37162281_1_slaves-george-washington-liberty-bell-center.

110. See, for example, Gatewood and Cameron, "Battlefield" (207); Laurajane Smith, "'Man's Inhumanity to Man' and Other Platitudes of Avoidance and Misrecognition: An Analysis of Visitor Responses to Exhibitions Marking the 1807 Bicentenary," *Museum and Society* 8 (2010): 193–214; and Emma Waterton, "Humiliated Silence: Multiculturalism, Blame and the Trope of 'Moving On,'" *Museum and Society* 8 (2010): 128–157.

111. Doss, *Memorial Mania*, 264.

112. See http://www.tripadvisor.com/Attraction_Review-g60795-d2456252-Reviews-The_President_s_House-Philadelphia_Pennsylvania.html.

113. See http://www.philadelphiaspeaks.com/forum/architecture-urban-planning/18773-presidents-house-independence-mall-8.html.

114. In Peter Crimmins, "President's House Balances Noble Image with True Picture," *newsworks* [WHYY], December 16, 2010, available at http://www.newsworks.org/index.php/homepage-feature/item/9339-15pchouse.

115. Laurajane Smith, "Affect and Registers of Engagement: Navigating Emotional Responses to Dissonant Heritages," in *Representing Enslavement and Abolition in Museums: Ambiguous Engagements*, ed. Laurajane Smith, Geoffrey Cubitt, Ross Wilson, and Kalliopi Fouseki (New York: Routledge, 2011), 300.

116. Mark McPhail, "Stones the Builders Rejected: Freedom Summer, Kent State, and the Politics of Public Amnesia," in *Public Memory, Race, and Ethnicity*, ed. G. Mitchell Reyes (Newcastle upon Tyne, UK: Cambridge Scholars Publishing, 2010), 103.

117. See http://www.philadelphiaspeaks.com/forum/architecture-urban-planning/18773-presidents-house-independence-mall-6.html and http://www.philadelphiaspeaks.com/forum/architecture-urban-planning/18773-presidents-house-independence-mall-7.html.

118. See http://www.philadelphiaspeaks.com/forum/architecture-urban-planning/18773-presidents-house-independence-mall.html, http://www.philadelphiaspeaks.com/forum/architecture-urban-planning/18773-presidents-house-independence-mall-7.html, and http://www.philadelphiaspeaks.com/forum/architecture-urban-planning/18773-presidents-house-independence-mall-3.html, respectively.

119. See http://www.tripadvisor.com/Attraction_Review-g60795-d2456252-Reviews-The_President_s_House-Philadelphia_Pennsylvania.html.

120. McPhail, "Stones," 103.

121. Michael's extended commentary refers primarily to the Liberty Bell, but he seems to have regarded the President's House site as part of the Liberty Bell exhibition, especially considering that he posted his lament on the IHA's website about the President's House.

122. Savage (*Monument Wars*) noted the proliferation of victim memorials, observing that they have no ideological or demographic boundary—"Victims are everywhere, crossing boundaries of nation, class, race, and gender"—and worried that "our own victim monuments will simply be matched by others" (295).

123. See, for example, Danielle Allen, *Talking to Strangers: Anxieties of Citizenship since Brown v. Board of Education* (Chicago: University of Chicago Press, 2004); David A. Frank and Mark L. McPhail, "Barack Obama's Address to the 2004 Democratic National Convention: Trauma, Compromise, Consilience, and the (Im)possibility of Racial Reconciliation," *Rhetoric & Public Affairs* 8 (2005): 571–594; Mica Pollock, *Colormute: Race Talk Dilemmas in an American School* (Princeton, NJ: Princeton University Press, 2004); and Beverly Daniel Tatum, *Can We Talk about Race? And Other Conversations in an Era of School Resegregation* (Boston: Beacon Press, 2007).

124. A. Susan Owen and Peter Ehrenhaus ("Communities of Memory, Entanglements, and Claims of the Past on the Present: Reading Race Trauma through *The Green Mile*," *Critical Studies in Media Communication* 27 [2010]: 131–154) write of the anxiety about "whether any narrative representation can ever fully express" the overwhelming legacies of race and slavery in the United States (135).

CHAPTER 8

1. In Stephan Salisbury, "Slavery Laid Bare: A Historic Platform for Dialogue on Race," *Philadelphia Inquirer,* May 20, 2007, available at http://www.ushistory.org/presidentshouse/news/inq052007.htm, and Salisbury, "Remaking History," *Philadelphia Inquirer,* June 30, 2008, available at http://www.ushistory.org/presidentshouse/news/inq063008.htm.

2. See http://www.philadelphiaspeaks.com/forum/architecture-urban-planning/18773-presidents-house-independence-mall-12.html.

3. See http://planphilly.com/eyesonthestreet/2012/03/01/presidents-house-compromised.

4. Davis Buckley, in discussion with the author, June 3, 2013.

5. In Kellie Patrick Gates, "Making of the President's House," *PlanPhilly,* February 23, 2009, available at http://planphilly.com/articles/2009/02/23/8311. "PlanPhilly.com is [an] alternative media news website dedicated to covering design, planning and development issues in Philadelphia" (http://planphilly.com/about-us).

6. In discussion with the author, July 3, 2013.

7. Despite the inaccuracy in thinking of the passageway as solely a means of keeping the enslaved invisible (as noted in Chapter 6), its role as an underground passageway possesses significant symbolic power, especially when considered in light of the nearby executive office.

8. See, for example, "Susan Harrison Wolffis, Reflections on the Vietnam Veterans Memorial—from Both Sides of the Wall," *Muskegon [MI] Chronicle,* May 23, 2013, available at http://www.mlive.com/opinion/muskegon/index.ssf/2013/05/susan_harrison_wolffis_93.html; and Josh Noel, "The Countryside of 9/11," *Chicago Tribune,* August 15, 2013, available at http://www.chicagotribune.com/travel/ct-trav-0818-flight-93-memorial-20130815,0,633409.column?page=1.

9. Kirk Savage, *Monument Wars: Washington, D.C., the National Mall, and the Transformation of the Memorial Landscape* (Berkeley: University of California Press, 2009), 287.

10. See Charlene Mires, *Independence Hall in American Memory* (Philadelphia: University of Pennsylvania Press, 2002), 88–99.

11. The Visitor Center, however, offered a compelling installation during my visit titled *Seizing Freedom: The Roots of the Underground Railroad in Philadelphia,* which integrated different times and places within the park.

12. Nancy Fraser, "Rethinking Recognition," *New Left Review* 3 (2000): 108.

13. Kenneth Foote, *Shadowed Ground: America's Landscapes of Violence and Tragedy* (Austin: University of Texas Press, 1997), 293.

14. Michael Calvin McGee, "The Origins of 'Liberty': A Feminization of Power," *Communication Monographs* 47 (1980): 45.

15. Kenneth Burke, *A Grammar of Motives* (New York: Prentice-Hall), 514.

16. Michael Calvin McGee, "The 'Ideograph': A Link between Rhetoric and Ideology," *Quarterly Journal of Speech* 66 (1980): 15.

17. Only the Slave Memorial plaque ("The devastating effects of slavery continue to affect race relations to this day") refers to the contemporary legacy of slavery. I recognize that my desire to address contemporary issues suggests the possibility of even more interpretation at the President's House. I'd prefer to see less interpretation, of course, primarily through a reduction in the redundancies now present.

18. Robert E. Terrill, "Irony, Silence, and Time: Frederick Douglass on the Fifth of July," *Quarterly Journal of Speech* 89 (2003): 230.

19. J. Christian Spielvogel, *Interpreting Sacred Ground: The Rhetoric of National Civil War Parks and Battlefields* (Tuscaloosa: University of Alabama Press, 2013), 80.

20. The location of the lab in the foreseeable future remains in flux. It was supposed to move into the park's First Bank of the United States building, but engineering concerns postponed the move indefinitely while the bank building is renovated. See Stephan Salisbury, "Philadelphia Public Archaeology Lab at Independence National Historical Park Closed for Up to Two Years," *Philadelphia Inquirer,* August 6, 2010, available at http://articles.philly .com/2010-08-06/news/24969529_1_archaeological-work-park-building-lab. As of 2014, the park had not made any definitive plans to move the lab to the bank building.

21. Inga Saffron, "For Tourists and City, Not Re-created Equal," *Changing Skyline,* December 26, 2010, available at http://www.ushistory.org/presidentshouse/news/inq122610 .htm.

22. Mark McPhail, "Stones the Builders Rejected: Freedom Summer, Kent State, and the Politics of Public Amnesia," in *Public Memory, Race, and Ethnicity,* ed. G. Mitchell Reyes (Newcastle upon Tyne, UK: Cambridge Scholars Publishing, 2010), 116.

23. The panel titled "A Brief Timeline of Freedom and Slavery" has an entry for each of the three, noting in one sentence when they resided in the house.

24. A. Susan Owen and Peter Ehrenhaus, "Communities of Memory, Entanglements, and Claims of the Past on the Present: Reading Race Trauma through *The Green Mile,*" *Critical Studies in Media Communication* 27 (2010): 135. They cite James Jasinski's explanation of the Greek notion of *aporia,* paraphrasing his definition: "*Aporia* concerns anxiety about the adequacy of representation" (135). See Jasinksi's *Sourcebook on Rhetoric: Key Concepts in Contemporary Rhetorical Studies* (Thousand Oaks, CA: Sage, 2001).

25. Nathan Irvin Huggins, *Revelations: American History, American Myths,* ed. Brenda Smith Huggins (New York: Oxford University Press, 1995), 169.

26. Edward T. Linenthal, "Epilogue: Reflections," in *Slavery and Public History: The Tough Stuff of American Memory,* ed. James Oliver Horton and Lois E. Horton (New York: New Press, 2006), 216.

27. Dell Upton, "African American Monuments and Memorials," in *Commemorative Landscapes of North Carolina,* digital collection hosted by the University of North Carolina at Chapel Hill Library, available at http://docsouth.unc.edu/commland/features/essays/upton/.

28. Kirt H. Wilson, "Rhetoric and Race in the American Experience: The Promises and Perils of Sentimental Memory," in *Sizing Up Rhetoric,* ed. David Zarefsky and Elizabeth Benacka (Long Grove, IL: Waveland Press, 2006), 23.

29. Ibid., 37.

30. Salisbury, "Remaking History."

31. Posted by MarketStEl on February 19, 2013, at http://www.philadelphiaspeaks.com/ forum/architecture-urban-planning/18773-presidents-house-independence-mall-13.html.

32. In discussion with the author, October 1, 2013.

33. Derek H. Alderman and Rachel M. Campbell, "Symbolic Excavation and the Artifact Politics of Remembering Slavery in the American South: Observations from Walterboro, South Carolina," *Southeastern Geographer* 48 (2008): 343.

34. *Advancing the National Park Idea: National Parks Second Century Commission Report* (Washington, DC: National Parks Conservation Association, 2009), 22.

35. Ibid., 23.

36. Erika Doss, *Memorial Mania: Public Feeling in America* (Chicago: University of Chicago Press, 2012), 258.

37. Anne Mitchell Whisnant, Marla R. Miller, Gary B. Nash, and David Thelen, *Imperiled Promise: The State of History in the National Park Service* (Bloomington, IN: Organization of American Historians, 2011), 29. These suggestions are among twelve statements identified by the OAH, in a report invited by the NPS, as "basic approaches to historical research and interpretation" (27); the twelve statements are found on pp. 27–29.

38. Sharon Macdonald, *Difficult Heritage: Negotiating the Nazi Past in Nuremberg and Beyond* (New York: Routledge, 2009), 189.

39. In "Non-white Birth Rate May Inspire Policy Changes," *Talk of the Nation*, National Public Radio, May 17, 2012, available at http://www.npr.org/2012/05/17/152927636/non-white-birth-rate-may-inspire-policy-changes.

40. Marouf Hasian, Jr., "Remembering and Forgetting the 'Final Solution': A Rhetorical Pilgrimage through the U.S. Holocaust Memorial Museum," *Critical Studies in Media Communication* 21 (2004): 88.

41. James E. Young, "The Counter-monument: Memory against Itself in Germany Today," *Critical Inquiry* 18 (1992): 273.

42. Joshua Gunn, "Review Essay: Mourning Humanism, or, the Idiom of Haunting," *Quarterly Journal of Speech* 92 (2006): 83.

43. From a statement included in November 7, 2006, letter from Richard Tustin to the three finalist design teams, obtained on appeal of a FOIA request submitted to the NPS and Department of the Interior.

Index

Roger C. Aden is a Professor in the School of Communication Studies at Ohio University. He is the author of *Popular Stories and Promised Lands: Fan Cultures and Symbolic Pilgrimages* and *Huskerville: A Story of Nebraska Football, Fans, and the Power of Place.*